new media

an introduction

To Jack and Gloria Flew,

*for always appreciating the value of
an education and of knowledge.*

To Charlotte Sophia Flew.

*My writing of this book has been her introduction
to the 'very busy' world that she is now a part of.*

new media

3 edition

an introduction

terry flew

OXFORD

UNIVERSITY PRESS

OXFORD

UNIVERSITY PRESS

253 Normanby Road, South Melbourne, Victoria 3205, Australia

Oxford University Press is a department of the University of Oxford.
It furthers the University's objective of excellence in research,
scholarship, and education by publishing worldwide in

Oxford New York

Auckland Cape Town Dar es Salaam Hong Kong Karachi
Kuala Lumpur Madrid Melbourne Mexico City Nairobi
New Delhi Shanghai Taipei Toronto

With offices in

Argentina Austria Brazil Chile Czech Republic France Greece
Guatemala Hungary Italy Japan Poland Portugal Singapore
South Korea Switzerland Thailand Turkey Ukraine Vietnam

OXFORD is a trademark of Oxford University Press
in the UK and in certain other countries

10064758 302·231

Luton Sixth Form Co... ge
Learning Resources Cen... e

National Library of Australia Cataloguing-in-Publication data

Flew, Terry.
New media : an introduction.
3rd ed.
Bibliography.
Includes index.
ISBN 9780195551495 (pbk.).
1. Mass media—Technological innovations. 2. Mass media—
Influence. 3. Mass media—Social aspects. 4. Mass media—
Political aspects. I. Title.

302.23

Edited by Venetia Somerset
Cover design by Mason Design
Text design by Patrick Cannon
Typeset by Cannon Typesetting, Melbourne
Proofread by Anne Mulvaney
Indexed by Jeanne Rudd
Printed in Hong Kong by Sheck Wah Tong Printing Press Ltd

contents

tables

figures

preface

'I get by with a little help from my friends.'

Indulging in 1960s baby boomer nostalgia can certainly be a dangerous way to commence a book about new media in the 21st century. But it does need to be noted that this third edition of *New Media* was absolutely dependent on the contribution of four people in particular:

- Adam Swift, for his comprehensive copy editing of my chapter drafts from a remote work station in creative Wellington
- Barry Saunders, for his work on recording and transcribing interviews, as well as his contributions as someone who 'lives the life' of new media (he has a blog and watches TV programs from his computer)
- Sal Humphreys, for her co-authorship of the Games chapter (Chapter 7), from a no less remote work station in Adelaide
- Angela Romano, my partner, who gave me critical space to complete the manuscript at vital times, and whose insights into journalism and democracy in Asia inform the analysis developed in Chapter 8.

An important innovation in this third edition of *New Media* has been the inclusion of interview transcripts with leading thinkers and practitioners in the new media field. My special thanks to Vinton Cerf, sometimes referred to as a 'Father of the Internet', for giving us his time and insights into how the Internet has evolved, from someone who has been integrally involved from the 1960s to the present. I am also particularly appreciative of the contribution of Professor Zhang Xiaoming of the Chinese Academy of Social Sciences, who I believe provides valuable insights into how creative industries are developing in China that will be very important to the predominantly English-speaking readership of this text. Thanks to Weihong Zhang for her work in organising and then translating this interview. Thanks to interviewees Mark Bahnisch, founder of the *Lavartus Prodeo* collaborative blog site and lecturer at Griffith University, Graham Young, the editor and founder of *On Line Opinion*, and Professor Brian Fitzgerald from the School of Law at Queensland University of Technology, and an internationally renowned academic on Internet law. Thanks also to Leanne Blazely for her work on transcribing the Brian Fitzgerald interview.

The other major innovation in this edition of *New Media* is the extensive use of case studies. Feedback from the first two editions indicates that it is not enough to know theory about new media; it needs to be supported by practical applications of the ideas and concepts being considered. There are 11 case studies in this edition that deal with the global Internet; Marshall McLuhan and Raymond Williams as pioneer media theorists; postmodernism and new media; the transformation of telecommunications; social network analysis; digital storytelling; theories of creativity and their relevance to business; citizen journalism from a news editor's perspective; the Korean online news site *OhMyNews*; *YouTube* and *Joost* as online video distribution outlets; and the Creative Commons socio-legal movement. I hope that these will provide valuable learning resources, and I welcome feedback on possible future case studies to be included in subsequent editions of the text.

Thanks also to those who made more intangible contributions to the knowledge that informs this book. These include (in alphabetical order) Debra Adams, John Banks, Axel Bruns, Jean Burgess, Sue Carson, Christy Collis, Stuart Cunningham, Mark Gibson, Gerard Goggin, Phil Graham, Joshua Green, Melissa Gregg, Brad Haseman, Caroline Hatcher, John Hartley, Greg Hearn, Joanne Jacobs, Michael Keane, Helen Klaebe, Don Lamberton, Georgie McClean, Jason Potts, Kerry Raymond, Darren Sharp, Christina Spurgeon, Jason Sternberg, Martin Stewart-Weeks, Sue Street, Peter Thomond, and Jason Wilson. The English cricket team also warrant some retrospective thanks, as their generally mediocre performance during the Ashes tour of 2006–07 gave me plenty of opportunity to think through new media developments in the absence of other forms of stimuli during the hot, dry summer in Brisbane.

Thanks to the team at Oxford University Press who have overseen this project to fruition. Thanks to Lucy McLoughlin for keeping the faith after I missed the contractual deadline for first draft copy, and for her ongoing work in liaising with those who have used previous editions of this book. Thanks to Venetia Somerset for her copy editing of the book, Tim Campbell for his oversight of the final production process and Shalini Kunahlan for her work on assisting with permissions.

I would conclude this Preface with two observations. The first is that if we are moving towards an era of more collaborative social production models, as I argue in *New Media*, then this has implications for the nature of academic writing and publishing. Writers such as Henry Jenkins and Charles Leadbeater have provided important examples of how an academic work can benefit from the circulation of chapter drafts and other thoughts and relevant materials during the writing process, as aids to developing the ideas of the book through an active feedback loop with their user constituency. I see this as a valuable practice for subsequent work of my own, and would recommend it to other researchers in this field, as it actively applies the value-adding possibilities of content co-creation to academic publishing.

My second point would relate to work–family balance. I differentiate this from work–life balance, which frequently involves employer-subsidised gym classes, long walks during the lunch break, and other relatively peripheral add-ons for the 'always on' 21st-century service, knowledge and creative industries workforce. This book was written during the life of Charlotte Flew, who is two at the time of publication. Writing this book has been a challenge to my partner, Angela Romano, and to Charlotte herself. Recent parents who are also academic publishers may attest to the value of what are known in the television industry as the 'interstitials', which are those periods between doing something (e.g. putting a child to sleep) and something else (e.g. being with the child when they wake up). Charlotte may well already be a digital native; she is certainly adept at using a mouse at a very young age. At the same time, if we are to give children like Charlotte the opportunities in life that they so richly deserve, there is a need at the highest levels of government and industry to think about the balances that we achieve, and the choices that we make, so that academic research and scholarship does not become a surrogate or an alternative to these brief but pleasurable experiences.

abbreviations

AIMIA	Australian Interactive Multimedia Industry Association
APEC	Asia Pacific Economic Co-operation grouping
API	Applications Programming Interface
ARPA	Advanced Research Projects Agency
ASEAN	Association of South East Asian Nations
AT&T	American Telephone and Telegraph Company
B2B	business-to-business
B2C	business-to-consumer
BBC	British Broadcasting Corporation
CAR	computer-assisted reporting
CBAA	Community Broadcasting Association of Australia
CBF	Community Broadcasting Foundation
CC	Creative Commons
CCI	Creative Industries and Innovation
CCTV	closed-circuit television
CDS	Centre for Digital Storytelling
CED	Committee for Economic Development
CERN	*Conseil Européen pour la Recherche Nucléaire* (European Organisation for Nuclear Research)
CMC	computer-mediated communication
DARPA	Defense Advanced Research Projects Agency
DRM	Digital Rights Management

EA	Electronic Arts
ECI	Entertainment-Communication-Information
EFF	Electronic Frontier Foundation
ESA	Entertainment Software Alliance
EULA	End-User Licensing Agreement
FPS	first-party shooter
GATS	General Agreement on Trade in Services
GII	Global Information Infrastructure
GPL	General Purpose Licence
GUI	Graphical User Interface
HCI	human–computer interaction
HTML	Hypertext Markup Language
HTTP	Hypertext Transfer Protocol
ICANN	Internet Corporation for Assigned Names and Numbers
ICTs	information and communication technologies
IGO	international governmental organisation
INGO	international non-governmental organisation
IP	Internet Protocol
IPR	intellectual property rights
ISOC	Internet Society
IT	information technology
ITCP	IT-related creative practice
ITU	International Telecommunications Union
LAN	local area network
MIT	Massachusetts Institute of Technology
MMOG	massive multiplayer online game
MNC	multinational corporation
MOO	Multi-User Object-Oriented Domain
MPPW	massively populated persistent world
MUD	Multi-User Dungeon
NAFTA	North American Free Trade Agreement
NCSA	National Centre for Supercomputer Application
NES	Nintendo Entertainment System
NGO	non-government organisation
NII	National Information Infrastructure
NLS	oN-Line-System
NTIA	National Telecommunication and Information Administration
P2P	peer-to-peer

PBS	Public Broadcasting Service
PDA	personal digital assistant
RPG	role-playing game
RSS	Really Simple Syndication; Rich Site Summary
RTS	real-time strategy
SME	small and medium enterprise
SMS	short message services
TCP/IP	Transmission Control Protocol/Internet Protocol
TPM	Technological Protection Measure
TRIPS	Trade-Related Aspects of Intellectual Property Rights
UNCTAD	United Nations Committee on Trade, Aid and Development
WAIS	Wide Area Information Service
WAN	wide area network
WIPO	World Intellectual Property Organization
WSIS	World Summit on the Information Society
WTO	World Trade Organization

introduction
to new media

Why 'new' media?

In any discussion of new media, a question that needs to be addressed is why some media are considered to be 'new'. There is a temptation to simply list the latest developments in media technologies and call these new. Yet this approach is inadequate, partly because the rate of change in media technologies, services, and uses is so rapid that any list of this sort will quickly become dated. It also conflates the new and the novel. At one extreme, 'newness' can simply refer to the variants on long-established commodities, as when car manufacturers reveal their 'new' line of vehicles for the coming year, television networks present the 'newest' situation comedy or game show, or mobile phone companies announce a new model that is jewel-encrusted or locates the camera in a new place on the device.

Such an approach is also inadequate because, just as media technologies that we now consider to be 'old' were once 'new' (Marvin 1988; Gitelman & Pingree 2003), so too do media technologies that were once 'new' become 'old'. To many of those born after the 1980s, who Marc Prensky (2001) termed the *digital natives*, the idea of even a world without the Internet, email, mobile phones, computer games, digital cameras, and instant text messaging is simply preposterous: it is only the folk on reality TV shows such as *Big Brother* and *Survivor* who don't have access to such devices, and that was their choice. Indeed, networked personal computers and other digital media technologies are now so pervasive in our work, our home lives, and the myriad everyday interactions we have with each other as well as with social institutions, that they are ceasing to be 'new' in any meaningful sense of the term. As a result, any approach to new media that simply catalogues the technologies themselves, and fails to ask broader questions about the contexts of their use and their broader social and cultural impacts, ignores the central question of why there is a need to look at new media in the first place.

So should we still be speaking of 'new media'? There is a need, as Sonia Livingstone has noted, to ask 'what's new for society about the new media?' rather than simply 'what are the new media?' (1999: 60). This takes us to the larger question of whether, and how, technologies can act as factors in wider social change, yet at the same time be already embedded in a social context (Cowan 1997; Flichy 2005a). In *Novum Organum*, first published in 1620, the English philosopher Francis Bacon proposed that three discoveries had been central to marking out the period in which he lived as one that was markedly different from that preceding it:

> It is well to observe the force and effect and consequences of discoveries. These are to be seen nowhere more conspicuously than in those three which were unknown to the ancients, and of which the origin, though recent, is obscure: namely, printing, gunpowder, and the magnet. For these three have changed the whole face and state of things throughout the world; the first in literature, the second in warfare, the third in navigation; whence have followed innumerable changes. (Quoted in Graham 1999: 26–7)

One way of defining new media, which I have used in previous editions of this book (Flew 2002, 2005a), has been that it involved the combination of the three Cs—computing and information technology (IT), communications networks, and digitised media and information content—arising out of another process beginning with a 'C', that of convergence (cf. Miles 1997; Rice 1999; Barr 2000). As a first approximation, convergent media can be seen as combining computing, communications and media content in the way shown in Figure 1.1.

New media can also be thought of as digital media. Digital media are forms of media content that combine and integrate data, text, sound, and images of all kinds; are stored in digital formats; and are increasingly distributed through

Figure 1.1 The three Cs of convergent media

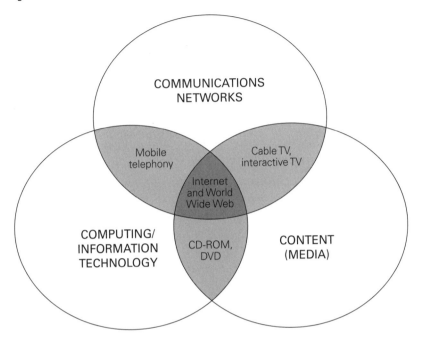

Source: Barr, *Newmedia.com.au*

networks such as those based on broadband fibre-optic cables, satellites, and microwave transmission systems. Such media, or forms of digital information,[1] have the characteristics of being:

- manipulable: digital information is easily changeable and adaptable, at all stages of creation, storage, delivery, and use
- networkable: digital information can be shared and exchanged between large numbers of users simultaneously, and across enormous distances
- dense: very large amounts of digital information can be stored in small physical spaces (e.g. USB flash discs) or on network servers
- compressible: the amount of capacity that digital information takes up on any network can be reduced dramatically through compression, and decompressed when needed
- impartial: digital information carried across networks is indifferent to what forms it represents, who owns or created them, or how they are used.

This still leaves open, however, the question of what is new for society from the new media. The broad social focus taken in this book towards new media is consistent with a study of media technologies that stresses the need to be aware of how the mediation of communications through technological forms renders communications a form of social practice. We follow Lievrouw and Livingstone (2005: 2) in their observation that any approach to thinking about new media needs to take account of three elements: the artefacts or devices that enable and extend our ability to communicate; the communication activities and practices we engage in to develop and use these devices; and the social arrangements and organisations that form around these devices and practices.

Lievrouw and Livingstone also make the point that these three elements should not be thought of as being linear or layered—the technologies influence communications practices, which in turn shape social arrangements and institutions—but rather as constituting an *ensemble* characterised by 'dynamic links and interdependencies among artefacts, practices, and social arrangements that … guide our analytic focus' (2005: 3). In this way, critical analysis of new media also has wider implications for how the media are studied more generally, since media studies as it emerged in the 20th century understood media production, texts, and audiences as discrete forms, which emerged in a linear fashion at different 'moments' of the media production-consumption cycle.

Internet history

The concept of new media is integrally bound up with the history of the Internet and the World Wide Web. While convergence has now spread across a range of platforms and devices, it was the emergence and mass popularisation, of the Internet that heralded the rise of new media, understood as bringing together computing and information technologies, communications networks, and media content. When we refer to the Internet, we are referring both to a technical infrastructure of computers and other digital devices (e.g. servers, routers) permanently connected through high-speed telecommunications networks, and to the forms of content, communication, and information sharing that occur through these networks. In their analysis of the social implications of the Internet, sociologists DiMaggio, Hargittai, Neuman, and Robinson define the Internet as 'the electronic network of networks that links people and information through computers and other digital devices allowing person-to-person communication and information retrieval' (DiMaggio et al. 2001: 307). A more technical definition has been developed by the Internet Society (ISOC), which in 1995 resolved that the Internet:

> refers to the global information system that: (i) is logically linked together by a globally unique address space based on the Internet Protocol (IP) or its subsequent extensions/follow-ons; (ii) is able to support communications using the Transmission Control Protocol/Internet Protocol (TCP/IP) suite or its subsequent extensions/follow-ons, and/or other IP-compatible protocols; and (iii) provides, uses or makes accessible, either publicly or privately, high level services layered on the communications and related infrastructure described herein. (Leiner et al. 2003)

The history of the Internet has been well documented, and will not be presented in detail here. It is vitally important, nonetheless, to observe that the history of the Internet, while developing in parallel with the general development of personal computers and other devices for digital information processing and retrieval, is both a history of the common networking protocols for the transfer of digital information, and a history of systems for the publication, organisation and distribution of this information.[2] Three elements of this history are particularly worth dwelling on. First, while the commitment to developing an integrated communications network arose in the USA as a consequence of the Cold War with the Soviet Union, the priorities of the Advanced Research Projects Agency (ARPA)—established in 1957 after the Soviets launched the Sputnik satellite—were arguably driven as much by the desire of the American scientific community to perfect mechanisms of communicating with one another as by the demands of the military.[3] The most significant development to come from ARPA in the 1960s was packet switching. Packet switching meant that long messages could be broken down into smaller 'packets'; messages could be rerouted if there was a blockage at one message route or point of connection between two computers; and messages would be sent in an asynchronous mode, meaning that the receiver would not receive the message until some time after the message was originally sent. Not only did packet switching overcome limitations of the telephone system, such as the potential for access to be blocked by heavy use by others, but it also established the principle of a decentralised network with no single point from which control can be exercised, which has been so central to the Internet's development (Gillies & Cailliau 2000: 18–25). With the establishment of

ARPANET as a national long-distance computer network in the USA in 1969, packet switching became central to this network, with the transfer of electronic mail being perhaps the major communications innovation arising from this development. In 1972, ARPANET demonstrated to the public its capacity to retrieve, access, and send data at the International Conference on Computer Communication in Washington, DC, where perhaps the world's first email was sent (although not called this at the time!) (Hassan 2004: 13).

The second major development in Internet history was the development of a common set of networking protocols, which enabled researchers in the various local area networks (LANs) to communicate with one another, through the interconnection of these LANs into a wide area network (WAN). The major breakthrough came in 1974, with the proposal developed by Robert Kahn and Vinton Cerf to develop a common switching protocol that could meet the needs of an open-architecture network environment, which came to be known as TCP/IP (Transmission Control Protocol/Internet Protocol). The quasi-privatisation of ARPANET in 1983, which allowed universities and commercial interests to play an increasing role on the network and which marked the commencement of the Internet proper, was premised on the adoption of TCP/IP as a common interconnection protocol. In sharp contrast to other media, the Internet would become both a public and a global communications medium, as all computers and computer networks could communicate with one another in a common language, whether they were Apples, PCs or mainframes, or whatever local or national computing network they were operating within. As Internet use spread in the 1980s from outside its core constituency of the US government and military, scientists, and defence contractors, the significance of TCP/IP being established as a common Internet protocol would be of increasing significance to more and more people worldwide.

The development of the World Wide Web in the 1990s was the third major development that has made the Internet what it is today. While developments such as TCP/IP and packet switching provided the means by which networks could connect with networks, and computers could connect with computers, the question of how people could connect with other people through such electronic networks had not received as much attention. The conception of the World Wide Web by Tim Berners-Lee in 1989, and its development by Berners-Lee and colleagues at CERN (*Conseil Européen pour la Recherche Nucléaire*, or European Organisation for Nuclear Research) from 1991 onwards would dramatically change the communications capabilities of the Internet. The significance of developing the World Wide Web became even more apparent in 1992 when Marc Andreesen of the National Centre for Supercomputer Application (NCSA) developed Mosaic as the first Web browser. Andreesen went on to become one of the founders of Netscape Communication, which developed Netscape, the first major commercial Web browser, in 1994. Microsoft quickly followed suit in 1995 with its Internet Explorer browser, released as part of its Windows 95 software suite to much fanfare and to the sounds of the Rolling Stones' 'Start Me Up'.

The ability to use Web browsers such as Netscape and Internet Explorer to access online content through the World Wide Web saw the mass popularisation of the Internet, with the number of Internet users worldwide growing by over 1300 per cent between 1994 and 1998 (see Table 1.1). Four features of the World Wide Web were particularly important in this popularisation. First, it allowed for the display of colourful pictures, music, and audio as well as data and text, and introduced multimedia capability to the Internet. Second, it was based on hypertext principles. Hypertext allows for the linking of information, where links from one information source provide simple point-and-click access to related information available from other sources. The concept of hypertext had circulated in various domains since the publication of Vannevar Bush's article 'As We May Think' in 1945, which proposed the development of a computational machine (the 'Memex') that not only could store vast amounts of information, but could allow users to create ancillary 'thought trails' (Bush 1996). Ted Nelson's experimentations with hypertext through 'Project Xanadu' in the 1960s and early 1970s pointed to the possibilities of interconnected electronic writing, and both the French Minitel system (developed as a national teletext system in 1983) and the Hypercard storage system (available on all Apple computers from 1987 to 1990) drew on hypertext principles in different ways. Third, the value of hypertext became even more apparent with the development not only of Web browsers such as Netscape Navigator and Microsoft Explorer, but search engines such as Yahoo! and Google, which provided vast and easy-to-use databases that gave users easy access to information stored on the Internet. Finally, the World Wide Web was associated with the development of both the common Hypertext Transfer Protocol (HTTP), which provided a platform-independent means of interconnection between websites, and Hypertext Markup Language (HTML) as a relatively straightforward means of writing source code for the World Wide Web. As a result, a much wider range of people could become producers as well as consumers of content on the World Wide Web. This trend would accelerate as commercial software for developing Web pages became increasingly available, such as Adobe InDesign, Macromedia Dreamweaver, and Microsoft Front Page, and has been further accelerated with the development of programs associated with what is known as Web 2.0.

The Internet has thus become the fastest growing medium ever recorded. It is estimated that as of December 2006 there were 1.076 billion Internet users worldwide, or about 16.6 per cent of the world's population, having grown from 30.6 million users in 1995, or by almost 2000 per cent over an 11-year period (Internet World Stats 2006). Table 1.1 indicates the number of Internet hosts worldwide, or the number of sites from which the Internet is accessed, as well as the rate of growth of Internet use over time.[4]

Table 1.1 Estimated Internet hosts worldwide

Year	Estimated number of Internet hosts worldwide	Annual rate of growth (%)
1991	376,000	
1992	727,000	96.4
1993	1,313,000	80.6
1994	2,217,000	68.8
1995	4,852,000	188.5
1996	9,472,000	95.2
1997	16,416,000	73.3
1998	29,670,000	80.7
1999	43,230,000	45.7
2000	72,398,092	67.5
2001	109,574,429	51.3
2002	147,344,723	34.4
2003	171,638,297	16.5
2004	233,101,481	35.8
2005	317,646,084	36.2
2006	394,991,609	24.3

Yearly figures are for January.

Source: Internet Software Consortium <www.isc.org>, accessed 3 December, 2006

THE GLOBAL INTERNET

In the 2000 US presidential election campaign, the Democratic Party candidate Al Gore (now a leading global warming campaigner) made the claim, on the *Jay Leno Show*, that as Vice-President in the Clinton Administration, he had 'invented the Internet'. Gore was roundly criticised for his hubris, particularly as the collaborative nature of the Internet meant that no one could claim to have invented it, let alone a senior politician. Yet there is a subtext to Gore's otherwise hyperbolic claim that cannot be ignored. At the time of its mass popularisation in the mid-1990s, the bulk of the major initiatives that led to the Internet's emergence came from the USA, its user base was predominantly North American, and policies of the Clinton Administration—such as the promotion of a National Information Infrastructure (NII) and a Global Information Infrastructure (GII) modelled on the US NII—played a key formative role in the way in which the Internet evolved globally.

By contrast, the Internet today has a far more globally diverse user base. Of the estimated 1.076 billion Internet users in December 2006, the majority are now from Asia and Europe, and the fastest growing regions for Internet take-up are Africa, Latin America, and the Middle East:

Table 1.2 World Internet usage and population statistics

World Regions	Population (2006 est.) (million)	Population % of world	Internet Use Dec. 2006 (million)	% of Population as Internet Users	% of World Internet Users	User Growth 2000–06 (%)
Africa	915.2	14.1%	32.76	3.6%	3.0%	625.8%
Asia	3,667.8	56.4%	378.6	10.3%	35.2%	231.2%
Europe	807.2	12.4%	311.4	38.6%	28.9%	196.3%
Middle East	190.1	2.9%	19.02	10.0%	1.8%	479.3%
North America	331.4	5.1%	231.0	69.7%	21.5%	113.7%
Latin America & Caribbean	553.9	8.5%	85.04	15.4%	7.9%	370.7%
Australia/ Oceania	33.9	0.5%	18.36	54.1%	1.7%	141.0%
WORLD TOTAL	6,499.7	100%	1,076.2	16.6%	100%	198.1%

Source: Internet World Stats, 2006

THE GLOBAL INTERNET (*cont.*)

To get a sense of the significance of such a change over time, we can compare this data on the global distribution of Internet users to that found in Flew (2005), which contained data from 1997 and 2002 respectively.

Figure 1.2 Global distribution of Internet users 1997–2006

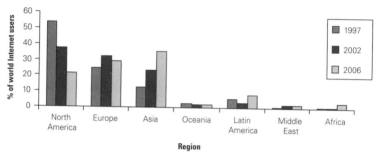

Source: Flew 2005: 73; Internet World Stats, 2006

While this data certainly provides considerable evidence of a global '*digital divide*', both between wealthier and poorer nations, as well as within nations, it nonetheless also highlights how the world's Internet-using population is becoming more globally diverse. A good indicator of the change is in the top ten languages used on the Web. While English

Figure 1.3 Internet world users by language

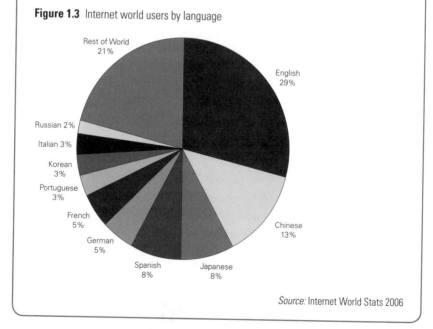

Source: Internet World Stats 2006

remains the dominant language, accounting for 29.7 per cent of languages used globally in 2006, it is challenged not only by languages such as Chinese and Spanish, which are the written and spoken languages of about 30 per cent of the world's population, but by languages such as Korean, Portuguese, and Russian, which are not as widely used worldwide, but are the languages of some of the world's fastest growing Internet-using populations, in South Korea, Brazil, and Russia. There is also a 'long tail' of languages used, with over 30 languages used by at least a million people on the Internet (Figure 1.3).

The conduit and the content

The development and popularisation of the Internet marked a high-water mark in the process of convergence. Through the World Wide Web, a rapidly growing number of Internet users were able to access a dramatically increased range of forms of digitised content (text, images, sound, video), delivered across telecommunications networks, via their personal computers, which increasingly became a single media platform able to deal with multiple media forms. This process of technological convergence, or the bringing together of computing, communications networks and media content, was matched by the development of convergent products and services, and processes of industry convergence, or the range of takeovers, mergers and strategic alliances that strengthened links between the computing and IT industries, the large telecommunications companies, and media corporations (Barr 2000; Flew 2005: 11–12).

At the same time, early Internet content was frequently quite impoverished in terms of the capabilities of the new media form. Indeed, the imperative to provide 'content' was often the problem, as it frequently led to the 'dumping' of already existing text online with little consideration of how such material was viewed and used differently from its print-based variants. The much-publicised initiatives of the time to digitise the entire contents of the US Library of Congress envisaged not only a veritable army of information workers on minimum wages undertaking endless document scanning, but also an Internet whose content was largely synonymous with that of the world of print media. One problem was, of course, download speeds; with most domestic users being reliant on 28.8 Kilobyte per second modems for much of the 1990s, access to audio and video was bound to be slow for many. Interestingly, it was also the case that media artists had to proceed slowly in developing their content for online access. To take one example, the Australian Film Commission's *Stuff-Art* initiative, developed in 1998 to promote the use of the Internet for the distribution of new media artworks, required participants to 'make innovative and entertaining interactive works that are small enough to fit on a floppy disc … and that download quickly over the Internet' (quoted in Tofts 2005: 141).

The development of the World Wide Web gave a renewed focus to the nature of the *interface*, or the 'front page' from which users access websites, typically through a Web browser and search engine. The quality of interface design draws attention to the nature of *human–computer interaction*, which is at one level a consequence of technical design and computer programming aspects of the interface, but which can only operate effectively when, as Anne Cranny-Francis observes, it recognises 'the cultural practices that enable users to engage with the technology', since it constitutes the 'hidden engine of the user's interaction with the text' (2005: 120). The importance of interfaces to the usability, and hence the popularity, of computers was apparent well before the advance of the Web. The success of Apple Computers in the 1980s was strongly related to its development of a Graphical User Interface (GUI) which, in simulating the environment of a desk top—with files, folders, in-trays, trash cans etc.—was intuitively usable to a vast array of users when compared with the PC-DOS system that was the leading personal computer interface at the time. Indeed, Apple fought a long, bitter, and ultimately unsuccessful legal case against Microsoft between 1994 and 1998 over its claim that Microsoft had incorporated the desktop metaphor into its Windows software, raising the question of whether the 'look and feel' of a GUI and software generally is copyrightable.

The question of the technical *conduit*, or the means by which online content is distributed, delivered, and accessed by the user, has become considerably more complex in the age of new media. With broadcast media, access to a suitable reception device (a television set or radio) gave its audiences content that looked and/or sounded more or less the same regardless of the device being used to access it (except in instances such as the transition from black-and-white to colour televisions). With the Internet, by contrast, a variety of factors come into play in terms of both the accessibility and the quality of the user experience in accessing online content, including:

· the age of the computer being used, and the software installed on that computer

- whether the user is accessing the content from a dial-up or broadband connection, and the speed of downloads available from that connection
- the overall quality of service and the available modes of delivery (dial-up, broadband, wireless broadband etc.) in the physical location from which the content is being accessed
- the type of computer being used (e.g. some material is not available for PCs or Mac computers)
- the software being used to access the content (e.g. the Web browser)
- the nature of the user themselves; for example, they may have a disability or other physical or mental condition that makes certain types of Web design inappropriate.

Sites such as Vincent Flanders' *Web Pages That Suck* (www.webpagesthatsuck. com) delighted in demonstrating the principles of good Web design by drawing attention to examples of bad Web design in a highly amusing manner. In response to the often baroque features of many early websites, where the designers managed to forget about both their users and the means by which they would access such sites, there was a turn towards *usability* in Web design, led by writers such as Jakob Nielsen (2000) and Donald Norman (1998).

The paradox of convergence, and the reason why the concept becomes more problematic over time, is that as the computing and IT, communications and media industries are brought further together by technological and industry changes, the disparities between and across content forms become more significant. If we simply consider computer-based media, two examples illustrate this. The first is *interactive online games*, which require content that is sufficiently rich and compelling to provide an immersive experience for the games player as user. What gamers seek from online media is, therefore, considerably more complex than the functionality and usability sought in Web-based user interfaces. Second, there is the case of electronic mail, or *email*, which is the world's most widely used Internet tool. With very few exceptions, emails themselves tend to be simple, text-based forms, even if they provide attachments or links that are more graphically complex. Indeed, to refer to emails as media content is certainly to stretch the definition of the term; as communications data that is based in the technical media of information and communication technologies (ICTs), they are media content, but they very rarely involve the kinds of production processes that we typically associate with the media content industries.

While the discussion of new media has thus far tended to focus on the Internet and computer-based digital media, a range of wireless technologies and applications have been developed that are increasingly shifting the locus of ICTs from the desktop to a range of portable, handheld devices. At the forefront of this has of course been the *mobile telephone*. The global take-up of mobile telephones has been considerably greater than that of the Internet, and it is estimated that there are now 2 billion mobile phone users worldwide, which is double the number of Internet users, and greater than the number of main telephone lines worldwide (ITU 2004; MobileTracker 2005). There have also been important transformations in how the mobile telephone is used, with devices being increasingly used for short message services (SMS) or text messages, taking and sending pictures, viewing video, playing games, listening to music, and accessing email and the Internet. These developments have meant that the question of media content that users will seek to access from mobile devices has added further layers of complexity to the question of media content in the context of convergence, pointing to the paradox of convergence: as the proliferation of interconnected digital media technologies and devices is accentuated, the question of developing content that works across multiple media—in both a technical and a consumer demand sense— becomes more and more complicated.

INTERVIEW: VINTON CERF, 'FATHER OF THE INTERNET'

Vinton Cerf has commonly been referred to as one of the 'founding fathers of the Internet'. Along with Robert Kahn and others, he was centrally involved in the development of packet switching and TCP/IP protocols, through his work on ARPANET in the 1960s and early 1970s and, from 1976 to 1982, his work with the US Department of Defense's Advanced Research Projects Agency (DARPA). Cerf's activities within ARPANET and DARPA were central to what remain two of the central defining characteristics of the Internet: its indifference to the content of data that is digitally encoded, and the capacity for differently configured computer systems to communicate with each other through the sharing of common protocols.

Vinton Cerf was founding president of the Internet Society from 1992 to 1995, and has served in various capacities as an advisor on Internet development, including membership of the Board of Directors of the Internet Corporation for Assigned Names and Numbers (ICANN) since 1999 (for more detail, see www. icann.org/biog/cerf.htm). He received the US National Medal of Technology from President Bill Clinton in 1995, and the Presidential Medal of Freedom from President George W. Bush in 2005.

He is currently a Vice-President of Google, where he has an additional position of Chief Internet Evangelist. His current interests include the development of an 'Interplanetary Internet'. He visited Brisbane, Australia in March 2007 as a guest of the Australian Interactive Multimedia Industry Association (AIMIA), and Barry Saunders was able to interview him via email during this period.

Did you think the Internet would be as popular as it ultimately proved to be?

[VC:] Well, I was already pretty excited about the experience with the ARPANET and a thriving community of academics were making good use of that. Email was a popular thing and when Gopher and the Wide Area Information Service (WAIS) popped up around 1992, you could see some very good potential. Tim Berners-Lee's WWW triggered huge popular interest of course. Many of us who have used Doug Engelbart's NLS (oN-Line-System) in the 1960s could see the potential (he invented the mouse, portrait mode display, hyperlinking, computer-aided knowledge work, and much more).[5] I did not anticipate the result of cheap computers and later Internet-enabled mobiles that has triggered a vastly larger level of interest than one would have anticipated in the 1970s when the initial work was being done.

In what ways do you think the Web changed as it became popular? For example, in the 1990s some saw it as a licence to print money.

[VC:] It triggered production of a vast amount of information contributed by users. Digital cameras and video-cams have exacerbated that trend: the consumers have become the producers. I think it has also expanded to support many new business models (Yahoo!, Google, eBay, Amazon, Skype, *YouTube*, Second Life, etc.—the list is endless). It is a stunningly good medium for collaborative work and play, and it aggregates thin markets into dense ones regardless of location.

Can you tell us something about your association with Google, and the Google approach to the Web?

[VC:] I am Google's Chief Internet Evangelist. Part of my job is to encourage the creation of more Internet access. Google sees the Web as a vast ocean of information that needs organising or at least indexing so that its content can be quickly searched and accessed. I anticipate many, many new applications that structure information by location, by time, by other organising principles.

I think Google will persist in developing new tools for information sharing and collaborative work.

Is Web 2.0 a significant development? Why? Why not?

[VC:] The term is more marketing hype than real but there is an underlying opportunity to use new Web services standards to allow the business processes of different companies to automatically interact—accounts payable interaction with accounts receivable; order entry interacting with inventory and fulfilment, and so on. The protocols associated with Web 2.0 will support such innovations.

How do you see the future of the Web?

[VC:] It will continue to absorb content. It will become increasingly integrated into day-to-day business operations. It will incorporate new information structures that can be more readily searched.

Will Web-based services increasingly migrate to mobile devices?

[VC:] Yes, there is no question that many people will first be introduced to the Internet through appropriately equipped mobiles.

What is your role in the Interplanetary Internet project?[6]

[VC:] I am one of the founders of the project and I continue to work with the engineering team on planning, protocol development, funding, and deployment.

What does the Interplanetary Internet project seek to do?

[VC:] We want to standardise the protocols used in deep space so as to allow missions to support each other. One mission's assets may be very useful for new missions and standards allow for interoperability that is so vital to the success of the Internet itself and can be used to leverage investments in previous mission's assets.

Web 2.0

The concept of Web 2.0 is centrally important to understanding new media in the 21st century. The term first began to be circulated in 2003, and the first conferences were held on Web 2.0 through O'Reilly Media (formerly O'Reilly & Associates) in 2004. Tim O'Reilly (2006), who has been a key thinker and promoter of Web 2.0, defined it as 'the business revolution in the computer industry caused by the move to the Internet as platform, and an attempt to understand the rules for success on that new platform. Chief among those rules is this: *Build applications that harness network effects to get better the more people use them ...* [or] harnessing collective intelligence' (emphasis added).

There are both Web 2.0 evangelists and sceptics—as seems to be the case with most new media concepts. *TIME* magazine drew particular attention to the Web 2.0 phenomenon when it declared that its 'Person of the Year' for 2006 was 'YOU', for each person's collective contribution to Web 2.0 (Grossman 2006). Not surprisingly, such prognoses generate equal doses of scepticism about both the sustainability of the phenomenon and the extent to which it is really marketing *hype* or what Steve Woolgar (2002) has called '*cyberbole*'.

Nonetheless, the concept of Web 2.0 has caught on for two particular reasons. First, it has embedded within it a range of the features that have long been seen as central to the Web as a communications infrastructure, such as the scope for participation, interactivity, collaborative learning, and social networking (*social networking media* is a commonly used alternative term to Web 2.0), as well as positive networking effects from harnessing collective intelligence; in other words, the quality of participation increases as the numbers participating increase, and this in turn attracts more new users to the sites. Second, some of the fastest growing websites of the 2000s have been based on Web 2.0 principles. These include sites such as the photography site *Flickr*, the online encyclopedia *Wikipedia*, the online user-generated video site *YouTube*, aggregated Web log (blog) sites such as *Blogger*, *Livejournal* and *Technorati*, and the various personalised Web space sites such as *MySpace*, *Facebook*, *Friendster* and *Bebo*.

The core principles of software programs and Internet sites that conform to Web 2.0 principles are that they are:

· many-to-many in their connectivity
· decentralised in terms of control
· user-focused and easy for new users to use
· open in terms of their technology standards and their Applications Programming Interface (API)
· relatively simple and 'lightweight' in their design, their administrative requirements and their start-up and ongoing development costs

- expected to evolve and change over time, as users make new modifications to the sites.

In their overview of design and application principles that underpin and drive Web 2.0, Musser and O'Reilly (2007) identified the following principles (Table 1.3).

Table 1.3 Principles of Web 2.0

Principle	Examples
Harnessing collective intelligence—deriving the benefits of large-scale ongoing participation and user co-creations and peer review of content to continuously improve the quality of the service	Google Wikipedia Flickr Amazon Del.icio.us
Data as the next 'Intel inside'—new wealth from online enterprises to be derived from database management	Amazon eBay Craigslist
Innovation in assembly—open APIs that allow for online remixing of content ('mash-ups') and the use of RSS (Really Simple Syndication)	Google Maps Yahoo! Flickr
Rich User Experiences, that promote user interaction and immersive engagement with the available online content	Google Maps GMail Netflix
Software above the level of a single device—services that can span across media devices, particularly mobile media such as mobile phones and PDAs	iTunes TiVo
Perpetual Beta testing—software is incrementally released, and understood as a service rather than as a final product	Google Flickr Open source software more generally
Leveraging the 'long tail'—recognising that there is a move from mass markets to niche markets, but that niche markets can be sustainable over a long period of time (cf. Anderson 2006)	Amazon eBay Google
Lightweight models and cost-effective flexibility—Web 2.0 marketing works off word of mouth rather than high up-front costs in business set-up and marketing	Digg.com (allegedly established with an up-front investment of $US2800) Flickr

Source: Musser & O'Reilly 2007

The concept of Web 2.0 clearly implies a relationship to an earlier form of the Internet (Web 1.0). O'Reilly (2005) identified some of the differences as being about a move from personal websites to blogs and blog site aggregation, from publishing to participation, from Web content as the outcome of a large up-front investment to an ongoing and interactive process, and from content management systems to links based on tagging, or what is known as *folksonomy*. A significant factor in its promotion has been lessons learnt from the dot.com crash of 2000, where very large numbers of small investors lost wealth from the unrealistic business models of a plethora of Internet start-ups which, in contrast to the Web 2.0 model, had high initial costs in developing infrastructure, personnel, and marketing strategies.

Bloggers such as Carr (2005) and Shaw (2005) have expressed scepticism about Web 2.0, arguing that such a term is simply marketing bait that will promote over-capitalisation in a new Internet capital-raising bubble (Bubble 2.0), on the basis of poorly defined understandings of the nature of the Internet as a social technology. Moreover, the decision by News Corporation to buy *MySpace* in July 2005 raises a series of questions, yet to be resolved, about the relationship between established, incumbent media and the emergent start-up enterprises that arise in the Web 2.0 space, in a controlled and commodified manner.

 USEFUL WEBSITES

Internet Society, *All About the Internet* <www.isoc.org/internet/history>. Excellent collection of papers on the early development of the Internet and World Wide Web. It includes Vinton Cerf's Brief History of the Internet, Tim Berners-Lee on the past, present and future of the World Wide Web, and the website for the series *Nerds 2.0.1*, produced by the US Public Broadcasting Service (PBS) in 1998.

Internet World Stats—Usage and Population History <www.internetworldstats.com/>. This site has the most up-to-date information on how many Internet users there are worldwide and where they are geographically located.

Web 2.0
Some of the most popular Web 2.0 sites worldwide include:

- *YouTube* <www.youtube.com>—user-generated videos
- *MySpace* <www.myspace.com>—social networking site
- *Flickr* <www.flickr.com>—online photo sharing
- *Blogger* <www.blogger.com>—'how to' site for creating Web logs (blogs)
- *Livejournal* <www.livejournal.com>—blog site creation and aggregation
- *Technorati* <technorati.com>—site that aggregates and monitors blog activity worldwide

- *Bebo* <www.bebo.com>—rival social networking site to *MySpace*
- *Friendster* <www.friendster.com>—social networking site with an emphasis on friendships
- *Facebook* <www.facebook.com>—social networking site that was initially focused on high school and college students.

twenty key
new media concepts

In considering the broader socio-cultural impacts of new media, there are some recurring concepts that come into play in identifying what it is to be 'new'. A review of the summary literature on new media (e.g. Elmer 2002; Gauntlett & Horsley 2002; Burnett & Marshall 2003; Lister et al. 2003; Cranny-Francis 2005; Flew 2005; Lievrouw & Livingstone 2005) points to themes and key concepts that act as organising principles for arguments about the specifics of new media and why it is justified to refer to such media as new. This is not to say that these authors present an argument that all that is 'old' is *passé* and of no relevance to understanding the nature of new media; far from it. It is rather to say that, in so far as it is legitimate to talk about new media, there are some key organising themes and concepts. The 20 key concepts are listed in alphabetical order rather than in any perceived order of significance, and they will all be recurring through this book.

1. Collective intelligence

Collective intelligence is a term used by Lévy (1997) and de Kerckhove (1998) to refer to the capacity of networked ICTs to exponentially enhance the collective pool of social knowledge by simultaneously expanding the extent of human interactions enabled by communications networks that can generate new knowledge, and the greatly enhanced capacity to codify, store, and retrieve such knowledge through collective access to networked databases. This new capacity to collaboratively develop, distribute, share, and communicate knowledge is central to arguments that we are now in a *knowledge economy*. The concept of collective, self-organising knowledge *networks* is also central to claims that *open source* software development will generate superior outcomes to proprietary software developed within corporations, as there is the scope to 'harness the hive' of knowledge that exists within a participating user community (Raymond 1998; Herz 2005).

2. Convergence

Convergence refers in the first instance to the interlinking of computing and IT, communications networks, and media content that occurred with the development and popularisation of the Internet, and the convergent products, services, and activities that have emerged in the digital media space. Many see this as simply the tip of the iceberg, since all aspects of institutional activity and social life—from art to business, government to journalism, health and education, and beyond—are increasingly conducted in this interactive digital media environment, across a plethora of networked ICT devices. The Australian Research Council Centre of Excellence for Creative Industries and Innovation (CCI) presents this trajectory for convergence as shown in Figure 2.1.

For writers such as Thomas Friedman (2005), this is in turn generating a global 'flat earth', where activities conducted through digital media can occur in any part of the world. It is noted in Chapters 9 and 10 of this book that there are reasons to question this claim, and that culture, policy and other variables remain critical to the geographical location of new media activities, particularly with the shift towards a global knowledge economy.

Figure 2.1 Trends in convergence, 2006–16

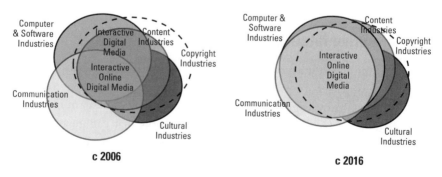

c 2006

c 2016

Source: CCI 2005

The second element of convergence is the morphing of devices (computers, mobile phones, televisions, etc.) as they become multi-purpose conduits for a range of activities involving digital media. It was observed in Chapter 1 that trends towards convergence coexist with trends towards divergence in terms of ICT devices (Zetie 2004).

3. Creative industries

While the term 'creative industries' has its origins in a policy initiative of the Blair Labour government in the United Kingdom to link the arts, media, and ICT sectors more explicitly in economic and export growth strategies (DCMS 1998), it has gained wider currency as a result of the growing opportunities to link creativity and wealth generation through new products and services developed and distributed using ICTs. Hartley defines the term as describing 'the conceptual and practical convergence of the creative arts (individual talent) with cultural industries (mass scale), in the context of new media technologies (information and communication technologies or ICTs) within a new knowledge economy, for the use of newly interactive citizen-consumers' (Hartley 2005: 5). As this definition makes clear, the rise of the creative industries is seen not simply as an outgrowth of public policy to support creative activities, but rather, as being inextricably linked to new media, globalisation, and the knowledge economy. While there has been much discussion of what are (and are not) creative industries, and how to measure their size and growth, and the term itself is in some dispute (see Hesmondhalgh 2007 for a dissenting perspective), it usefully captures the extent to which individual creativity is increasingly seen as a core intangible asset in the development of new and compelling content in interactive digital media environments, and the extent to which networked ICTs offer a democratising of the capacity for *participation* in media production.

4. Cyberspace

Arguably the most influential new media concept of the 1990s, *cyberspace* became the metaphor used to describe the 'sense of a social setting that exists purely within a space of representation and communication … it exists entirely within a computer space, distributed across increasingly complex and fluid networks' (Slater 2002: 535). The term was first used by the science fiction writer William Gibson in his 1984 novel *Neuromancer*, where it was an abstract concept that eluded concrete definition, but referred variously to a 'dataspace', the 'world in the wires', and 'the matrix', in which transnational corporations trade information in a space that is visual, ordered, and electronic (Kitchin 1998: 2). Popularised in the early 1990s by Internet activists such as John Perry Barlow and Mitchell Kapor (apparently first used in a 1993 speech given by Barlow to CIA operatives, according to Streeter [2004: 288–9]), the term took off as both metaphor and myth because it came to capture four core elements of the Internet as a digitally networked environment.

First, it described the flows of digital data through the network of interconnected computers that was both not 'real'—since one could not spatially locate it or feel it as a tangible object—and clearly 'real' in its effects. The popular phrase 'Cyberspace is where your money is' captured the extent to which global financial institutions had been leaders in the development of such digital data networks, and decisions made within these institutions of *digital capitalism* could have great impacts on people yet not be located in an identifiable place where such decisions could be controlled. Second, cyberspace was the site of *computer-mediated communication* (CMC), in which online relationships and alternative forms of online identity were enacted, raising important questions about the social psychology of Internet use, the relationship between 'online' and 'offline' forms of life and interaction, and the relationship between the 'real' and the *virtual*. Third, it drew attention to the *remediation* of culture through new media technologies, and the extent to which the Internet has never simply been a communications tool, but a cultural form and 'a social space in its own right ... [which] means looking at the forms of communication, sociality and identity that are produced within this social space, and how they are sustained using the resources available within this online setting' (Slater 2002: 533). Finally, because cyberspace was presented as a qualitatively new space, it was seen as providing new opportunities to reshape society and culture, whether through disembodied identities, borderless communication and culture, or the rediscovery of powerful myths such as the 'American Dream' and frontier civilisation (Mosco 2004). Cyberspace as myth and metaphor was thus integrally linked to the *hype* surrounding the Internet that has been such a recurring feature of new media discourse.

5. Digital capitalism

Political economists such as Dan Schiller (2000, 2006), Robert McChesney (1999, 2003), Vincent Mosco (1996, 2004) and Philip Graham (2000, 2006) have used this term to argue that new media and the 'Internet revolution' mark the rise of the Entertainment-Communication-Information (ECI) sector to prominence in the global capitalist economy, constituting the core infrastructure of global commerce and the fastest growing sectors of international capitalism. Rather than seeing this as heralding a 'new economy', they argue that such trends mark the consolidation and intensification of capitalist relations on a global scale, as information is increasingly commodified as intellectual property through *digital copyright*. Political economists have stressed the key role played by traditional 'Big Media' corporations such as News Corporation and Time-Warner in the new media environment, and argue that there is in fact a further concentration of media ownership and control occurring, alongside a growing international digital divide between information 'haves' and 'have-nots'.

6. Digital copyright/Creative Commons

A central paradox of new media has been the way in which digitisation as a technological process has made the copying, distribution, reuse, and repurposing of all forms of media content almost infinitely simpler and quicker, while at the same time the laws that govern the ownership, use, access, and financial payment for such content have become progressively stricter. While copyright law has always contained tensions between reasonable compensation for its original creators and fair use for non-commercial purposes in the public domain, developments in copyright law in the 1990s and 2000s have seen new systems for managing the ownership and use of intellectual property that many critics argue unduly benefit the owners of existing copyrightable material, to the detriment of new applications of creativity that reuse existing digital content in new and innovative ways (Lessig 2001, 2004; Vaidhyanathan 2001; Perelman 2002). As an alternative to this use of law to establish monopoly rents through intellectual property rights (IPRs) as a part of digital capitalism, the Creative Commons movement has sought to enable authors, artists, scientists, educators, and other creators of original content to establish more flexible yet legally sound principles through which their work can be used and repurposed to serve non-commercial, public good principles (Creative Commons 2007).

7. Digital divide

The National Telecommunication and Information Administration (NTIA) used this term in its *Falling Through the Net* reports in the late 1990s into the differential access to networked personal computers. It has been defined as 'the differential access to and use of the Internet according to gender, income, race, and location' (Rice 2002: 106). The term has also been important in the context of globalisation, in clarifying the extent to which, as the United Nations observed in 1995, 'more than half of the world's population lives more than two hours away from a telephone' (quoted in Couldry 2002: 186). In an overview of digital divide research, Norris (2001) has proposed that it is important to distinguish between: (1) the 'global divide', or differential Internet access between nations based on access to networked ICT infrastructures, computers, information transmission capacity, local website hosts etc.; and (2) the 'social divide', or the gaps within nations in terms of access to the Internet as a means of social engagement. Critics of the digital divide concept argue that inequalities related to new media involve far more than access, but also include opportunities to participate effectively in online environments (Gandy 2002). Murdock and Golding (2004) have argued that because the computing hardware, software, and skills required change so quickly, and opportunities to learn these new skills are unequally distributed, inequalities in the digital environment continue to reflect other sources of social inequality, such as those arising from income, occupation, or geographical location.

8. Globalisation

One of the most widely used concepts in social theory today, globalisation is a term used to both describe and make sense of a series of interrelated processes such as the rise of multinational corporations (MNCs); international production, trade, and financial systems; international communications flows; global movements of people and the increasingly multicultural nature of societies; developments in international law; global social movements such as the environmental movement; the development of international governmental organisations (IGOs), regional trading blocs, and international non-governmental organisations (INGOs); and global conflicts such as the 'war on terror' after the attacks on the World Trade Center and the Pentagon on September 11, 2001. While many of these developments are not new—trade and empire have been a feature of the world system at least since Columbus crossed the Atlantic in 1492—their speed, intensity, and interconnectedness are seen by many as marking a new stage in human social development. As technologies that enable 'borderless' communication, new media are central to debates about globalisation and its impacts. Globalisation has both its advocates (e.g. Cairncross 1998; Legrain 2002; Friedman 2006) and critics (e.g. Mander & Goldsmith 1996; Barber 2000; Klein 2000). For many of its critics on the political Left in particular, the issue is not globalisation per se, but rather the extent to which the term is used as a cover to extend the power of multinational corporations in an age of digital capitalism; as the Marxist writer Alex Callinicos puts it, 'the enemy is not globalisation, but global capitalism' (2001: 111). This raises a related question, which is the extent to which the trends associated with globalisation mark a *qualitative* shift in the pattern of economic, social, political, and cultural relations within and between states and societies, or whether they constitute a *quantitative* change, or a continuation of long-established trends. Arguments that propose that globalisation marks out a fundamental shift in social relations have been termed *strong globalisation* arguments (Flew & McElhinney 2005); by contrast, there are those who can be described as *globalisation sceptics* (e.g. Hirst & Thompson 1996), who point out the extent to which many of the developments associated with globalisation are not historically new, and question the political motives that lie behind globalisation hype (for an overview of these debates, see Flew 2007).

9. Hype

A recurring feature of the development of the Internet and the popularisation of digital media technologies has been their capacity to generate hype about how these technologies will change everything, typically for the better. Lister and colleagues (2003: 11) observed that this is an inherent feature of discourses surrounding new media being linked to the modernist belief in technology as being socially progressive. The "new" is "the cutting edge", the "avant-garde", the place for forward thinking people to be'. Such prophetic hype certainly characterised many analyses of the Internet in the 1990s (e.g. Dyson et al. 1994; Rheingold 1994; Negroponte 1995; Kelly 1997; Dyson 1999), which in turn tended to generate debunking responses that looked at the downsides of the new technologies and sought to reveal that the digital emperor had no clothes (Postman 1993; Sale 1995; Stoll 1995; Robins & Webster 1999). This 'polarisation between narrow suspicion and uncritical enthusiasm' (Woolgar 2002: 3–4) that characterised new media studies in the 1990s has to some extent given way to more empirically grounded research into new media, its uses, and impacts (Silver 2000; Flew 2001; Wellman 2004; Livingstone 2005). The dot. com crash of 2001 also revealed very starkly the dangers of investing in hype around new media companies that rested on fatally flawed business plans. At the same time, the extent to which hype surrounds new media remains pervasive, partly because it helps to boost share prices, persuade politicians and sell product, but also because it taps into what Vincent Mosco (2004) has referred to as the *digital sublime*. Mosco referred to the extent to which cyberspace possesses not only technical, political, and economic properties, but is also constituted as a form of cultural myth, offering possibilities of transcending the limits of contemporary society and the material world.

10. Information overload

The Internet has given its millions of users worldwide unprecedented access to a plethora of information. It was estimated that that there were about 30 billion Web pages worldwide in February 2007 (Boutell 2007), while the *Wikipedia* at the end of 2006 had over 1.5 million entries in English alone. Yet the availability of so much information, and the increasing *speed* with which information is sent to users, generates the problem of *information overload*. The problem is not simply dealing with well-known 'Net nuisances' such as spamming or the making of fraudulent claims online, but relates to a problem inherent in the Internet as a source of information. The philosopher Gordon Graham has pointed out that when the term 'information' is used of online content, it refers only to the capacity to access digital data from a computer or other networked device. The fact that this bears no relation to the quality or usefulness of the data generates the problem, since we typically understand information as an epistemologically normative term, because 'to be newly possessed of information implies that we know something we did not know before. But "digital information" can store *misinformation* ... as much as it can store the truth, so that the text or images it generates may be wholly misleading and produce erroneous belief rather than knowledge' (Graham 1999: 89). This tendency to conflate information in the form of digital data with knowledge is, for Graham, an example of misleading hype, and he argues for the need 'not to confuse the power of the Internet as a form of communication with its value as a conveyer of (epistemologically significant) information ... All the undeniable advantages of the Internet make it as powerful an instrument for deception and misinformation as for knowledge and learning' (1999: 90).

11. Interactivity

Interactivity is generally seen as a central feature of new media, although there is considerable debate about its meaning. It is typically presented as a feature of new media that distinguishes them from 'old media', which could only offer passive consumption. Lister and colleagues (2003: 20) observe that interactivity 'stands for a more powerful sense of user engagement with media texts, a more independent relation to sources of knowledge, individualised media use, and greater user choice'. While many forms of media offer some form of interactivity (e.g. digital television, DVDs), the unique features of the Internet in this regard relate to the distinctive elements of interconnectivity and interoperability. *Interconnectivity* refers to the capacity to easily connect interactions across different networks, while *interoperability* refers to the capacity to access all available forms of information and media content using different operating systems. One of the unique achievements in the history of the Internet was the way in which the adoption of Transmission Control Protocol/Internet Protocol (TCP/IP) as a common switching protocol for interconnecting networks promoted both interconnectivity and interoperability.

Interactivity can occur at many levels and degrees of engagement. McMillan (2005) argues that it is important to differentiate three levels of interaction: (1) user-to-user interaction, or the ways in which computer-mediated communication intersects with, or is at odds with, other rules, codes, and conventions of interpersonal communication; (2) para-social interaction, where online media generate new forms of user engagement with the content, which may range from the navigational practices of accessing and organising content to generate *hypertext* 'pathways', to the immersive practices associated with engagement with 'rich media' content such as multiplayer online games; and (3) user-to-system interactivity, or the ways in which users engage with the devices they are using, as studied in fields such as human–computer interaction (HCI) (cf. Reeves & Nass 2002).

Whether enhanced interactivity is synonymous with enhanced forms of participation with new media remains an open question. Tim Berners-Lee, one of the original developers of the World Wide Web, saw the concept of interactivity as it had developed on the Internet by the late 1990s as too constrictive, since it focused on the ability to access and choose content and not on the capacity to create and distribute new content. Berners-Lee (2000: 183) argued instead that the Web needed to be about *intercreativity*, or 'the process of making things or solving problems together. If interactivity is not just sitting there passively in front of a display screen, then intercreativity is not just sitting there in front of something "interactive"'.

12. Knowledge economy

The claim that the 21st century is marked by the rise of the knowledge economy points to the increasingly important role played by information, technology, and learning in wealth creation and economic competitiveness (e.g. OECD 1996). Three related observations lie behind this argument. First, there is the structural shift in employment from agriculture and industry towards the services and information sectors. Nora and Minc (1981) observed that the number of people employed in agriculture and manufacturing industries in the USA fell from 55 per cent in 1940 to 30 per cent by 1980, and that employment in information-related industries rose from 20 per cent to over 405 per cent over the same period. Similarly, Castells and Aoyama (1994) found that the proportion of the population involved in the handling of information, as distinct from the handling of goods, grew by 80 per cent in the USA between 1920 and 1990. Second, new media and ICTs greatly accelerate the production of new knowledge (David & Foray 2002). They do this by enhancing access to existing knowledge through networked data-bases, promoting online interaction between designers, producers, and users, and dramatically increasing the speed with which new knowledge can be disseminated into the public domain. In these ways, they promote not only new knowledge, but the pooling of *collective intelligence* across all knowledge domains. Finally, it is argued that innovation, or the development of new products and services, now 'comes closer to being the sole means to survive and prosper in highly competitive and globalised economies' (David & Foray 2002: 11). As knowledge is not synonymous with information, this presents the question of how to promote individual creativity and foster knowledge networks among people within and outside organisations, as the evidence on knowledge creation and knowledge transfer indicates that 'there are advantages to working together, however well people may be connected by technology' (Brown & Duguid 2000: 146). One consequence of the increas-ingly interactive as well as networked nature of digital media environments is the rise of *user-led innovation*, as users of online products and services are not simply consumers, but innovators in their own right.

13. Networks

The centrality of networks and networking to new media needs to be under-stood at three levels. First, the Internet is itself a *technical network*, or a global 'network of networks'. At the core of its physical infrastructure are the wires, cables, wireless transmission systems, and so on that provide the capacity to carry large amounts of information to a series of interconnected points. The Internet has exceeded the possibilities of earlier networked communications systems, such as the telephone system, as a result of its matrix structure, where all senders and receivers are interconnected through a sub-network of routing systems or servers, which distribute messages as a series of 'packets', regardless of the initial representational form encoded by the signal and decoded by the end-user. Second, there is the importance of *social networks*, understood in social network analysis as emphasising the interdependent and relational nature of links between people and institutions, and their importance in managing resource flows, providing opportunities, presenting constraints, and maintaining durable forms of social infrastructure (Thompson 2003: 54–6). The third level is that of *socio-technical networks*. In the work of Manuel Castells in particular, networks 'constitute the new social morphology of our societies' (Castells 1996: 469), to the point where the *network society* is 'the social structure characteristic of the Information Age' (Castells 2000a: 5). In Castells' work, the technological revolution associated with the Internet and networked ICTs and the social transformation to a global informational economy based around networks are fundamentally linked, since it has only been with the technological advances associated with new media that the capacity of networks to operate at a scale, speed, and level of complexity to become the dominant mode of social organisation. In particular, networked forms of organisation are seen as being the central drivers of processes of globalisation at the economic, geopolitical, and cultural levels and in terms of media use and identity formation (Castells 2001, 2004).

14. Participation

In the new media literature, participation is a concept used in three ways. First, in the context of the digital divide, it refers to inequalities in access to new media and the opportunity to use ICTs to participate as a user, worker, citizen, or consumer. At a global level, it refers to the difficulties faced by developing countries in being involved in decision-making concerning the development of ICTs (see e.g. WSIS 2003). The second use identifies the distinctive properties of new media that make it more open and interactive than traditional communications technologies. Kenney and colleagues (2000) argue that new media requires a rethinking of traditional sender–receiver models of communication, since 'Interaction ... demands a two-way (or multi-directional) model of communication. With the interactive features of new media, the receiver is recognised as an active participant.' The extent to which different forms of new media invite user participation is highly variable, and authors such as Berners-Lee have been critical of claims that *interactivity* is synonymous with participation. At the user level, Mayfield (2006) has developed the *power law of participation* (Figure 2.2), observing that the model of collective intelligence associated with Web 2.0 is not necessarily at the high end of potential user engagement with different forms of online media.

The third use of the term relates to the second, and concerns the question of whether the *participatory culture* that is promoted by new media (Jenkins 2006a,b) is connected to wider processes of democratisation of media access and use in the context of the rise of the *creative industries*, and what Hartley (1999b, 2005) has referred to as 'DIY citizenship' and Bruns (2005) describes as the rise of the 'prod-user' (cf. Deuze 2006).

Figure 2.2 The power law of participation

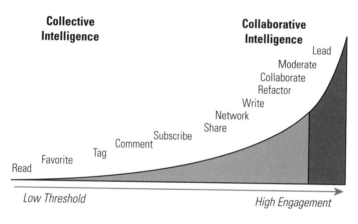

Source: Mayfield 2006

15. Remediation

Bolter and Grusin (2000) have proposed remediation as a way of thinking about the relationship between media forms that is not couched in terms of a transition from 'old media' to 'new media'. Arguing that the relationship between media forms is a 'genealogy of affiliations' rather than a 'linear history', they propose that 'no medium ... can now function independently and establish its own separate and purified space of cultural meaning' (2000: 55). They observe two apparently contradictory features of digital media design and new media content. First, there is the desire to establish immediacy in the relationship between the user and the content, to generate a sense of 'being there' that seeks to efface the extent to which this interaction is technologically mediated in order to enhance its realism and immediacy. While Web cams, Web logs (blogs), and *YouTube* video feeds are an example of this in the new media environment, contemporary reality TV programs such as *Big Brother* represent a similar tactic from 'old' media, offering their audiences a more unmediated, more real form of access to the show's contestants, along with the opportunity to shape the reality of the contestants through technologically mediated interaction. Second, there is the extent to which digital media content is generated by the combination and collage of already existing media content that is reassembled in the digitally networked environment. Examples such as the online 'repurposing' of print and broadcast media content on websites are obvious examples, but Bolter and Grusin (2000: 96–9) also draw attention to more distinctive and innovative modes of remediation, such as the appropriation of a range of well-established filmic techniques related to character, narrative, plot devices and *mise-en-scène* in computer games.

16. Security and surveillance

The Internet has generated a plethora of new information and personal *security* issues, which range from email spamming, computer virus proliferation and online harassment to forms of cyber-fraud and identity theft. The fact that the law nearly always lags behind new issues related to information security has meant that the ICT industry itself has frequently taken the lead in developing technological solutions to such problems. This has in turn raised issues about government sovereignty, democratic participation, corporate uses of personal information, and the scope for new forms of *surveillance*. At the heart of many questions about information security are the tensions between visions of the knowledge economy that are grounded in notions of digital copyright and information as private property, and the Internet as a creative commons based around the social sharing of knowledge in order to build collective intelligence. The ambiguous position of the *hacker* in these debates, whose activities in accessing computer systems and reproducing and altering data on them are both highly illegal yet possibly essential in exposing design flaws in such systems, is indicative of the complex legal and political environment in which such information security questions arise (Dyer-Witheford 2002).

Lyon (2002) has argued that a combination of interconnected digital technologies, from the 'cookies' left on personal computers by Web browsers to mark accessed sites, to closed-circuit televisions (CCTVs) in various urban spaces, have led to the rise of a *surveillance society*. Lyon locates the four key elements of surveillance society as being the growing use of ICTs to mark and locate where people are at particular times in order to coordinate activities better; the management of risk of various forms, from the comparatively low-level—welfare fraud, shoplifting, street crime—to the risks associated with large-scale terrorist actions; the balance between personal privacy and the use of personal information by various sources, from governments to insurance agencies and marketers; and the questions of power associated with who has access to such information, and whose information is accessed, or who watches and who is watched (2002: 5–8). As Lyon notes, one of the great paradoxes of the use of ICTs to address security concerns is that 'the applications of technology to risk management in the social sphere may themselves be read as a risk' (2002: 7). This point has been made by many in relation to various forms of anti-terrorism legislation, such as the US *PATRIOT Act*[1] passed by both Houses of the US Congress in the immediate aftermath of September 11. The issue has also been raised in relation to new media companies such as Google and Yahoo! agreeing to cooperate with government authorities in the People's Republic of China around Internet censorship provisions.

17. Speed

New media enable us to do things more quickly. Activities such as transferring funds between bank accounts, enrolling in a course, or buying an airline ticket can now be completed in minutes, whereas before they could often take hours. Search engines such as Google also give us instant access to easily downloadable information from our personal computers. The Internet has also generated a 24-hour news cycle, where it is expected that online sites are constantly updated as new information emerges, rather than relying on the traditional time routines of print or broadcast news production. Microsoft founder Bill Gates (1999) identified 'business at the speed of thought' as the key to success in the digital economy, while popular texts such as *Faster: The Acceleration of Just About Everything* (Gleick 2000) and *The Future Just Happened* (Lewis 2001) draw attention to the connections made between speed and new media. Cranny-Francis (2005) has noted that one of the key ways in which we evaluate ICTs and Web content sites is by their speed: how quickly can relevant material be uploaded, downloaded, distributed, and modified. The question of whether this emphasis on speed is having a corrosive impact on politics, culture, and social life was initially raised by the

Canadian communications theorist Harold Innis (1951) in his critique of the spatial *bias of communication* in 20th-century media. Contemporary theorists such as Paul Virilio have questioned the impact of new media in terms of *accelerated modernity* (Redhead 2004), while Mattelart (2003) has referred to 'informational neo-Darwinism', which fetishes speed at the expense of critical and reflective thought.

18. Ubiquity

In the context of new media, *ubiquity* refers to the extent to which the proliferation of digital devices, the density and interconnectedness of networks, and both the multiplicity of forms of use and the routine nature of uses of new media see new media increasingly embedded in all aspects of everyday life. While new media in the 1990s was largely associated with the Internet as accessed from computers, and for most people computers were largely boxy devices with screens that sat on desks, in the 2000s the range of digital devices that enable access to information and communication services in ways that maximise speed and *mobility* has proliferated. At the same time, the idea that ICT capabilities were always tied to computers was always something of a myth: to take one example, the microwave oven has always essentially been a computer used for the purposes of cooking food, but is designed as it is to appeal more to consumers as a food preparation device. Donald Norman's (1998) work on the *invisible computer* has drawn attention to the centrality of design and usability in the appeal of new technologies to consumers, in relation to questions of human–computer interaction and interaction design. Recent initiatives around the *disappearing computer* have raised the question of what will it mean for the future development of ICTs and new media as 'computers disappear from the scene, become invisible, and disappear from the perception of the users', who nonetheless seek their communication affordances and capabilities (Streitz & Nixon 2005: 34; cf. Disappearing Computer 2004).

19. User-generated content/user-led innovation

At one level, all Internet content is user-generated, as the medium by its very nature promotes *interactive*, many-to-many modes of communication. The phenomenon of user-generated content, however, refers specifically to the ways in which users as both *remediators* and direct producers of new media content engage in new forms of large-scale participation in digital media spaces. Massive multiplayer online games (MMOGs), for instance, derive their particular dynamism as media forms from the productivity of the players themselves, and the investments they make in the evolution of the game itself (Humphreys 2004). They represent a model of media production that is recursive, non-linear, and ongoing, leading to the emergence of what Bruns (2005: 23) has termed, in relation to online news sites, the rise of the 'prod-user', who engages with such sites interchangeably as both a producer and a consumer, often simultaneously. Such an understanding of the online user as participant in co-production points in the direction of the open source movement in the software development realm, and its championing of collective intelligence as the cornerstone of better software in the software realm. This in turn links to what von Hippel (2005: 1) has described as user-led innovation, and the *democratisation of innovation*, where 'users of products and services—both firms and individual consumers—are increasingly able to innovate for themselves' and, through digital networks in the knowledge economy, these innovations can be distributed, shared, and improved upon by user communities.

20. Virtuality

One of the features of new media is that it enables forms of interaction through computer-mediated communication that are separated in both time and space and have a potentially global reach through digital networks. The Internet has also promoted the *convergence* of modes of communication from one-to-one (e.g. email), one-to-many (e.g. websites), and many-to-many (interactive 'real time' online spaces) that challenges traditional hierarchies between senders and receivers of communication and between producers and consumers of media content. The 1990s saw a plethora of works that drew attention to this 'virtual' nature of communication and discussed the emergence of virtual communities (e.g. Rheingold 1994), virtual identities (e.g. Turkle 1995), virtual reality (e.g. Lévy 1998), and ways of 'being digital' (e.g. Negroponte 1995; Tapscott 1998) that offered newer and better possibilities of life and experience in the 'online' world than in reality, or what was fashionably referred to at the time as the 'offline' world. While it was not hard to identify a strong degree of unsubstantiated hype behind such propositions (see e.g. Lockard 1997; Robins & Webster 1999; Slater 2002), and elements of the 'digital sublime' (Mosco 2004), the question of how participation in virtual environments intersects with the everyday experience of those involved in sustained CMC remains an important one. Woolgar (2002) has proposed 'five rules of virtuality' that draw on extensive research in the United Kingdom on uses of new media:

1   Both the uptake and uses of new media are critically dependent on the non-ICT-related contexts in which people are situated (gender, age, employment, income, education, nationality).
2   Fears and risks associated with new media are unevenly socially distributed, particularly in relation to security and surveillance.
3   CMC-mediated or 'virtual' interactions supplement rather than substitute for 'real' activities.
4   The introduction of more scope for 'virtual' interaction acts as a stimulus for more face-to-face or 'real' interaction.
5   The capacity of 'virtual' communication to promote *globalisation* through communication that is spatially disembedded encourages, perhaps paradoxically, new forms of 'localism' and the embedding, rather than the transcendence, of identities grounded in a sense of place, belief, experience, or practice.

 USEFUL WEBSITES

Wikipedia <en.wikipedia.org/wiki/Main_Page> and *Google* <www.google.com>. The world's largest online encyclopedia and the world's largest Internet search engine are the two obvious starting points for getting information on new media concepts, who uses them, and the debates surrounding them.

New Media Studies <www.newmediastudies.com>. David Gauntlett, Professor of Media and Communications at the University of Westminster, has maintained this lively and quirky site since 2000. It is particularly focused on the relationship between media, theory, identity, and the Web, and it accompanies his two books on Web studies (Gauntlett 2000, 2004) as well as other works.

Voice of the Shuttle <vos.ucsb.edu>. First developed by Alan Liu at the University of California in 1994, this site provides a remarkably rich range of academic resources in the humanities, including cyberculture and media studies.

approaches to
new media

Beyond hype and counter-hype

Writing in 1998, Kitchin (1998: ix) observed that 'cyberspace is probably one of the most universally over-hyped terms of the latter part of the twentieth century'. Any survey of popular writing about the Internet and cyberspace in the mid-1990s finds no shortage of pronouncements of a utopian, almost transcendent nature about the implications of the new media. Nicholas Negroponte's *Being Digital* (1995) was one of the most influential examples. As founding director of the Media Lab at Massachusetts Institute of Technology (MIT) and a founder and columnist for *WIRED* magazine, Negroponte championed the idea that digitisation had reached a point where the transition from an economy and society based on 'atoms' (tangible physical assets) and the production of goods, to one based on 'bits' (intangible wealth based on knowledge), meant that 'computing is not about computers any more. It is about living' (1995: 6). Negroponte concluded *Being Digital* by proclaiming that 'the empowering nature of being digital' meant that 'like a force of nature, the digital age cannot be denied or stopped. It has four very powerful qualities that will result in its ultimate triumph: decentralizing, globalizing, harmonizing and empowering' (1995: 229, 231). Electronic Frontier Foundation (EFF) co-founder John Perry Barlow argued that 'with the development of the Internet, and with the increasing pervasiveness of communication between networked computers, we are in the middle of the most transforming technological event since the capture of fire' (1995: 36). George Gilder (1994: 49) hopefully predicted that the Internet would mean the death of television, which he saw as being 'a tool for tyrants … [whose] overthrow will be a major force for freedom and individualism, culture and morality'. In 1994, through the Progress and Freedom Foundation (www.pff. org), Esther Dyson, George Gilder, George Keyworth, and pioneering new media thinker Alvin Toffler (1970, 1980) published *Cyberspace and the American Dream: A Magna Carta for the Knowledge Age*, which found in the Internet both a concrete expression of uniquely American values of entrepreneurship and rugged individualism and identified cyberspace as 'the land of knowledge, and the exploration of that land can be a civilisation's truest, highest calling', the basis for the 'creation of a new civilisation, founded in the eternal truths of the American Idea' (Dyson et al. 1994).

Examples of such digital and cyberspace hype could be multiplied. Another example would be the then US Vice-President Al Gore's speech to the International Telecommunications Union in 1994 proclaiming that the US-led Global Information Infrastructure initiative would promote 'robust and sustainable economic progress, strong democracies, better solutions to global and local environmental challenges, improved health care, and—ultimately—a greater sense of shared stewardship of our small planet' (Gore 1994). John Brockman's anthology of interviews with and short pieces by the *digerati*, defined as those who 'evangelize, connect people, adapt quickly … [and] give each other permission to be great' (1996: xxvi) is an excellent primer on mid-1990s cyberbole for anyone who didn't happen to be around for the first adventure.

Not surprisingly, such hype surrounding new media, the Internet, and cyberspace generated counter-hype, or a debunking of how reality does not match the claims of the cyberspace advocates, as part of what Knights and colleagues (2002) refer to as the '"emperor's-new-clothes" story'. Former cyberspace advocate Clifford Stoll (1995: 13) had second thoughts about cyberspace, warning that 'life in the real world is far more interesting, far more important, far richer, than anything you'll ever find on a computer screen'. Critics of the digital age such as Brook and Boal (1995) and Sale (1995) reinvoked the spirit of the Luddite opposition to industrial technologies in early 19th-century Britain to warn of the need to 'resist the virtual life', with Sale going as far as to smash a computer on stage while promoting his book

(Silver 2000: 20). Barbrook and Cameron (1995: 1) argued that the new media discourse promulgated by *WIRED* magazine was part of a *Californian ideology* that constituted 'a bizarre fusion of the cultural bohemianism of San Francisco with the hi-tech industries of Silicon Valley', combining political libertarianism with a belief in free markets in a world where 'everybody can be both hip and rich'. Postman (1993) critiqued the entire relationship of culture to technology in modern societies as one of *technopoly*, defined as 'the deification of technology, which means that the culture seeks its authorisation in technology, finds its satisfactions in technology, and takes its orders from technology' (1993: 71). The collapse of many of the dot.com enterprises that started up in the late 1990s with the sharp decline of the NASDAQ index in April 2000 generated a veritable cottage industry of corporate *mea culpas* about the dangers of attaching too much belief to new media hype (Kuo 2001; Malmstein 2001; cf. Lovink 2002).

In their review of the social implications of the Internet, DiMaggio et al. (2001) present a fivefold typology of Internet impacts that identifies positive and negative assessments (Table 3.1).

Table 3.1 Social implications of the Internet

Internet Impact	Positive	Negative
1. Inequality	New access to information based upon computer use and availability (digital opportunity)	Patterns of access, availability and use of ICTs reflect other social inequalities (digital divide)
2. Community	New forms of social interaction and community formation through 'virtual communities' that are not space-bound	Online activities become an obstacle to 'real-life' interactions; declining commitment to locality-based social capital formation
3. Politics	New opportunities for online political engagement, information exchange and deliberation; a 'virtual public sphere'	Isolation from others in politically effective geographical locales; management of participation by political and economic elites
4. Organisations	Flexible organisations; networked inter-action among those within and outside of the organisation; more 'horizontal' channels of online communication	New forms of internal surveillance; online communication remains hierarchical; online as a low-trust communications environment
5. Culture	'Demassification' of access to and use of media content; new opportunities for users to become media producers ('produsers' [Bruns 2005])	Hyper-segmentation and 'I media' as a barrier to communication with others; fragmentation and dilution of a 'common culture'

Source: DiMaggio et al. 2001

Overly optimistic or pessimistic accounts of the impact of new media, or 'cyberbole', have been countered by approaches that seek to identify a middle ground between extreme positions. Silver (2000) and Flew (2001) observed the need for a 'new empiricism' in Internet studies that went beyond utopianism and critique, and engages with new media users and the environments, both technological and socio-cultural, in which they make use of networked ICTs.

We will return to current themes and tendencies in new media research in the later part of this chapter. It is, however, worth noting three possible limitations of an empirical approach to understanding new media that identifies optimistic and pessimistic accounts and aims to find a moderate, middle ground position between them. First, such an approach lends itself more readily to some research and theoretical traditions than to others; it particularly lends itself to forms of statistically based sociology that is linked to advice to government policy-makers on managing technological change such as the quantitative, survey-based research methodologies of the Pew Centre's *Internet and American Life Project* (Rainie & Bell 2004). These empirical approaches exist alongside others, such as speculative media theory, that have tended to approach the interaction between technology and culture in more future-oriented terms, and *critical political economy*, which has questioned the extent to which policy-making organisations possess sufficient distance from the most powerful private interests to be able to act in the public interest. Second, empirical new media tends to have an 'after-the-event' element to it; it is a research practice of those who seek to manage change, rather than of those who make change. This in itself may be an artefact of ways of thinking associated with the 20th-century one-to-many broadcast media systems. Kress (1997: 78) has made the observation that, just as the binary opposition between producers and consumers of media is challenged by new media technologies, so too is the distinction between *design* and *critique*, where 'some individuals set the agenda and others either follow or object'. One of the recurring themes of new media developments is the extent to which critique of existing systems happens through design— such as open source software, open publishing, citizen journalism, and participatory media systems—so that the politics of new media is as often enacted through the relationships between large-scale corporate media and those who pursue alternative forms of *digital creativity*, as it is between those who analyse the power relations of new media from an academic or research perspective.

Finally, it is important to consider the recurring significance of optimism about new media as a form of myth that is historically grounded. In his critical genealogy of the 'cyberspace myth', Mosco (2004) observes that his interest in this topic stemmed in part from his experience as a graduate student in 1973, when he was employed by Daniel Bell to look at claims that multichannel cable television in the USA, with the potential for back-channel interactivity, would 'bring about ubiquitous two-way communication, and ... usher in a Wired Society governed by Electronic Democracy' (2004: 1; cf. Streeter 1987). Mosco's point is not simply that these claims about the democratising potential of cable television look silly with the benefit of over 30 years of hindsight, but that many of the claims bear a striking resemblance to those made about the transformative impact of the Internet 20 years later. His argument is that identifying myths as falsehoods is not sufficient, since myths about new media technologies arise in part out of the possibility that 'they offer an entrance into another reality, a reality once characterised by the promise of the sublime' (2004: 3). In doing so, Mosco draws attention to the pioneering analysis of Carey and Quirk (1992), who noted the ways in which contemporary prophecies about an 'electronic revolution', based on new ICTs, have parallels in the utopian projections for the future of humanity with electrical power in the late 19th century, particularly around the idea that industrial machinery and electrical technology could be harnessed in harmony with nature to provide both material prosperity and social peace. In observing the role of myth in relation to new media, therefore, we need not only to 'unmask ... fiction' (Mosco 2004: 3), but to draw out the lessons of history for understanding processes of technological innovation and diffusion, and to understand the complex and interconnected relationship between technology and culture in the formation of contemporary social realities.

Approaches to technological change

Many of the utopian propositions noted above, and elsewhere in this book, can be seen as being marked by *technological determinism*. While technological determinism is not a theory of technological change as such, it marks out a way of thinking (or perhaps not thinking) about the relationship between new technologies and society that has been quite pervasive. Williams (1974: 13) defined technological determinism as marking a view that 'research and development have been assumed as self-generating. The new technologies are invented ... in an independent sphere, and then create new societies or new human conditions'. The literature on the impact of the Internet is rich with examples of such arguments, as noted in this chapter. In relation to new media, Buckingham (2000: 45) has observed that in such arguments, 'the computer is predominantly seen as an autonomous force that is somehow independent of human society, and acts on it from the outside'.

Historical analysts of technology such as Winner (1986a,b), Cowan (1997) and MacKenzie and Wacjman (1999) have demonstrated the flawed logic of technological determinist arguments, and how these have played themselves out in practice. Recent examples relevant to new media include:

- the VCR/Beta wars of the 1980s, where the adoption of a common standard for video recorders had less to do with the inherent superiority of one format over another (some suggested that Beta was a superior format), than with the capacity of other video recorder hardware manufacturers to squeeze Sony (the principal promoter of Beta) out of the crucial US market
- the legal battles between Apple and Microsoft in the late 1990s over ownership of the 'desktop' graphical user interface, which indicated that GUIs did not simply 'evolve' from earlier to newer versions but that they might constitute highly lucrative forms of intellectual property
- the over-investment of telecommunications companies in '3G' wireless broadband spectrum in the early 2000s, driven by an assumption—largely untested—that users sought to access Internet content through their mobile phones
- the continued difficulties in developing digital television in many parts of the world, as the implications of a more economical use of spectrum come up against the resistance of incumbent broadcasters to the potential to develop new television services (Galperin 2004).

The approach taken in this book questions arguments about the relationship between new media technologies and society that can be seen as technologically determinist in nature. In doing so, there are two important caveats to be noted. The first surrounds the question of whether a cluster of related technologies have come to shape historical development over the long term. Heilbroner (2003) has argued that the generalisation of particular technological forms over time contains within it implicit forms of social organisation that are difficult to reverse through socio-political change. Castells (1996) develops a similar argument in his claims about the relationship of ICTs to a 'network society', which is that the development of the

Internet has enabled networks to become a generalised 'social morphology' of 21st-century society and culture. Second, it is important to observe that the 'partial truth' of technological determinism is that once particular technologies are widely adopted and used, they acquire a degree of 'lock-in' that shapes society and culture in a wider sense. Winner (1986a,b) made this point in relation to what he termed 'inherently political technologies' such as nuclear power, whose very existence requires hierarchical, command-and-control forms of internal organisation and high levels of external surveillance. In a different but related vein, Arthur's (1999) concept of *increasing returns to adoption* points to the extent to which a preferred commercial model—his example is the QWERTY typewriter keyboard and how it achieved dominance in the early 20th century—generates processes of adaptation by other large organisations, and skills development among prospective workers leads to technological 'lock-in' since the costs of change for individuals and organisations become too great to contemplate.

The major alternative to technological determinism is the *social shaping of technology* approach. This points to the need to analyse 'the socio-economic patterns embedded in both the *content of technologies* and the *processes of innovation*' (Williams & Edge 1996: 866). It is argued that social, institutional, economic, and cultural factors shape the choices made about which forms of technological innovation are advanced, the content of technological artefacts and practices, and the outcomes and impacts of technological change for different groups in society. This in turn requires a broader understanding of technology than simply its commonsense level of the *tools and artefacts used by humans to transform nature, enable social interaction, or extend human capacities*. As MacKenzie and Wacjman argue, this definition of technology as 'hardware' needs to be extended to a consideration of the uses to which such technologies are put, or their *contexts of use*, and the *systems of knowledge and social meaning that accompany their development and use*. This three-dimensional understanding of technology is apparent in French and German, where the words *la technique* and *die Technik* convey a meaning of technology that involves the tools, their uses, and associated forms of knowledge, as well as in the origins of the word 'technology' in Ancient Greek, as combining *techne*, or practical or applied arts and skills, and *logos*, or systematic reason, knowledge, or discourse (MacKenzie & Wacjman 1999: 7).

The broad framework of social shaping of technology approaches has within it three distinctive strands: the diffusion of innovations model; the political economy model; and theories of culture and technology. The *diffusion of innovations* model is particularly associated with the communications theorist Everett Rogers (2003), who sought to model the rate of adoption and eventual spread of an innovation in the social system through the communication via particular channels—influential individuals, related businesses, social networks—over time. Rogers' model identifies different categories of user, including early adopters, and the adoption threshold at which an innovation becomes a mature technology. In *The Invisible Computer*, Norman (1998) draws on Rogers' work to argue that there is a change in market focus from the attributes of the technology to its ease of use and ability to solve problems as it evolves through the diffusion cycle (Figure 3.1). The 'innovator's dilemma', discussed in Chapter 10, draws upon this framework to observe the dangers of developing more complex technological solutions at the stage in the product cycle where a technological product is becoming a mass-market commodity.

Whereas the diffusion of innovations approach tends to focus on social uptake of new technologies and have what Rogers acknowledged was a 'pro-innovation bias' (2003: 106), the *political economy* approach focuses much more specifically on the politics and power relations embedded in technological development. MacKenzie and Wacjman (1999) argued that an understanding of how technologies developed both historically and in the present era required that close attention be paid to dominant economic relations, social relations of production, military priorities, the role of the state, and gender relations. Similarly, Sholle (2002: 6) rejects the 'technology-as-tool-kit' approach in favour of a *critical theory of technology* which argues that 'technologies are

Figure 3.1 Consumer demand and the diffusion cycle

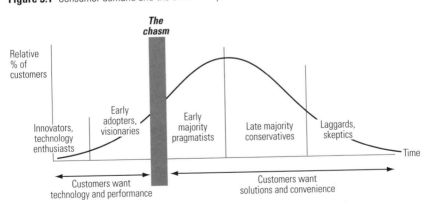

Source: Norman 1998: 30

... processes that structure the world in particular ways ... we should not see technology and the social as separate domains'. The political economy approach, and critical theories of technology more generally, draw attention to the ways in which politics, power, and economic relations are embedded in the process of scientific and technological research itself. This can occur directly, through the capacity of large corporations, government agencies, and the military to shape the research and training priorities of academic research through their provision of large-scale funding at a time when government funding and other traditional sources are being squeezed; Schiller (2000) argues that this has become increasingly central to Internet and other new media research. Less directly, but perhaps more profoundly, it is argued by Feenberg (2003) and others that 'Technological development is constrained by cultural norms originating in economics, ideology, religion, and tradition'. We are typically oblivious to this, since it is taken as given that there is an underlying *technological rationality*, or what Feenberg terms a 'technical code', that is 'not merely a belief, an ideology, but is effectively incorporated into the structure of machines' (2003: 657, 658). Picking up on Feenberg's critical theory of technology, Sholle (2002: 7) argues that:

> A technology such as the computer is a product of social processes from the beginning. The particular construction of knowledge in institutions of science and engineering, the economic interests of companies, the cultural patterns of consumption, the spatial arrangements of communities and nations, the political *motifs* of government policies are inscribed into the technology from the very beginning.

PIONEER MEDIA THEORISTS: MARSHALL McLUHAN AND RAYMOND WILLIAMS

The relationship between new media technologies and media content raises a series of complex issues about the social and cultural impacts of media themselves. While the new media discussed in this book have largely been developed and popularised since the 1990s, it is important to observe that the wider question of whether media technologies have the power to transform society and culture has a much wider and more longstanding provenance (cf. Lister et al. 2003: 72–92). Two of the key thinkers from the 1960s and 1970s were the Canadian communications theorist Marshall McLuhan and the British cultural theorist Raymond

Williams. In many ways, their respective approaches to the question of how media technologies relate to the wider society and culture have constituted two competing poles of thought about new media.

Marshall McLuhan was a controversial, original, and eclectic theorist whose work stressed the extent to which cultural content was embedded within specific technological forms, meaning that the media influence not only *what* we think but *how* we think. His work, developed in key texts such as *Understanding Media* (McLuhan 1964) and *The Medium is the Massage* (McLuhan & Fiore 1967), has always polarised opinions, with his advocates arguing that 'his was the first coherent interpretation of the electric world' (McLuhan & Zingrone 1997: 6), while his critics maintained that his writings had assumed 'an importance which has nothing to do with their worth' (Ricks 1968: 59). McLuhan's ideas became unfashionable during the 1970s and 1980s, particularly in light of the critique of technological determinism levelled by Raymond Williams and others (see below), but the rise of the Internet saw him championed as a visionary (see e.g. Wolf 1996; Levinson 1997; de Kerckhove 1998).

Central to McLuhan's theory of communications media is his well-known aphorism that 'the medium is the message'. What this meant was that technologies are first and foremost extensions of our human selves, which extend our human capacities: 'The personal and social consequences of any medium—that is, of any extension of ourselves—result from the new scale that is introduced into our affairs by each extension of ourselves, or by any new technology' (McLuhan 1964: 23). At the same time, the impact of any medium on the conduct of human affairs is neither transparent nor obvious. For McLuhan, the key to understanding electronic culture is not in the technologies themselves, such as machines or computers, nor in the uses of their content or alleged 'effects', but rather in the ways in which they subtly alter the environment in which humans act and interact. He proposed that the logic of the 'electric age' can be found in electric light, since it is pure information, 'a medium without a message', which can only have content when it is used in conjunction with another medium, for example the use of electric light to spell out a neon sign:

> The electric light escapes attention as a communication medium just because it has no 'content'. And this makes it an invaluable instance of how people fail to study media at all … The message of the electric light is like the message of electric power in industry, totally radical,

PIONEER MEDIA THEORISTS (*cont.*)

pervasive and decentralised. For electric light and power are separate from their uses, yet they eliminate time and space factors in human association exactly as do radio, telegraph, telephone and TV, creating involvement in depth. (McLuhan 1964: 24–5)

One implication of McLuhan's analysis was that 'the impact of the communication media on sensory perception influences not only what we think but how we think' (McPhail & McPhail 1990: 69). For McLuhan, the 'grammar' of a medium structures human sensory responses to it, fundamentally altering perceptions of social reality: 'All media work us over completely. They are so persuasive in their personal, political, economic, aesthetic, psychological, moral, ethical and social consequences that they leave no part of us untouched, unaffected, unaltered … Any understanding of social and cultural change is impossible without a knowledge of the way media work as environments' (McLuhan & Fiore 1967: 26).

In contrast to McLuhan's focus on how media technologies reshape society and culture, Raymond Williams was primarily interested in the question of how technologies are *shaped* by social, cultural, political, and economic forces. This stress on the *social shaping of technology* meant that Williams focused on the social forces, power relations, and conflicts between competing interests that led to some options being pursued while others are not developed or are actively foreclosed upon. For Williams, a failure to focus on the social dimensions of how technologies are developed and how they are used is an example of *technological determinism*, which he accused Marshall McLuhan of and which Williams believed was an ideology used by the powerful to support their own interests:

> If the effect of the medium is the same, whoever controls and uses it, and whatever apparent content he may try to insert, then we can forget ordinary political and cultural argument, and let the technology run itself. It is hardly surprising that this conclusion has been welcomed by the 'media-men' of the existing institutions. (Williams 1974: 131)

Using the historical development of television as his principal case study, Williams argued instead that the medium's development needed to be understood as arising from a series of primarily commercial investment decisions in the technologies of mass broadcast communication, which had been shaped by the development of radio and which promoted a relationship between technology and the wider society that was based around 'centralised transmission and privatised reception' (1974: 24). It both shaped, and was shaped by, a wider set of developments in industrial capitalist societies, such as mass production, the rise of consumer society, large-scale commercial investments in communications technologies, and the development of suburban housing that saw a spatial separation of home from places of work. Given these general features, Williams nonetheless also emphasised the significance of different institutional forms to the forms of broadcast television content which emerged, contrasting in particular the American commercial broadcasting system to the role played by the BBC as a public service broadcaster in the United Kingdom.

In the context of new media, the frameworks developed by Williams and McLuhan generate important differences in focus. The social shaping of technology approach that Williams championed draws attention to the decisions made in the development and adoption of new media technologies, which people, groups, and social institutions have the power to make such decisions, and what are the possible alternative uses of these technologies (cf. Winston 1998 for an extension of such themes). It thus draws attention to the political economy of communications media and technology. By contrast, McLuhan's approach stresses the extent to which societies and cultures become so immersed in modes of being and behaving that are shaped by their wider technological environment that our very ways of being human are inherently linked to the technological forms through which we extend our capacities and senses. Such an approach therefore questions the extent to which we can seek to understand culture independently of the technological forms through which it is always already mediated.

Further reading
Stevenson 1995; Levinson 1997; Winston 1998; Burnett & Marshall 2003; Lister et al. 2003: 72–92

Social psychology: Identity and interpersonal relations online

There has always been a strong interest in the social psychology of new media use, or what is also termed computer-mediated communication or CMC. Reasons for this range from the well-established interests of corporations in how best to target marketing to new consumers and governments and how to manage concerns about access to new media, to the interests of those who have seen CMC as harbingers of new forms of community, sociality, and identity formation. A curious feature of debates about new media and CMC has been the extent to which the concern has been about ensuring that children in particular have access to the new media, which has coexisted with *moral panics* about the dangers of access to pornography, violent video games, cyber-stalkers, and so on. While concerns about the adverse impacts of a new medium on children have been common (see Critcher 2006 for an overview of moral panic literature), new media debates have also been marked by a particular *visionary utopianism* (Buckingham 2000: 46), whereby the young—variously termed the 'N-Gen' (Tapscott 1998), the 'screenagers' (Rushkoff 1996), and the 'digital natives' (Prensky 2001)—are seen as being already immersed in a digital environment that promises a better world— more interactive, democratic, and communicative—than that of one-way broadcast media. This highly positive spin on the social psychology of the Internet had deep roots in the most influential literature of the 1990s.

Two of the most influential books of the 1990s on the social psychology of Internet use were Howard Rheingold's *The Virtual Community* (1994) and Sherry Turkle's *Life on the Screen: Identity in the Age of the Internet* (1995). To many, one or both of these books were their introduction to thinking about the world of CMC in any systematic way. Before then, CMC had tended to be viewed sceptically by communications specialists, concerned that the absence of visual and other non-verbal cues in online communication when compared to face-to-face interaction would make CMC a risky business (Baym 2005). What both Rheingold and Turkle brought to bear was a perspective that saw CMC as playful, fun, interactive, socially progressive, and very possibly a better world than that of your 'real' or 'offline' social experience. More-over, both developed their arguments from intellectually well-grounded and theoretically sophisticated positions that were, nonetheless, readily accessible to the lay reader.

In perhaps the most famous early account of CMC-based online cultures, Rheingold defined virtual communities as 'social aggregations that emerge from the Net when enough people carry on those public discussions [using the Internet] long enough, with sufficient human feeling, to form webs of personal relationships in cyberspace' (1994: 5). While recognising that the origins of the Internet lay in the US military-industrial-governmental complex, Rheingold observed that the democratic potential of CMC lay in the decentralised nature of such networked communications, which presented, in a way very different from one-to-many mass media, the possibility to 'piggy-back alternative networks on the mainstream infrastructure', and 'use CMC to create alternative planetary information networks' (1994: 14). Rheingold was enthusiastic about the development of virtual communities, seeing in them the possibility of a reinvigorated sense of community-building and citi-zen participation in public life. This potential arose from three interrelated attributes of CMC: the building of social networks and social capital; the sharing of knowledge and information; and the enabling of new modes of democratic participation in public life. With an optimism that was drawn from experiments in virtual community developed in the USA such as the Free-Nets and other community networks in cities such as Cleveland, Santa Monica, and Seattle (cf. Schuler 1996), Rheingold emphasised the elements of social choice and political activism that would be involved in the achievement of such outcomes:

> The technology that makes virtual communities possible has the potential to bring enormous leverage to ordinary citizens at relatively little cost—intellec-tual leverage, social leverage, commercial leverage and, most importantly, politi-cal leverage. But the technology will not in itself fulfil this potential—this latent technical power must be used intelligently and deliberately by an informed popu-lation. More people must learn about that leverage and learn to use it, while we still have the freedom to do so, if it is to live up to its potential. (1994: 4–5)

Turkle (1995) identified virtual communities as sites of play and perfor-mativity through the creation of online identities that were indicative of the transition from modernity to postmodernity. Turkle presented a detailed argument about how participants in various forms of online commu-nications—most notably MUDs (Multi-User Dungeons) and MOOs (Multi-User Object-Oriented Domain)—were engaged in forms of performativity online that differed significantly from their personas in 'real life' forms of social interaction. Drawing on psychoanalysis, Turkle found that participants in virtual communities increasingly came to view 'real life' as simply one 'window' through which a personality is developed and expressed, and that CMC constitutes a constructive and potentially liberatory space through which 'the obese can become slender, the beautiful plain, the "nerdy" sophisticated' (1995: 12). Turkle found in this possibility for the multi-plicity and performativity of identities in online environments a parallel both to postmodernist and post-structuralist arguments about the fluidity and fragmented nature of contemporary subjectivity, and to developments in human–computer interface interaction that promote 'surface' interaction over deep engagement with the technology. Turkle argued that through both identity play within CMC and the simplification of GUIs seen with Apple and Microsoft Windows, 'we are moving toward a culture of simulation in which people are increasingly comfortable with substituting representations of reality for the real' (1995: 23).

Like many of the prophetic enthusiasms of early Internet culture, the passage of time has seen the puncturing of some of these speculative balloons in favour of more empirically nuanced accounts of the nature of community and identity in CMC. It must be noted that they had their critics at the time. To take one example, Lockard (1997: 225) argued that 'cyberspace is to community what Rubber Rita [an inflatable sex toy] is to human companionship'. The novelty of CMC has also decreased over time, Herring (2004: 33) observed that many current students 'do not relate to the utopian and dystopian speculations of earlier decades, and find the debates of the 1990s about online democracy, identity and virtuality hyped and vaguely silly'. This point is not simply technological or generational. It also reflects a strong tendency in the 1990s Internet literature to counterpose the 'virtual' to the 'real', understanding the two as almost parallel universes into which people entered and left with varying degrees of personal commitment and intensity. Wellman and Haythornthwaite (2002) argued that speculative accounts of the Internet in terms of hype and counter-hype, as compared to more everyday forms of communication and interaction, were both poorly grounded empirically and deeply unhelpful in understanding how users integrate both into their everyday lives. Slater (2002: 544) argued that this dichotomy emerged at a transitional stage of new media research more generally, and that it is not surprising to find that, since a medium such as the Internet evolves in terms of technologies, user behaviours, questions of access, and legal and commercial environments, we would find a 'process of disaggregating "the Internet" into its diversity of technologies and uses, generating a media landscape in which virtuality is clearly not a feature of the media but one social practice of media use among many others'. This is not to reject the utility and importance of research into the social psychology of Internet use and CMC. It is, rather, to make the more modest claim that forms of community formation, civic engagement, and social interaction through CMC are likely to be diverse and contradictory, and 'it is better to ground this understanding of the complexity … in research than in speculation and assertion' (Rice & Haythornthwaite 2005: 108).

Technology and culture

Feenberg's (2003) observation that technology and culture are mutually constitutive has also been developed in work from a cultural studies perspective that understands new media as *cultural technologies*, or as assemblages of technology, content, context, power relations, and social knowledge. Berland (1992: 40) proposed that media as cultural technologies produce not only content (media texts), but also spatial arrangements and modes of consumption that 'are material practices with their own structural effects and tensions'. The concept of *technocultures* has been used by Penley and Ross (1991), Menser and Aronowitz (1996), and Green (2002) to refer to 'tools of mediated communication through which cultural material is created and circulated' (Green 2002: xxx–xxxi). Green makes the important point that, while all technologies have cultural impacts (think, for instance, of the myriad cultural implications of the automobile), media technologies have a particular significance in this regard. Media technologies enable the circulation of what Thompson (1991: 132) termed 'symbolic forms … by virtue of which individuals communicate with one another and share their experiences, conceptions and beliefs'.

The significance of this conception of culture as communication mediated through technologies becomes apparent when we recognise that, just as the concept of technology has three levels of meaning, so too does culture. First, there is the level of aesthetics, which equates culture with the arts, and both with schemata of cultural value (cf. Frow 1995). Cultural studies have drawn attention to a second, more *anthropological* definition of culture as *the whole way of life, or forms of lived experience, of people, communities, and social groups.* Such an expanded definition of culture draws attention to the significance of forms of communication, social relations, and practices of everyday life to an understanding of culture, as was observed by Raymond Williams in *The Long Revolution*:

> Culture is the description of a particular way of life, which expresses certain meanings and values not only in art and learning but also in institutions and ordinary behaviour … Such analysis will … include analysis of elements in the way of life that to followers of the other definitions are not 'culture' at all; the organisation of production, the structure of the family, the structure of institutions which express or govern social relationships, the characteristic forms through which members of the society communicate. (1965: 57–8)

In addition to artistic and intellectual activity, and the ways of life of communities or groups, there is a third level of meaning of culture, derived from semiotics, structural anthropology, communications theory, and theories of ideology, which is what Thompson (1991: 136) refers to as the *structural conception of culture*. This conception of culture 'emphasizes *both* the symbolic character of cultural phenomena *and* the fact that such phenomena are always embedded in structured social contexts'. Noting the observation of the famous semiotician Umberto Eco (1976: 9) that 'every act of communication … presupposes a signification system as its necessary condition', this structuralist approach to culture draws attention to the ways in which individuals are 'produced' as social beings within a given system of social, cultural, linguistic, and psychological relationships, which possessed an underlying structural 'code' not necessarily accessible to those individuals who were expected to adopt and conform to such codes. Drawing out the implications of this for new media studies, Poster (2005: 136) observes that 'computer-mediated communication fundamentally shifts the registers of human experience as we have known them in modern society … Time and space, body and mind, subject and object, human and machine are each dramatically transformed by practices carried out on networked computers'. Table 3.2 provides a summary of these perspectives.

Table 3.2 Defining technology and culture: A three-level approach

	Definition of technology	Definition of culture
First level, 'common sense' definitions	Technology as physical objects, tools, artefacts	Culture as 'the arts' and aesthetics excellence
Second level, 'contextual' or user-based definitions	Technology as content or 'software', defined by how it is used	Culture as 'ways of life' or lived experience of peoples, communities, or groups
Third level, 'Communicative' or 'structural' definitions	Technology as systems of knowledge and social meaning	Culture as underlying 'structural system'

Political economy and cultural studies

The wider relationship between political economy and cultural studies approaches to media has been discussed in detail in Flew (2007). Putting it simply, *political economy approaches* tend to start from the perspective of *economic and industrial dynamics*. They focus on the extent to which *access to resources* at various levels influences the directions that new media developments take, and on those possibilities and affordances that are not adopted because those proposing them lacked sufficient power resources. These include access to investment capital to participate in new media ventures, access to political influence on the basis of economic power and significance as a decision-maker, and access to the technologies themselves on the part of potential users, with the focus on inequalities of access across all of these levels, which are seen as mapping on various indicators of social inequality, such as class, gender, race, ethnicity, and other markers of disadvantage.

Theorists such as McChesney (1999, 2000, 2002), Schiller (2000; cf. McChesney & Schiller 2003), Mosco (1996, 1997, 2000, 2004), Gandy (2002), and Murdock and Golding (2004) have been among the most influential contributors to developing a political economy approach to new media. For the most part, this work is sceptical about claims that new media have led to fundamental changes in the socio-economic structures into which they are seen as being embedded. In an essay debunking claims that the rise of the Internet presages new forms of democratic media politics, McChesney (2000: 33–4) has observed that 'despite its much-ballyhooed "openness" … [the Internet] will likely be dominated by the usual corporate suspects. Certainly a few new commercial players will emerge, but the evidence suggests that the content of the digital communications world will appear quite similar to that of the pre-digital commercial media world'. Similarly, Kumar (2005: 154) argued that developments associated with new media and the knowledge economy have not produced a radical shift in the dynamics of capitalist societies since 'the imperatives of profit, power and control seem as predominant now as they have ever been in the history of capitalist industrialism. The difference lies in the greater range and intensity of their applications … not in any change in the principles themselves'.

Cultural studies approaches start from the perspective of *communications and culture*, and the complexities that arise and the power relations that emerge in the relationship between the production, reception, interpretation, and use of messages arising from technologically mediated forms. While they have a common lineage with political economy in their historical relationship to neo-Marxism and critical theory, the *active audience* tradition within this field has seen it tend towards more positive assessments of the transformative potential of new media. Jenkins (2006a) captures the extent to which, from a cultural studies perspective, the relationship between producers and users of new media constitutes a contested space akin to earlier work in cultural studies on the relationship between popular culture and hegemony (cf. Hartley 2003; Flew 2007: 39–43):

> We are entering an era of prolonged transition and transformation in the way media operates. Convergence describes the process by which we will sort through these options ... Media producers will only find their way through these current problems by renegotiating their relationship with their consumers. Audiences, empowered by these new technologies, occupying a space at the intersection between old and new media, are demanding the right to participate within the culture ... The resulting struggles and compromises will define the public culture of the future. (Jenkins 2006a: 24)

The general rule of thumb has been that those working from a more cultural studies-oriented perspective have tended to be more optimistic about the potentialities of new media. By contrast, those working from a more political economy-based perspective have tended to be more sceptical about the transformative capacities of new media, stressing more strongly the continuities between 'old' and 'new' media. At the same time, this correlation is complicated at several points. The work of Manuel Castells, for instance, seeks to fuse the insights of political economy and cultural studies around an argument that new media technologies have been transformative in ways that have not been seen since the 'print revolution' of the 16th century.

From a perspective grounded in Marxist political economy, Graham (2006: 16) has argued that the current phase of what he calls *hypercapitalism* has transformed the dynamics of capitalist economies so fundamentally that 'use-values and exchange-values are not necessarily separable in a knowledge economy'. Similarly, the work of Tiziana Terranova emphasises the extent to which a strategic response to what she terms the 'cultural politics of information' requires a break with conceptions of information that see it simply as communications content that requires subsequent critical decoding, or as 'immaterial' and of a second order to the dynamics of industrial production (2004: 3).

At the same time, there has been debate within cultural studies over its relationship to new media. Bassett (2007) has noted the extent to which the focus of cultural studies on the *politics of signification* found in critical interrogation of the sender-text–message-receiver relationship often effaced the significance of the media technologies themselves as drivers in their own right of systems of meaning. Drawing on Terranova's (2004: 9) argument that in the context of ubiquitous and ever expanding new forms of digital media derived from informational networks 'there is no meaning ... outside of an informational milieu that exceeds and undermines the domain of meaning from all sides', Bassett proposes that a cultural studies practice oriented towards new media needs to engage with the forms of political engagement that are specific to digitally networked media, such as 'tactical media' (Cubitt 2006) and 'hacktivism' (Dyer-Witheford 2002; O'Neil 2006), while also requiring the '(re)incorporation of the political economy of new media into cultural studies' (Bassett 2007: 234).

 ## USEFUL WEBSITES

H2O Playlist: Political Economy of New Media <http://h2obeta.law.harvard.edu/78774>. Compiled by Vincent Reynauld of Carleton University, this is a blog site housed with the Berkman Center for Internet & Society at the Harvard Law School.

McLuhan Program in Culture and Technology <www.mcluhan.utoronto.ca>. Provides useful resources, and contemporary applications, of the work of Marshall McLuhan.

MIT Communications Forum <http://web.mit.edu/comm-forum>. A site that captures many of the leading international contributions on new media, particularly through the papers from MIT's annual *Media-in-Transition* conferences.

04

ten key contemporary new media theorists

Is 'new media theory' a useful and relevant concept?

There are two questions central to any consideration of the relevance of new media theory. The first is whether there is a need for theory at all in the design and application of new media. In relation to film, the British filmmaker Alan Parker once said that 'film needs theory like it needs a scratch on the negative' (quoted in Lapsley & Westlake 2006: 1), suggesting that 'theory' is something that only gets in the way of media production. The 'Media Wars' debates in Australia, which revolved around the relationship between journalism and media and cultural studies, saw writers arguing that requiring journalism students to do courses in media and cultural studies marked a detour through academic theory that would be of no practical relevance to their future careers (Flew & Sternberg 1999; Windschuttle 2000; Flew et al. 2007). The large number of new media, digital media, and multimedia courses that are offered by commercial providers, which focus on learning how to use software applications and develop programming skills without any reference to 'theory', is a clear indication that this is also a wider sectoral view that privileges production, and learning the tools of digital media production, over new media theory.

The second question is whether there are any innate characteristics of new media that require the development of new media theory. In other words, what is the *new* component of new media theory? Robert McChesney (2000: 33), as we saw in Chapter 3, proposed that the World Wide Web would be dominated by the 'usual corporate suspects'. This approach, which has been a common one in political economy, sees new media as marking out the latest stage of capitalism, whose principal theoretical concepts are seen as largely given (e.g. monopoly capitalism, commodification, corporate power). The communications theorist Dennis McQuail, in his widely used text *Mass Communication Theory*, observed that 'although "new media theory" does open the way for the decline or end of mass communication, it has not really introduced any fundamentally new issues of communication theory' (2002: 19).

This chapter takes issue with these claims that new media theory is irrelevant to creative or professional digital media practice, or that its developments are largely explicable within existing social and media theory paradigms. The sheer quantitative growth of all things related to new media, and the extent to which they are generating significant qualitative changes in society, culture, and the economy more generally, suggest the need for new modes of thinking to accompany these developments, and it remains the role of theory to provide us with signposts to guide us through such new questions. At the same time, this is not to suggest that a qualitative change in media technologies requires the dismantling of prior systems of thought. As the work of authors such as Castells, Flichy, Livingstone, Schiller, and Miller and Slater shows, the insight from disciplines such as history, sociology, media and communications studies, and political economy continue to provide necessary anchor-points that can challenge some of the more utopian imaginings of new media theory.

The term 'new media' points to some interesting changes in the way in which the relationship of theory to practice, or to its object of study, also needs to change. First, Kress (1997) has argued the need for theories seeking to develop media literacy in the digital media context to move from critique, or the critical scrutiny of media texts in order to reveal their rules of formation and their limitations as representations of social reality, to design, with a focus on how multiple representational forms can be combined, orchestrated, and remade in order to generate new forms of meaning. While the capacity for critique is a necessary element of effective design, the social role of the designer is different from that of the critic and, Kress argues, one that becomes more important in periods of transformative technological and cultural change. As a result, critique that seeks wider influence will need to work much more directly with new media designers than was the case with 20th-century mass media. Terranova (2004) and Bassett (2007) have argued that new media theories have been strongly influenced by fields such as cybernetics and information theories, rather than the more conventional coordinates of critical theory and cultural studies. McNair (2006) has also observed that insights associated with 'chaos theory' in the natural sciences, such as the importance of non-linear change, disruptive technologies, learning objects, and generic mutation, are highly relevant to the study of global news and journalism.

Manuel Castells

Manuel Castells has been the most significant social theorist of new media in the last two decades. With his three-volume *The Information Age: Economy, Society and Culture* series (1996, 1998, 2000a), he aimed to develop an understanding of the 21st-century 'Information Age' that parallels the foundational social theories of Karl Marx of 19th-century capitalism, and Max Weber of 20th-century modernity. The central organising concept of this work is the idea that we now live in a global network society that is decisively shaped by new media and ICTs as the dominant *techno-economic paradigm*, and this has been a foundational contribution to new media theory.

Castells' early work was in Marxist urban sociology, where he sought to understand class struggles as they developed in urban spaces, developing the concept of *collective consumption* as a way of understanding new forms of social conflict based around forms of urban social amenity such as housing, transport, health, and public space (1977, 1978). In the 1980s, his work branched out into two new and distinct directions. First, he became increasingly interested in *new social movements* such as feminism, environmentalism, gay and lesbian rights movements, and movements of racial and ethnic minorities, as well as the changing politics and cultural geography of cities (1983). Second, in his work on the informational city (1989) he began to develop an analysis of the role of information technologies in economic restructuring, and their relationship to the globalisation of economic activity and the reorganisation of urban and regional spaces.

Four themes can be derived from Castells' early work that can be seen as central to his later work in the *Information Age* trilogy. First, he argues that the development of network structures and architectures is a core feature of the contemporary social condition. These networks are not controlled by anyone but extend outward from computing and ICTs to all forms of social, economic, and cultural relations, and to the realm of human biology through genetic engineering and biotechnology. Second, networks as a *social morphology* and globalisation as an economic and cultural experience are inextricably interconnected, but they do not imply greater global homogenisation. Third, all aspects of the self—identity, experience, relationships—are bound up with the network society, but the implications of this are neither uniformly utopian nor uniformly dystopian. They promote, on the one hand, new forms of inclusion and exclusion from systems of power, production, and engagement with systems of meaning (media as culture), whose impacts are increasingly uneven both within and between societies. On the other hand, they also generate a diverse range of *resistance identities*, which may be deemed 'progressive' or 'reactionary' on a traditional Left–Right political spectrum, but tend to focus on a recapturing of control over something that is local and tangible, in the face of forms of networked power that appear increasingly remote and intangible, while also—and perhaps ironically—using the technologies, techniques, and symbols of new media in such struggles. Finally, Castells identifies what he terms *statism*, or the ability to regain control over these networked systems of power, production, and experience through political control over nation-states, as a political strategy that is no longer tenable in the transition from 20th-century industrial society to the 21st-century *informational mode of development*.

Patrice Flichy

The work of Patrice Flichy has been vital to addressing the seemingly paradoxical topic of new media history. It seems odd at first sight to be doing histories of new media, since the nature of the technologies and the patterns and contexts of their use are constantly changing. At the same time, as was noted in Chapter 3, the absence of a historical perspective in relation to new media frequently generates the unproductive cycles of hype and counter-hype that so often punctuate new media discourse.

Flichy (2005a: 188) has argued that a historical perspective on media technologies draws our attention to the fact that 'there is never a single technical solution' to how to develop a new media technology, but rather 'several solutions are studied in parallel [and] the historian has to study these solutions and analyse both successes and failures'. He identifies two concepts as being central to understanding the dynamics of new media history, and why some forms are diffused and proliferate, whereas others stagnate and wither. The first is that of *boundary objects*, or objects that can be 'situated at the intersection of several social worlds', and can therefore bring together the diverse communities involved in decisions about technical innovation, ranging from scientists and engineers to financiers, marketers, suppliers, and end-users. The second is that of *path dependency*. Drawn from the work of economic historian Paul David (1985), path dependency refers to the extent to which, once certain choices are made about the development and diffusion of a technological form, there is a degree of lock-in that leads to a generalisation of that technological form as it is adopted by multiple users and relevant agents, as there are costs associated with not adopting the existing form.

These two concepts are vital to understanding how Flichy constructs the history of the Internet around what he terms an *Internet imaginaire*. He proposes that, from the initial thinking about networked computing in the 1960s to the present, there has been a driving myth around the Internet as both the product and harbinger of collective intelligence and imagination. This utopian vision has animated decision-making about its development to the point where the Internet became a 'self-realising prophecy', since 'by repeatedly convincing ourselves and others that it is going to be the main tool of a new society, we actually make it happen. Talking about the technology often amounts to doing it, or at least diffusing it' (Flichy 2007: 2).

Form the 1960s to the development of the World Wide Web in the early 1990s, Flichy argues that the continuous development of the Internet, and ARPANET in particular, was driven by the ideals and values of what he terms the 'republic of computer specialists'. Central to this value system were a belief in interaction and cooperation between a community of specialists, or a computing 'cyber college'; a merit-based system derived from continuous peer review and feedback; a belief in cooperation and transparency as being at the core of network development; and the Internet as a 'world apart' from other areas of society. These values held sway for as long as they did because these computer specialists were both the designers and the users of the network; generous access to public funding from the US government insulated them from the demands of industry and the commercial market.

In the 1990s, this of course changed with the mass popularisation of the World Wide Web and the Internet, and the growing role of business in the Internet's future development. The underlying 'network ideology' was, however, replicated in the popularisation of the Internet during this decade, through pioneering texts such as Howard Rheingold's *The Virtual Community* (1994), magazines such as the San Francisco-based *WIRED*, and associations such as the Electronic Frontier Foundation. In such ways, Flichy argues, a digerati (cf. Brockman 1996) emerged that could mediate relations between designers, users, the business community, governments, and the wider public, that preserved core foundational values of the *Internet imaginaire* even as the material conditions of its development and diffusion were being profoundly altered. Flichy's historical analysis has parallels in the work of Mosco (2004) on 'cyberspace myths' and the 'digital sublime' discussed in Chapter 3.

Henry Jenkins

Henry Jenkins has been a key theorist of new media and media convergence from the perspective of its users and participatory culture. His 2006 book *Convergence Culture: When Old and New Media Collide* builds upon his pioneering work on media fan culture in *Textual Poachers* (Jenkins 1992). In his early work, Jenkins used the concept of 'poaching', as developed in Michel de Certeau's *The Practice of Everyday Life* (1984), to understand the ways in which media fans reappropriate the content of popular media culture to serve their own needs, build communities, and develop their own practices of reading and systems of meaning through these media texts. Jenkins' analysis of 'Trekkies' (*Star Trek* fans) is particularly well known in this respect, and the analysis builds on subcultural theories as well as ethnographic audience research.

Convergence culture is based around the relationship between three concepts: media convergence; participatory culture; and collective intelligence. It understands *media convergence* as 'the flow of content across multiple media platforms' (Jenkins 2006a: 2), but differs from other approaches to convergence by seeing this not so much as a consequence of the merging media forms themselves through digital technologies, but rather as a new level of engagement with media by its users, as 'consumers are encouraged to seek out new information and make connections among dispersed media content' (2006a: 3).

Participatory culture draws attention to the transformation of media communication in the early 21st century from a system of mass communication, based on one-to-many message transmission and a structural separation between the producers and consumers of media, to one where both now constitute 'participants who interact with each other according to a new set of rules that none of us fully understands' (2006a: 3). Multiplayer online game cultures are perhaps the exemplars of such trends, but they are occurring across media forms such as television (*YouTube*, *connect.tv*) and media professions such as journalism (blogging and citizen journalism). Again, the point for Jenkins is that this is enabled rather than driven by the technologies themselves: reality television programs such as *Big Brother* and *Survivor* are powerfully driven by the intersection between media convergence and participatory culture, even if they appear on what has been considered by some to be the 'old' medium of broadcast television.

Collective intelligence refers to the power of networked communities in developing knowledge systems that are not only greater than the sum of their individual parts, but that grow, evolve, and collectively learn through ongoing interaction. The impact of new media, and particularly Web 2.0, on such processes can be understood if we contrast an icon of print-based knowledge, the *Encyclopedia Brittanica*, to the *Wikipedia*. The first drew on the collective intelligence of multiple authors to develop a definitive information system, but was limited by both cost (most people accessed *Brittanica* through public libraries) and interaction (readers could agree or disagree with the text's contents, but could not change them). The *Wikipedia* is also collectively authored, but is freely available to all who have a networked personal computer, and gives its readers the capacity to comment on, revise, or question its content.

Jenkins' work is grounded in a cultural studies-based approach to new media that focuses on the perspective of its users. It connects up with the arguments of authors such as Stephen Johnson (2005) that, contrary to the dire predictions of many that popular media culture is 'dumbing down' those who consume it, there is instead a cyclical relationship between audience demand for more complex media forms, the growing textual sophistication of media producers, and more interactive new media technologies, which is producing more complex forms of popular culture that engage the brain more systematically. Importantly, Jenkins' work consistently stresses that it is the 'work' performed by media users themselves, rather than the technological innovations, that is the driver of such transformations.

Scott Lash

In *Critique of Information* the sociologist and critical theorist Scott Lash argued that the rise of the global information order is marked by a fundamental blurring of the distinction between technology and culture. This means that critiques of relations of power, inequality, and domination of such a technological and informational culture can no longer operate outside it, but rather must operate within the networks and flows of this informational culture. In relation to academic work, this means that 'socio-cultural theory itself at the turn of the twenty-first century increasingly must take on the form of information, increasingly take on the form of media ... theory will be increasingly in the same genre as information, as media' (2002: 65).

For Lash, three shifts are critical to understanding global information culture. First, there is the extent to which global flows are challenging national economic, political, and cultural relations. Second, there is the shift in the dominant economic sectors from manufacturing to services and information, which entails not only the rise of the ICT and new media industries, but also the increasingly information-based nature of commodities and production processes (cf. Lash & Urry 1989). Third, there is a decline in the role and significance of established social institutions, and a rise in more fluid, flexible, and less structured cultural forms of association grounded in affective relations mediated by electronic communication. As a consequence of these shifts, for Lash, 'the new economy is thus a *communications* economy. It is an economy less of accumulation of capital or information than one of flows. These flows ... are communications in the broadest sense' (2002: 205).

Lash argues that social and cultural theory thus increasingly become *media theory*. This is both in the sense of having to engage with a social order whose primary economic and interpersonal relations are increasingly driven by technological culture and where 'the cultural superstructure to which the media belong become part and parcel of the economic base' (2002: 76), and in the sense of needing to engage with the forms of 'immediacy' and global networks which characterise media culture in order to have any impact (2002: xii).

Lash has been critiqued by Milner (2006: 119), who argues that global information culture is presented here as 'a technological inevitability' rather than as a 'site of struggle'. Lash's argument is that what he refers to as media theory is 'only possible in an age in which social and cultural life have been pervaded by the media' (2002: 66).

> Media theory would not ... make a lot of sense without the spread of computing (information), the Internet (communication), the coming to a position of prominence of the culture industries ... and the proliferation of fast-moving consumer goods, of the global brands. It is all of these that make our society and culture a media society and a media culture. (2002: 67)

Lawrence Lessig

Lawrence Lessig is Professor of Law at the Stanford Law School, and director of the Centre for Internet and Society at Stanford. He is a prolific author, commentator, blogger, and Internet law activist, and his key books include *Code and other Laws of Cyberspace* (2000), *The Future of Ideas: The Fate of the Commons in a Connected World* (2001), and *Free Culture: How Big Media Uses Technology and the Law to Lock Down Creativity and Control Culture* (2004). He is also the founder and CEO of Creative Commons, a global movement dedicated to building 'a layer of reasonable, flexible copyright in the face of increasingly restrictive default rules' (see Chapter 11 on Creative Commons). As an Internet lawyer and activist on behalf of those who support greater openness of access to digital content, and oppose forms of copyright and other laws that serve to restrict such access artificially. He has also been a high-profile participant in relevant US Supreme Court cases relating to this, such as *Eldred v. Ashcroft*, to be discussed in detail in Chapter 11.

In *Code and Other Laws of Cyberspace* and *The Future of Ideas*, Lessig argued that law and legislation played a critical role in shaping the *architecture of the Internet*. Moreover, the code as it is developed in the most influential and widely used software packages governs user behaviour in ways that are akin to those of the legal system; to quote one of Lessig's more famous aphorisms, 'Code is Law' (2000: 6). Lessig described digital communications systems as having an architecture that consists of three layers:

1   A *physical* layer, which is the network through which communications travels, and communications devices are connected to one another.
2   A *code* layer, constituted by the code or software which operates communications hardware devices, as well as the protocols through which devices interconnect.
3   A *content* layer, which is the content that is delivered through the communications infrastructure.

For Lessig, the truly distinctive feature of the Internet was the way in which its end-to-end (e2e) architecture ensured that the network itself operated in a relatively simple manner that was indifferent to its various users, and whose intelligence was concentrated at the 'ends' of the network, rather than within the network itself. It was also reliant on a code (HTML) for content development that was easy to learn and easy to teach to others (in an age of Web 2.0, even this condition is now redundant). For Lessig, the result was that the Internet has evolved as a communications infrastructure where both its physical layers and its layers of code are free. They are neutral, non-rivalrous resources available to all without needing to seek the permission of others. As a result, the ability to produce content for the Internet can occur through processes that are almost infinitely decentralised. Lessig thus argued that the Internet's development has developed an *information commons* that promotes continuous innovation. For Lessig, the commons has three aspects:

> One is a commons of code—a commons of software that built the Net and many of the applications that run on the Net. A second is a commons of knowledge—a free exchange of ideas and information about how the Net, and code that runs on the Net, runs. And a third is the resulting commons of innovation built by the first two together—the opportunity, kept open to anyone, to innovate and build upon the platform of the network. (2001: 49)

The catch is the manner in which such technological and creative possibilities come up against the hard realities of corporate control, the seeking of monopoly rents through devices such as copyright law, and the capacity of powerful established corporate interests to hold undue influence over governments and legislators. In *The Future of Ideas*, Lessig discussed the potential for the 'code' layer of the Internet to be transformed from a relatively open to a proprietary environment, where dominant industry players can shape the direction of innovation in order to best protect their own interests, so that corporations such as Microsoft could use their 'power over the Windows platform to protect the Windows platform from innovation that would threaten it' (2001: 246).

Lessig's general argument has been that 'We as a society should favour the disrupters. They will produce movement toward a more efficient, prosperous economy' (2001: 92). In *Free Culture*, Lessig argues that creativity and innovation are best served by information and culture that is as widely available as possible, 'to guarantee that follow-on creators and innovators remain *as free as possible* from the control of the past' (2004: xiv). This idea of an 'information commons' or a 'creative commons' is, however, threatened by government and legal initiatives, backed by powerful corporate interests, to strengthen already existing intellectual property rights even as the technological foundations on which they have rested are continuously eroding. For Lessig, this creates the danger of a '"permission culture"—a culture in which creators get to create only with the permission of the powerful, or of the creators of the past' (2004: xiv), with a cost not only to personal liberties and creative capacities, but with significant adverse economic consequences.

Sonia Livingstone

Sonia Livingstone's work on new media provides a key link between audience/reception studies in relation to broadcast media and the Internet, and approaches derived from social psychology and emergent perspectives from political economy and cultural studies (see e.g. Livingstone 1998, 2002). Livingstone's work has sought to understand the epistemological foundations of 'new media studies' and how these relate to the methodological choices of new media researchers.

The field of new media studies is problematised from a research perspective in two ways that are quite distinct. First, the origins of the Internet and new media technologies have emerged at the interface of information technology systems, communications practices, information management, systems of social meaning, and creative practice, and the possibility of convergence across these domains remains difficult if nonetheless highly sought after. As a result, new media as an object of research can appear very different as approached from disciplinary paradigms as diverse as computer science, sociology, social psychology, political economy, applied economics, the applied humanities, and the creative arts.

The second problematic aspect of new media research is the shifting nature of the Internet as an object of research. Livingstone has argued that 'the case for asserting the existence of, and importance of, Internet studies lies ... less in the distinctiveness of its theories or methods than in the distinctiveness of its object' (2005: 12). The Internet of the late 2000s, with its ubiquitous video and audio feeds through sites such as *YouTube*, is for its users a different Internet from the overwhelmingly text-based medium of the late 1990s. At the same time, the question of whether the 'Internet experience' has changed depends critically on the social question of 'which users', which in turn refers us back to issues of access: in the first instance to the networked computer technologies themselves, and in the second to the high-speed broadband networks that enable access to new forms of online media content.

Livingstone has explored, from an applied and policy-oriented perspective, a range of issues including children's use of the Internet, media consumption and citizen engagement with public life and politics, the changing role of media regulation around perceptions of risk, and media literacy in a convergent new media environment. Livingstone (2005) has defined media literacy as 'the ability to access, analyse, evaluate, and create messages across a variety of contexts', and has identified its core components as involving questions of *access* to the media technologies themselves; the capacity for *analysis* of diverse media forms; the scope to develop capacities for *evaluation* of media content that do not simply reproduce existing hierarchies of taste and judgment; and the ability to move from consumption to *content creation*, and the analytical as well as technical skills connected to this.

Daniel Miller and Don Slater

Bracketing Daniel Miller and Don Slater together is not intended to deny their individual contributions to new media research (e.g. Miller 1998; Slater 2002) or the work undertaken with other collaborators (e.g. Horst & Miller 2006). The purpose is to draw attention to the significance of their ethnographic study of Internet use in Trinidad (Miller & Slater 2000) to the move from speculative theorising about the Internet towards more empirical culture as everyday life from culture as mediated communication. Miller and Slater's *The Internet: An Ethnographic Approach* (2000) is a key text in the move of new media studies towards a 'new empirics' (Flew 2001) that questioned notions such as 'cyberspace' and 'the virtual' in favour of grounded research into how new media use was embedded in the everyday lives and cultural practices of specific communities.

A key driver of Miller and Slater's work on Internet use in Trinidad was their rejection of Internet research that 'focuses on the way in which the new media seemed able to constitute spaces or places *apart from* the rest of social life ("real life" or offline life), spaces in which new forms of sociality were emerging, as well as bases for new identities' (2000: 4). Their empirical finding that Trinidadians had a '"natural affinity" for the Internet' (2000: 2) was, somewhat counter-intuitively, used to question assumptions about the allegedly 'disembedded' nature of CMC in cyberspace. They argued instead for 'the need to treat Internet media as continuous with and embedded in other social spaces, [and] that they happen within mundane social structures that they may transform but they cannot escape into a self-enclosed cyberian apartness' (2000: 5).

Miller and Slater's ethnographic work rejected the assumptions about the distinction between the 'real' and the 'virtual' that underpin this approach at all levels, arguing that 'this way of writing about the impact of the Internet seems to us quite wrong for the case of Trinidad' (2000: 8). The empirical propositions developed in *The Internet* that work against such a dichotomy between the real and the virtual include the widespread access to and use of the Internet across all sections of Trinidadian society; the use of the Internet to maintain diasporic relations among family and friends between Trinidadians in the national homeland and abroad (e.g. students in the USA and Canada); and the use of websites to represent Trinidad and promote Trini identity. Miller and Slater conclude their text by arguing that it 'has been a book about material culture—not about technology', and that 'it has been about an integral aspect of people's daily lives ... not about a virtual world that stands against and deifies or supersedes something else called the real' (2000: 193).

Mark Poster

Mark Poster has sought to analyse the implications of new media for the self, identity, culture, and social relations from a critical social theory perspective. Poster argues, however, that critical social and cultural theory has not dealt in sufficient depth with the implications of new media for relations between people, technology, and information. A recurring theme of Poster's work has been that, as a result, critical theorists have tended to underestimate the extent of the social and cultural changes arising from new media technologies.

The Mode of Information (1990) sought to apply post-structuralist theory to new modes of electronically mediated communication, and to illustrate how new media technologies served to decentre and reconstitute subjectivities through new ways of organising and presenting information. It linked the work of key post-structuralist and postmodernist theorists such as Jean Baudrillard, Michel Foucault, Jacques Derrida, and Jean-Francois Lyotard to media phenomena such as television advertising, computer databases, hypertext writing, and virtual communities.

The Second Media Age (1995) refined and sharpened some of these themes, as the popularisation of the Internet was giving clearer shape to what new communicative practices associated with new media might look like. The idea of a 'second media age' pointed to the differences between broadcast media as they had developed in the 20th century, with one-way communication flows, highly centralised control, and a clear distinction between producers and audiences, to those of the 21st century, 'characterised by a decentralized network of communications [that] makes senders receivers, producers con-sumers, rulers ruled, upsetting the logic of understanding of the first media age' (1995: 33). Poster's argument was that new media were reconstituting conceptions of the self and subjectivity, but also that the 'second media age' was not an overthrow of the first, but rather an extension of some of the structural tendencies associated with a growing 'mediatisation' of society and culture.

In *What's the Matter with the Internet* (2001) the concept of *underdetermination* was introduced by Poster as a way of understanding both how the Internet differed from other media forms and what that implied for the constitution of identity. He argued that subjective identities were not only already being formed and shaped by technology—the ways in which personal information is coded, mapped, and organised on computer databases is a clear example of this—but there was also the scope to 'play' with subjective identity, through the many-to-many, globally networked, and interactive communications apparatuses of new media.

Poster has argued that the Internet needs to be thought of less as a communications tool and more as a social space in which roles are played, identities are formed and re-formed, and meaning is reconfigured. As he puts it, 'the Internet is more like a social space than a thing, so that its effects are more like those of Germany than those of hammers' (2001: 176). A focus on the effects of Internet technology is therefore misplaced, because it misunderstands the extent to which culture and identity are already formed through technology.

POSTMODERNISM AND NEW MEDIA: A CASE STUDY IN CULTURAL STUDIES

There was a natural affinity between theories of postmodernism and new media as they co-developed during the 1990s. Both drew attention to discontinuities between the past and the present, between representational and post-representational forms, the implications of mass media for understandings of culture, the questioning of 'master narratives' of progress and the authority of scientific knowledge, and the significance of identity as a form of performativity and play that was not simply given by established social categories such as gender, race, sexuality, ethnicity, and social class. The implicit link between postmodernism as a category of cultural, political, and social theory was made explicit by theorists such as Poster (1990, 1995) and Turkle (1995), who saw developments in new media such as two-way communication and the development of 'virtual' identities in online environments as emblematic

POSTMODERNISM AND NEW MEDIA (*cont.*)

of emergent postmodern forms of identity formation, whereby the 'self on the screen' through CMC was in an ongoing relationship of game-play with the geographically distant others with whom they engaged.

Postmodernism has been a notoriously difficult concept to define. One reason for this is that it invariably sits in some relationship to modernism, so any attempt to explicate what is postmodern needs to engage in a critical dialogue with that deemed to be modern; as a result, debates about whether a particular cultural/symbolic form or practice exhibits 'modernist' or 'postmodernist' elements is endemic to the field (Frow 1994). The second is that a distinction is often made between *postmodernity* as a new stage of society and culture, and *postmodernism* as referring to particular artistic and cultural forms and processes (Bell & Kellner 1991; Kumar 1995). This parallels the distinction made between modernity as a socio-economic, political, and cultural condition, and modernism as a series of movements, strategies, and cultural activities—particularly in the arts—that sought to engage critically with modern societies.

Collins (1992) provided a useful summary of the principal elements of postmodernism, which included:

1 the emergence of a distinctive aesthetic style in areas such as art, design and architecture, based upon irony, self-referentiality, *bricolage* of elements of the past and present, and the absorption of a 'popular vernacular';

2 an intellectual reaction to modernism and its underlying assumptions about there being general and universal forms of knowledge, truth, subjectivity, value, progress, and the relationship between social reality and its modes of representation;

3 cultural developments associated with mass media culture, such as the explosion of information, the universalisation of access to media such as television, and the blurring of lines between 'truth', 'reality', and their representation through media forms such as advertising

The French philosopher and cultural theorist Jean Baudrillard was a major contributor to postmodern theory. Baudrillard developed the concept of *simulation*, arguing that the logic of simulation had overtaken claims to an underlying social reality, to the point where such simulacra come to constitute the real itself, through 'the generation by models of a real without origin or reality: a hyperreal' (1988b: 166). Baudrillard explained this concept by analogy, arguing that Disneyland was a simulacrum of the reality of America; that evidence of political corruption reveals not aberrations from normal politics, but the everyday functioning of the contemporary political system; and that attempts to fake a hold-up will fail because others will behave in a 'real' fashion, for example by giving you the money, or by shooting you. Baudrillard drew upon McLuhan in his essay 'The Masses: The Implosion of the Social in the Media', arguing that McLuhan recognised the significance of the means used to organise the public into mass forms through the media, such as opinion polls, publicity, and advertising. For Baudrillard, McLuhan also anticipated how such simulations of 'the public' would be responded to by people, not through forms of mass resistance, but rather by an ironic agreement to participate in such games, while at the same time refusing to believe in the truths they generate:

> The present argument of the system is to maximise speech, to maxi-mise the production of meaning, of participation. And so the strategic resistance is that of the refusal of meaning and the refusal of speech; or of the hyperconformist simulation of the very mechanisms of the system, which is another form of refusal by over acceptance. It is the actual strategy of the masses. (1988b: 219)

Many saw Baudrillard's contribution to these debates as too extreme in its rejection of the possibility of an emancipatory politics in an age of mass media. Theorists such as Lash and Urry (1989), Harvey (1990), and Jameson (1992) saw the rise of postmodern culture as linked to shifts within capitalism from an industrial, mass production-based, and predominantly national economic system to one based increasingly on information flows, flexible production networks, and globalisation. They nonetheless drew on political economy as the basis of understanding capitalism as a socio-economic system, but drew attention to the growing centrality of culture as technologically mediated symbolic forms to the contemporary global capitalist system. Jameson referred to postmodernism as being characterised by 'a prodigious expansion of culture throughout the social realm, to the point at which everything in our social life—from economic value and state power to practices and to the very structure of the psyche itself—can be said to have become "cultural"' (Jameson 1992: ix).

Further reading

Poster 1988; Lash and Urry 1989; Harvey 1990; Best and Kellner 1991; Jamesan 1992; Collins 1992; Frow 1994; Woods 1999; Cahoone 2003

Dan Schiller

Dan Schiller has been a leading theorist of new media from the perspective of critical political economy. Along with other critical political economists such as Robert McChesney (1999, 2000, 2002) and Vincent Mosco (1996, 1997, 2000, 2004), his work has emphasised the role of corporate power and influence in shaping the development of new media, and the role played by the USA at an international level in furthering a privatised, market-driven conception of the global media and communications environment. The critical political economy approach to media studies has characteristically emphasised four elements (Mosco 1996; Golding & Murdock 2000):

1 the interconnectedness between economic, political, cultural, and military power as they are related to the media and communications sphere

2 the importance of a historical perspective that locates developments in 'new' media in the wider evolution of media and communications systems, institutions, and policies

3 the shifting balance between commercial media industries and the government sector, and the argument that since the 1980s in particular, there has been a global shift towards more market-driven, neo-liberal communications policies, including the privatisation of public broadcasting and telecommunications

4 the need for a critique of corporate power that is grounded in an ethical commitment to more open and democratic forms of communication.

The critical political economy approach has also characteristically taken a global perspective, drawing on the pioneering argument of Herbert Schiller that the economic rise of the ECI sector in the USA was linked to cultural domination on a global scale, through the global circulation of Western media and cultural industries, commodities, and culturally embedded values and meanings (see e.g. Schiller, H. 1995; cf. Flew 2007: 30–7 for a more detailed overview of critical political economy).

In *Digital Capitalism* (2000), Dan Schiller argued that the key to understanding the Internet in its contemporary form lies in the evolution of corporate communications networks (Intranets) in the USA, and their integration with the US telecommunications infrastructure through common networking protocols (TCP/IP, see Chapter 1) for the carriage of digital data. Because these computing and communications industries increasingly operated on a global scale, they pushed US governments and supranational policy agencies such as the International Telecommunications Union (ITU) and the World Trade Organization (WTO) to promote the deregulation and opening up of national telecommunications systems worldwide to form an integrated Global Information Infrastructure that mirrored the US National Information Infrastructure. The result, as McChesney and Schiller (2003: iii) have argued, has been a 'transnational corporate-commercial communication system' based around a global neo-liberal policy regime that 'relaxed or eliminated barriers to commercial exploitation of media, foreign investment in the communication system, and concentrated media ownership'. One of the consequences of such developments, for Schiller, has been a hollowing out of public-sector information institutions, ranging from public broadcasters to libraries to schools and universities, alongside a massive growth in the scale, speed, and sophistication of privatised information sources, meaning that public institutions are increasingly reliant on corporate support for their ongoing activities, which in turn strengthens corporate control over information provision (Schiller 2006).

THE TRANSFORMATION OF TELECOMMUNICATIONS: A CASE STUDY IN POLITICAL ECONOMY

Between the 1980s and the 2000s, there was a dramatic transformation of the industrial and policy foundations of telecommunications worldwide. Prior to the 1980s, there was an assumption that telecommunications was delivered by a public monopoly provider, with universal service obligations to provide all national citizens with a plain old telephone service (POTS) (Westerway 1990: 48). The principles behind the POTS were that everyone in the country should have access to a basic, reliable telephone service on a reasonably equitable basis. This was achieved through the mechanism of *cross-subsidies*: large users (businesses) subsidised smaller users (domestic consumers), urban users subsidised users in rural and remote areas, international users subsidised local users, and users generally subsidised the telecommunications provider through higher prices in order to enable investment in further development of the network to ensure that the same service was available to all users. It was in the 1980s that the technological foundations were fragmenting, with the arrival of value-added services such as fax and data transmission.

THE TRANSFORMATION OF TELECOMMUNICATIONS (*cont.*)

Schiller (2000) observes that, the telecommunications paradigm was shifting from under the radar of the big phone monopolies from the 1960s onwards, as leading corporate users, most notably in the finance sector, were developing global corporate Intranets for data transfer across networks that piggybacked onto the public services but were separate from them. Moreover, telecommunications based on digital technology was being developed through DARPA that would form the basis of the Internet (see Chapter 1), even though the telecommunications industry remained sceptical. Nonetheless, the major driver of global change in telecommunications was not technology but policy, in particular the break-up of the giant American Telephone and Telegraph (AT&T) company in 1984, following the *AT&T v. Department of Justice* antitrust case, concluded in the US Federal Court in 1982. The 'break-up of the Bells' (AT&T's corporate symbol is a large bell, and it used to be known as 'Ma Bell'), triggered a wave of competition in the US telecommunications industry that not only increased competition, but greatly changed the expectations of what a telecommunications business provided for its users (Cortada 2006).

It was also a catalyst to privatisation of telecommunications, with the UK government privatising 51 per cent of British Telecom in 1985, and Japan breaking up its telecommunications monopoly through Nippon Telephone and Telegraph in the same year (Chakravartty & Sarikakis 2006: 62–3). Between 1984 and 1999, 110 telecommunications companies were partly or fully privatised (Winseck 2002a). This process involved the creation of new transnational telecommunications companies, and in 2003 nine of the world's 100 largest transnational corporations were in the telecommunications sector, including Vodafone (2), France Telecom (10), Deutsche Telekom (14), Telecom Italia (24), Telefónica (36), Singtel (66), Nokia (69), Verizon (82), and Motorola (97) (UNCTAD 2005: 269–71). The privatisation of telecommunications worldwide, which had strong support from the International Telecommunications Union and the World Trade Organization, also involved the takeover by major US and European telecommunications companies of providers in Africa, Asia, Eastern Europe, the Caribbean, and Latin America, as developing countries sought to sell off public telecoms monopolies in order to generate foreign investment revenues to finance government projects (Winseck 2002a,b).

Looking back from over two decades, there is no doubt that phones themselves are far more groovy, multi-functional, and ubiquitous than they were in the 1980s. It is also apparent that the degree of regulation of telecommunications has increased, not decreased, as a result of moves towards market-based competition, as seen in the number of countries with independent regulatory agencies with a specific responsibility for telecommunications, which grew from 12 in 1980 to 96 in 2000 (Intven 2000). This is indicative of the persistence of three problems of telecommunications that public monopoly sought to address, and which a more commercial and privatised policy approach has not eliminated. First, there is the ongoing capacity to exploit monopoly power in the provision of infrastructure and services. Second, there is the tendency for the most valuable communications services, such as high-speed broadband and wireless infrastructure, to cluster around the major economic hubs, to the detriment of other regions. Third, there is the issue of who pays for the provision of some form of universal access to basic communications services and infrastructure (Hudson 2002; Winseck 2002).

Further reading

Hudson 2002; Winseck 2002; McChesney & Schiller 2003; ITU 2004

Tiziana Terranova

Tiziana Terranova's *Network Culture: Politics for the Information Age* (2004) is a critical exploration of the relationship between culture, information, and politics, in the context of 'a cultural formation, a *network culture*, that seems to be characterised by an unprecedented *abundance* of informational output and by an *acceleration* of informational dynamics' (2004: 1). Proposing that there is a need to rethink the relationship between information and culture from earlier cultural studies models derived from semiotics, Terranova argues that 'information is no longer simply the first order of signification, but the milieu which supports and encloses the production of meaning. There is no meaning ... outside of an informational milieu that exceeds and undermines the domain of meaning from all sides' (2004: 9).

Drawing upon information systems theory and cybernetics, Terranova understands the Internet not so much as a new media form, but rather as 'an informational space that is driven by the biophysical tendencies of open systems (such as the tendency towards divergences, incompatibilities, and rising entropic levels of randomness and disorganisation) ... whose main feature is an openness which is also a constitutive tendency to *expansion*' (2004: 3). By its very nature, the informational space constituted by the Internet balances centrifugal and disorganising forces to the level of chaos and collapse with an underlying internal network architecture designed and conceived of from its inception 'as a heterogeneous network, able to accommodate in principle ... not only diverse communication systems, but also drifting and differentiating communication modes' (2004: 52).

Drawing out the implications of such an analysis for a critical cultural politics of information, Terranova's work draws attention to three further fundamental features of contemporary information culture within 21st-century capitalism. The first is that *free labour* is an endemic feature of the digital economy, because it is bound up with the desire of individuals to build digital networks and digital content because they believe at some level in what they are doing; it is a form of *affective labour*, which capital exploits and ultimately exhausts 'by undermining the means through which that labour can sustain itself: from the burn-out syndromes of Internet start-ups to under-compensation and exploitation in the cultural economy at large' (2004: 94). For Terranova, working in the digital media sectors (hosting chat rooms, designing code, animation for games, etc.) is always less glamorous and well renumerated for the hours worked than it first appears.

Second, the characteristic mode of control in network culture is that of *soft control*. Working from the application of biological metaphors to complex, computer-aided systems design, Terranova points to the importance to contemporary network cultures of abstract machines that can absorb complexity and difference, creating a vital 'middle zone' between local controls and determinations—an adaptive yet overarching global network that affords a vitally productive space for that which is autonomous, creative, and original. As Terranova puts it: 'The abstract machine of soft control is thus concerned with fine tuning the local conditions that allow machines to outperform their designers' specifications, that surprise the designers but spontaneously improve on them, while also containing their possible space of mutation' (2004: 119).

Terranova's third major point relates to the complex relationship between new media and network culture and notions of 'the mass', as found in mass media, mass communications theory, and various forms of political theory. The widely held proposition that the Internet means the 'end of mass media' is for Terranova a highly partial and particular reading of what is occurring. She instead argues that:

> The Internet … seems to capture (and reinforce) a feature of network culture as a whole—the way it combines masses, segments and microsegments within a common informational dimension in which all points are potentially even if unevenly affected by all other points. Within the Internet medium, this peculiar combination of masses and segments does not produce a peaceful coexistence of two different modes … In a network culture, the differentiating power of image flows achieves a kind of hydrodynamic status characterised by a local sensitivity to global conditions … A networked mass displays a kind of active power of differentiation. It is still a mass, but it cannot be made to form a stable majority around some kind of average quality or consensus. (2004: 153–4)

USEFUL WEBSITES

Association of Internet Researchers <www.aoir.org>. The website for the Association of Internet Researchers (AoIR) has been promoting cross-disciplinary research and international collaboration in Internet studies since 2000. Its website provides a range of useful materials, including papers from all of its annual conferences.

International Journal of Communication <http://ijoc.org/ojs/index.php/ijoc>. This is an online, multi-media, academic journal that was established in 2007 through the University of Southern California Annenberg School of Communication, and aims to be 'an interdisciplinary journal that, while centered in communication, is open and welcoming to contributions from the many disciplines and approaches that meet at the crossroads that is communication study.'

Mute: Politics and Culture after the Net <www.metamute.org>. A lively site dealing with question of art, culture, and politics in relation to 21st-century new media, which has a very extensive contributions base and discussion forums.

05

social networking
media

The nature of networks

Networks have been a central concept in social theories of new media. In perhaps the best known argument about the centrality of networks to 21st-century society and culture, Manuel Castells identified the network society as being the outcome of a historical trend where 'dominant functions and processes in the information age are increasingly organised around networks. Networks constitute the *new social morphology of our societies*, and the diffusion of networking logic substantially modifies the operation and outcomes in processes of production, experience, power, and culture' (Castells 1996: 469).

The rise of networks can be understood from two angles. One emphasises the growing significance attached to networks in other areas of social, cultural, political, economic, and, indeed, military relations. The other considers how the Internet as a technological form that is fundamentally grounded in networks comes to permeate all aspects of society in terms of the form as well as content of social relations.

Podolny and Page (1998: 59) observed that 'every form of organisation is a network', since the nature of an organisation requires ongoing processes of exchange between more than two social actors. At the same time, one of the distinctive features of a network is a set of ethical orientations around behaviours such as trust, reciprocity, goodwill, and mutual obligation that differ from the contractual basis of purely market-based transactions and the notion of authority based largely on designated forms of power that characterise hierarchical forms of organisation. Moreover, the focus of network analysis is as much on relations between organisations as it is on relations within organisations. Benefits of network forms of organisation include:

- the capacity for *collective learning* among agents across the network
- accrual of *legitimacy or status* for individual agents from being part of a larger network
- *greater adaptiveness to unanticipated changes* in the wider socio-economic environment
- *minimising forms of vulnerability* arising from resource dependency upon others (Podolny & Page 1998: 62–6).

In considering why the reliance on networking as a basis for an organisation's activities will vary, Podolny and Page note three key variables:

- the importance of *power* relations to the interactions between organisations—the more power is exercised to achieve organisational goals, the less significant network forms will be
- the *age of an organisation*—older organisations are typically less imbued with a 'networking culture' than newer ones
- *national cultural and legal differences*—network forms of organisation tend to be associated more with collectivist cultures than with more individualistic ones, they are, for example, more characteristic of Asian countries than they are of the USA or the United Kingdom (Podolny & Page 1998: 67–8; cf. Hofstede 1980; Scott 1986; Doremus et al. 1998).

In economics, an interest in networks has arisen from three sources. The first is the concept of *network externalities*. Shapiro and Varian (1999: 183) observed that an externality can be positive or negative, and involves activities that 'arise when one market participant affects others without compensation being paid'. Environmental degradation is an obvious example of a negative externality, as it primarily affects 'third parties' other than those directly involved in the transaction. Education is often cited as a positive externality, as the benefits to society of a better-educated population outweigh the benefits received by either the learner or the providing institution. Positive network externalities arise from the increasing scale of benefits that accrue from being a part of a larger network. These intersect with the benefits that accrue to corporations and other organisations from positive feedback, whose significance is amplified through networks as information travels more quickly, and is more difficult to manage by organisations themselves.

The second key factor has been what is known as the *new institutionalism*. The growing awareness of transaction costs and their significance in both inter-organisational and intra-organisational relations led authors such as Williamson (1975, 1985) to understand the corporation as a *nexus of contracts*, or an institutional means of managing transaction costs and pooling capabilities associated with organising interdependent relations in a context of market failure, imperfect information, and endemic uncertainty. The relationship between an economic organisation such as a corporation and other agents (e.g. suppliers, their workforce, consumers) is in turn governed by features such as *bounded rationality* (the difficulty of acquiring all forms of knowledge needed to make fully informed decisions); *asset specificity* (the idiosyncrasies of both the resources sought from others and the complexities of assets and skills offered); and *contingent uncertainties*, or the scope for opportunism, fraud, and exploitation based on inequalities of access to knowledge and resources (Thompson 2003: 67–8). An interest in networks arises here from an awareness of both the limits of contracts as a way of managing such ongoing relations, and the question of whether relations grounded in informal modes of cooperation and collaboration are economically superior to those that are based on contract and the management of antagonistic relations.[1]

The third source of interest in networks from an economic perspective arises more specifically from the shift that Benkler has identified where information, knowledge, and culture have moved to the centre of economic relations more generally. Benkler (2006: 37) makes the observation that information has tended to be viewed as a *public good* in so far as its consumption is 'non-rivalrous', that is, one person's use of the information does not diminish the access of others to the information. Added to this is the point that information is both the input and output of its own production process. Benkler has argued that a necessary condition of the production of information today is access to information produced by other people at other times. Both of these features of information—including here cultural and entertainment products as well as the products of formal knowledge systems—dovetail very neatly with the development of the Internet as a decentralised ICT-based digital network, because the Internet provides a historically distinct means of distributing information collectively and on a global scale.

The growing significance of networks to politics has long been documented. It has had clear manifestations since the 1960s in the rapidly declining membership of major political parties, declining participation in electoral politics and a growing sense of popular alienation from formal political institutions and processes (see e.g. Castells 1998: 342–53). Miller (2004: 208) draws attention to the rise of *network campaigns* pursued by social movements by extra-parliamentary means through loosely organised representative agencies and coalitions, and how this is enabled by new media:

> Network campaigns allow a diverse grouping of organisations and individuals to participate through commitment to a shared purpose, while remaining autonomous individual agents. In this way, it is possible to gain additional leverage over decision-making bodies through the 'multiplier effect' of a coherent message and more efficient deployment of resources and effort, while maintaining the flexibility and energy that more bureaucratic forms of co-ordination tend to squander.

The specific characteristics of network campaigns that generate such advantages include having a shared goal; being 'structure-light'; mobilising a diverse collation of skills and resources around shared goals; advanced use of new media technologies; embracing diversity and openness; the ability to draw upon, and develop, media celebrity; the ability to use media spectacle around specific targets; time-limited strategies; high levels of media visibility; and the ability to act cheaply and quickly (2004: 208–13).

Miller had in mind network campaigns conducted by peaceful means, such as the *Jubilee 2000* campaign for debt-reduction for Third World nations or the role played by environmental organisations such as Greenpeace. It is also the case, however, that network strategies are also the characteristics of terrorist organisations such as Al Qa'eda and leaders such as Osama bin Laden. Al Qa'eda's stated goal of the elimination of Western power and influence from Muslim states would have been a peripheral influence on world events had it been conducted solely from the mountains of Afghanistan and northern Pakistan. What has given Al Qa'eda its enormous significance in current world events is the alignment of such a goal to aspects of network politics such as the capacity to use new media to disseminate messages widely to current and potential supporters; the high level of visibility attached to events such as the terrorist attacks on the World Trade Center and the Pentagon in the USA on September 11, 2001 (9/11), as well as subsequent terrorist attacks in Bali in 2002, on the Madrid subway in 2004, and the London Underground rail network in 2005; and the inherently 'structure-light' nature of this organisation, which maintains itself through a dense and seemingly amorphous network of agents and activists. Al Qa'eda has continued to operate in spite of the massive growth in surveillance of activities and links that occurred in the aftermath of 9/11, the war in Afghanistan to depose the Taliban government, and the war in Iraq. Friel (2002) has observed the extent to which bin Laden has exemplified the 'network logic' of developing and running a global organisation:

> He decentralized decision-making authority and created a flat management structure to quickly respond to changes in his operating environment. He overcame turf battles by creating an overarching sense of mission and doctrine. He used the Internet and the globalisation of news and the revolution in telecommunications to advance his organisation's goals worldwide. He developed a complex organisational network in which information gets only to the right people at the right times. In his network, connections between individuals and groups are activated at key times to get work done and severed when they are no longer necessary.

The case of Al Qa'eda and Osama bin Laden reminds us of the dangers of reversing technological determinism to the point that it overturns 'technology controls society' arguments with arguments that the technologies themselves have no influence on shaping social outcomes. Castells (2004: 221) has insisted on this point in relation to the Internet and the network society, arguing that 'without specific technologies some social structures could not develop'. Benkler (2006: 17) makes a similar observation: 'Different technologies make different kinds of human action and interaction easier or harder to perform. All other things being equal, things that are easier to do are more likely to be done, and things that are harder to do are less likely to be done.' Elaborating on the link between the Internet and the network as social morphology, Wellman (2001) has argued that *a computer network is also a social network*. Proposing that both individuals and organisations socialise into communities through networks rather than groups, Wellman identified the many social affordances that the Internet and related ICTs provided for sustaining both geographically specific community ties and enabling new and potentially global networked ties, which included growing broadband access capacity (e.g. photos and videos could be exchanged, and not just text), as well as global connectivity. These were seen as part of a general process of modernity 'away from place-based inter-household ties to individualised person-to-person interactions and specialised role-to-role interactions' (2001: 231). Finding that 'cyberspace fights against physical place less than it complements it', Wellman observed that the relationship of new media to networking is that it 'has increased the importance of network capital in the fund of desirable resources, along with financial capital, human capital, and cultural capital' (2001: 247, 248).

SOCIAL NETWORK ANALYSIS

Social network analysis is a methodology developed in the social and behavioural sciences to map interpersonal linkages using statistical and graphical techniques. Wasserman and Faust identify the distinctiveness of social network analysis as being its view that 'the social environment can be expressed as patterns or regularities in relationships among interacting units' (1994: 3). The understanding of forms of self, activity, and behaviour as being *relational* is fundamental to this approach. Four key elements of social network analysis are identified by Wasserman and Faust:

1   Actors and their actions are viewed as interdependent, that is, formed through relationships to others.

2   Relational ties, or what are referred to as *linkages*, are channels for the flow of resources, which may be material (capital, commodities, etc.) or immaterial (power, influence, information, etc.) in nature.

3   Network models view the network structural environment as providing opportunities for, or presenting constraints upon, individual behaviour.

4   Network models conceptualise structure (social, economic, political, etc.) as lasting patterns of relations among actors. (1994: 4)

Social network analysis characteristically works from the bottom up, in that it aims to identify relationships that exist in a particular place and time, the mapping of which can contribute to wider hypotheses about social structure. It has seven core concepts (cf. 1994: 17–21):

1   *Actor:* an actor is a discrete unit of decision-making and action, which may be an individual, but may also be a corporation, a government

SOCIAL NETWORK ANALYSIS (cont.)

agency, or some other form of organisation such as an association, a trade union, a university.

2 *Relational ties*: this refers to the establishment of links between actors, which can include mutual admiration, shared membership of associations, regular meetings and other forms of communication, movement of actors between places, formal relationships of authority, and biological relationships based upon kinship and descent.

3 *Dyad*: this is the information used to establish a relational tie between two actors, so that they can be seen to constitute a pair.

4 *Triad*: this identifies probabilities of relationships between three actors based on knowledge of dyadic relationships.

5 *Subgroup*: if identification of the existence of dyadic relationships can be established, and these can be triangulated to the potential for triadic relationships, then this will form the basis for the existence of a subgroup of actors.

6 *Group*: the group in social network analysis is 'the collection of all actors on which ties are to be measured' (Wasserman & Faust 1994: 19). Such a group should be finite in its nature (i.e. the set of actors involved is already established) and there is a need to establish that these actors constitute a group as a bounded set.

7 *Relation*: this refers to the evidence of interaction and relationships among members of the group that indicate both durable ties and the capacity to act in response to a situation in the social environment.

Social network analysis has its origins in the development of the *'sociogram'*, as a way of illustrating the nature of interpersonal relations within a group. Two of the core elements of what was then termed 'sociometry', as a precursor to social network analysis, were the use of visual representations of group structure, and a probability-based model of structural outcomes. Particular questions within the social sciences and, more recently, theories of the creative economy and creative industries, have acted as trigger points for social network analysis. One longstanding question for social network analysis has been whether there exists a ruling class, or what C. Wright Mills (1956) referred to in the American context as a *power elite*, in capitalist societies. Simply identifying that there exist rich people who derive wealth from the control of economic property is insufficient; what is required is the ability to demonstrate that such a group may be able to act cohesively and collectively in order to pursue shared interests. Work on interlocking corporate directorships, and their relationship to other ties such as those based on corporate share ownership and investment financing, has been critical in clarifying some of these questions and in establishing points of difference between different capitalist models (e.g. comparisons between the American, Japanese, British, or German models) (Scott 1986, 1991; cf. Stokman et al. 1985).

A second and more recent example relates to the homology that the Internet creates between social networking and interconnections established through technology. Wellman's point that 'we find community in networks, not in groups' (Wellman 2001: 227) draws attention to the way in which forms of interaction that constitute the basis for social networks are increasingly developed through mediated communication (e.g. email correspondence), and provides clear points of intersection between the analytical concerns of social network analysis and the capacity to map 'data transfers' that the Internet enables. This is made explicit in the blogging process, as bloggers often provide a 'blog roll' of those other bloggers they consider to have opinions that are worth looking at.

A final example relates to the attention given to interpersonal networks, or what is referred to as soft infrastructure, in the literature on creative industries and creative cities. Charles Landry (2000: 133) has defined *soft infrastructure* as 'the system of associative structures and social networks, connections, and human interactions that underpins and encourages the flow of ideas between individuals and institutions'. The process of uncovering such interconnections is the *sine qua non* of social network analysis, and Hearn and colleagues (2004) provide an example of how such techniques can be applied to the music industry in Queensland.

Further reading
Wasserman & Faust 1994; Wellman 2001; Cross 2004

Castells' theory of the 'network society'

Manuel Castells argued in his three-volume work *The Information Age* that a 'network society' has emerged in the late 20th and early 21st century. For Castells, the network society is both cause and consequence of the shift from an industrial to an informational mode of development, which he defines in these terms:

> In the industrial mode of development, the main source of productivity lies in the introduction of new energy sources, and in the ability to decentralize the use of energy through the production and circulation processes. In the new, informational mode of development, the source of productivity lies in the technology of knowledge generation, information processing, and symbol communication ... What is specific to the informational mode of development is the action of knowledge upon knowledge itself as the main source of productivity ... I call this mode of development informational, constituted by the emergence of a new technological paradigm based on information technology. (1996: 17)

Castells proposed that the rise of a network society had its origins in five central elements of this new informational mode of development, or *information technology paradigm*, based on the mass diffusion of digitally networked ICTs:

1 Information becomes the raw material of economic activity, acting as both the input and the output of the new technologies.
2 New ICTs have pervasive effects through all realms of human social activity.
3 The logic of networking applies to all social processes and organisational forms, since uncertainty is inevitable and knowledge resides in multiple sources, and therefore needs to be collectively pooled in order to be effectively applied.
4 Processes, organisational structures, and institutional forms need to be flexible, in order that such activities and entities can be readily altered and transformed in light of uncertainty and unplanned changes.
5 The growing convergence of specific technologies into a highly integrated system means that all industries adopt the attributes of 'pioneer' ICT-based network enterprises such as Cisco, Apple, and Nokia, which include scalability of partnerships and relations, interactivity with suppliers and consumers, management of flexibility, growing customisation of products and services, and accumulation of brand-based market value (Castells 2001: 75–7).

For Castells, the *new economy* derived from the pervasive impact of networked ICTs and has three core characteristics. First, it is *informational*, in the sense that 'the capacity of generating knowledge and processing/ managing information determine the productivity and competitiveness of all kinds of economic units, be they firms, regions, or countries' (2000b: 10). Second, it is *global*, since 'its core strategic activities have the capacity to work as a unit on a planetary scale in real time or chosen time' (2000b: 10). Castells defines these 'core strategic activities' as the operation of financial markets, international trade of goods and services, science and technology, the activities of multinational firms, communications media, and the movements of highly skilled specialist labour. Finally, the new economy is *networked*. It is based on information networks such as the Internet, as well as the networked enterprise becoming the dominant form of economic organisation, at whose heart is no longer the capitalist firm, but global financial markets and business projects based on short-term strategic alliances and partnerships. For Castells, the networked enterprise is a logical corollary of electronic business, as it is based around 'the Internet-based, interactive, networked connection between producers, consumers, and service providers' (2001: 75).

The corollary of a network society, and a new economy based on information, globalisation, and networking, is that power is increasingly organised around the *space of flows*. These are constituted in three ways. First, they are constructed electronically through the communications networks themselves, as well as spatially through the existence of *global cities* as centres of global commerce and communications, such as New York, London, Tokyo, Paris, Los Angeles, and a number of others competing for ascendancy (cf. Sassen 1991, 2001; Taylor et al. 2002).[2] Second, *technopoles* such as Silicon Valley in California, Route 182 in Boston, Bangalore in India, the Pearl River Delta (Hong Kong/Guangzhou) in China, and Malaysia's Multimedia Super Corridor provide examples of how the global space of flows is constructed through its 'nodes and hubs', and how nation-states increasingly compete to establish locations within their territorial domain as central points in this global network. Finally, for Castells (1996: 410–18), the global space of flows is constituted *culturally*, through the shared experiences and practices of geographically mobile managerial and knowledge worker elites who, while still predominantly North American and European, are increasingly deracinated, with the rise of global elites from Asia, Latin America, the Middle East, and Africa, and the increasingly multicultural nature of the global metropolitan centres.

A central contradiction of the new economy arises from the fact that economic processes are increasingly global, whereas most jobs are local and most people are rooted to a particular place, unable or unwilling to migrate to new growth centres. Castells proposed that there is an increased bifurcation between self-reprogrammable labour and generic labour, which occurs alongside the rapid growth of small and medium enterprises (SMEs) that are connected into larger networks. *Self-reprogrammable labour* are those workers who possess what Pierre Lévy has termed 'a capacity for learning and innovation that is continuously improved and that can be actualised in an unpredictable manner within changing contexts' (1998: 77). By contrast, *generic labour*, or forms of semi-skilled and unskilled work that can be done by many people in many places, is particularly vulnerable to globalisation and technological change. In the industrial era, all workers could potentially benefit from the strong representation of trade unions, although this was in practice highly differentiated on the basis of gender, race, ethnicity, skills, and occupation. In the informational mode of development, for Castells, 'labor is disaggregated in its performance, fragmented in its organisation, diversified in its existence, [and] divided in its collective action'; as a result 'labor loses its collective identity, [and] becomes increasingly individualised in its capacities, in its working conditions, and in its interests and projects' (1996: 475).

The network society is a global capitalist society. Castells argued that the world has never been more dominated by capitalist economic relations than is presently the case, as nominally 'socialist' countries such as China and Vietnam are now pivotal to the global market economy. Strong contradictions face nation-states in the global network society, as they continue to be required to perform a series of vital economic, social, legal, and cultural functions, but do so in an environment where 'the instrumental capacity of the nation-state is decisively undermined by globalisation of core economic activities [and] by globalisation of media and electronic communication' (1998: 244). Globalisation has promoted the rise of a diverse range of oppositional movements based on resistance identities (1998: 356), which can range from radical anti-globalisation protestors, globally networked ecological movements, regionally based guerrilla movements, transnational fundamentalist religious movements, and conservative nationalists. He draws an interesting distinction between *resistance identities*, whose capacity for growth over time is limited by their dependence on the capacities and decisions of those they oppose, and *project identities*, which can extend beyond resistance to develop new forms of civil society that can in turn act to reshape or transform the nature and operation of those social institutions whose conduct is central to their own project (1998: 357–8; cf. Calabrese 1999).

One particularly interesting element of Castells' argument about the relationship between globalisation and networks is his analysis of how there are
clear dynamics of inclusion and exclusion within these networks, although
the nature of these shifts over time, while there are also forms of 'perverse
integration' into the globally networked economy, can be most clearly seen in
the rise of a 'global criminal economy'. Inequalities are also increasingly based
around the dynamics of inclusion and exclusion in relation to global networks.
Within countries there is the process of social exclusion, whereby particular
individuals, groups, and communities experience disconnection from the
workforce and social institutions, on bases as diverse as lack of formal education, personal circumstances (illness, addiction, criminal conviction), urban
or regional location, or discrimination based on race or ethnicity. At a global
level, Asian 'tiger' economies such as Singapore, Hong Kong, Taiwan, South
Korea, Malaysia, and China have become more integrated into the circuits of
global informational capitalism and have experienced rapid economic growth.
However, much of Sub-Saharan Africa, the Middle East, Central Asia, and,
since the early 1990s, Russia have become marginalised and disconnected
from this economy, leading to extreme poverty, famines, and epidemics, and
the rise of dysfunctional 'predatory states', such as the former Taliban regime
in Afghanistan and the government of Sudan. There is also what Castells
termed 'perverse integration' into the globally networked economy, most
clearly seen in the existence of a 'global criminal economy', which includes
the Russian *mafiyas*, the drug traffickers of Colombia, Peru, Bolivia, Mexico,
Ecuador, Burma (Myanmar), and Thailand, the diaspora of Chinese Triads,
and in the Western countries where drugs such as cocaine and heroin largely
find their consumer market.

Among the critical commentaries on Castells' work (see e.g. Calabrese
1999; Webster & Dimitriou 2003; Hassan 2004; Miège 2004; Stadler 2006; cf.
Flew 2007 on globalisation and the 'space of flows'), the issue I wish to focus
on is his treatment of new media and its broader cultural implications. Castells
proposes that the network society is one where 'reality itself ... is increasingly
captured, fully immersed in a virtual image setting ... in which appearances are
not just on the screen through which experience is communicated, but they
become the experience' (1996: 373). For Castells, this points to a *culture of real
virtuality*, since 'cultures are made up of communication processes. And all
forms of communication ... are based upon the production and consumption
of signs. Thus there is no separation between "reality" and symbolic representation' (1996: 372). Flew (2007) argues against such interpretations of culture,

on the grounds that there are levels of 'culture as lived experience' and 'culture as symbolic communication' that are ontologically distinct, even though media in all their forms continue to permeate cultures and lived experience globally. Garnham (2004) has argued that Castells' analysis is analytically flawed by a failure to recognise levels of mediation between technology and culture, and empirically flawed by his failure to recognise that 'media' encompasses a diverse range of forms, so that 'real virtuality' achieved through radio or television remains different to that drawn from the Internet. Miller and Slater (2000) argue that Castells' dichotomisation between 'the Net' and 'the Self' is misconceived, as it both overestimates the transformative impact of new media technologies on everyday life (culture as lived experience), and underestimates the extent to which new media are incorporated into an already existing repertoire of socio-cultural activities and relationships.

Networks and social production

Much of the work on the socio-economic role of networks has focused on the ways in which they transform organisational relations, as seen in the literature of network enterprises (Castells 2001: 64–116; Thompson 2003: 111–48; Barney 2004: 83–90). In *The Wealth of Networks* (2006), Yochai Benkler argues that the impact of networks runs more deeply than this. He says that the early 21st century has brought the rise of a *networked information economy*, whose core characteristic is that 'decentralised individual action—specifically, new and important cooperative and coordinated action carried out through radically distributed, non-market mechanisms that do not depend upon pro- prietary strategies—plays a much greater role than it did, or could have, in the industrial information economy' (2006: 3).

The key driver of such development is the generalisation of the Internet and networked personal computing, whose degree of connectivity continues to grow as the costs of accessing ICTs continue to fall, and the capacity of each networked computer to produce, retrieve, and store data of all sorts continues to rise. For Benkler, this 'removal of the physical constraints on effective information production has made human creativity and the economics of information … core structuring facts in the new networked information economy' (2006: 4).

The rise of the Internet and networked ICTs provides a necessary but not a sufficient explanation for the rise of the networked information economy. Benkler's work points to three subsidiary conditions. First, there is the rise of information, knowledge, and creative industries themselves, which even at their most 'industrialised'—as they were in the second half of the 20th century—needed to be more flexible and more reliant on non-market motives than traditional manufacturing industries. Second, the existence of the Internet itself has given a major boost to all non-market forms of production and distribution of information, knowledge, and culture, as there are *coordinate effects* to a multiplicity of individual actions that greatly enrich the networked information environment. When one superimposes the information retrieval capacity of an Internet search engine such as Google on the billions of Web pages that exist on the Internet, it is possible to see what Benkler terms the '"information good" that … is produced by the coordinate effects of the uncoordinated actions of a wide and diverse range of individuals and organisations acting on a wide range of motivations—both market and non-market, state and non-state' (Benkler 2006: 5). Third, there is the rise of peer production of information, knowledge, and culture through large-scale cooperative efforts. The conceptual and practical origins of this have lain in the free and open source software movement, but the rise of Web 2.0 and social software has seen its impact diffused across a range of domains.

This points to the rise of *social production*, or the rise of models of information, knowledge, and cultural production that are loosely collaborative, not necessarily driven by market criteria, and not directly proprietary in terms of who owns and controls the use by others of the final product. Observing that individuals have a variety of motives to act, to make information available to others, and to cooperate, Benkler argues that social production rises to prominence in the networked information economy from the confluence of two factors: the fact that knowledge as a uniquely valued input to production is always possessed uniquely by individuals, and that the majority of these individuals 'have the threshold level of material capacity [i.e. networked computers] required to explore the information environment they occupy, to take from it, and to make their contributions to it' (2006: 99).

Given that in any society an excess of useful human knowledge and creativity exists relative to what is required economically, Benkler identifies two features of those projects that can most successfully harness the human resources necessary for effective social production. The first is *modularity*, or the properties of a project that determine 'the extent to which it can be broken down into smaller components, or modules, that can be independently produced before they are assembled into a whole' (2006: 100). At one extreme, development and management of a nuclear power plant is extremely difficult to modularise, as the centre needs to be sure not only of the quality of all work (in order to avoid nuclear accident) and the loyalty and commitment of all staff (because of the dangers of trafficking nuclear products to third parties). By contrast, the *Wikipedia* (www.wikipedia.org) has drawn very successfully upon the degree to which the assembling of an online encyclopedia can occur through the agglomeration of a vast and diverse range of independent inputs. The second factor is that of *granularity*, or the size of the modules, in terms of the time and effort that an individual must invest in producing them, which sets 'the smallest possible individual investment necessary to participate in a project' (2006: 101). The *Wikipedia* is again a good example, as the investment of time and resources involved in making a single contribution is relatively small, or, in Benkler's terms, fine-grained. Table 5.1 indicates not only the growth in the number of contributors to the *Wikipedia* between 2001 and 2005, but also the degree of granularity that exists between those who have been occasional contributors and those who maintain an ongoing relationship to the site and its contents. Two notable features of the table are that while the number of contributors of all types grew exponentially over the period, the fastest rates of growth were in the number of occasional contributors (reflecting granularity) and the number of non-English language contributions (reflecting the globalisation of the Internet):

Table 5.1 Contributors to *Wikipedia*, January 2001 to June 2005

	Jan 2001	Jan 2002	Jan 2003	Jan 2004	July 2004	June 2005
Contributors[1]	10	477	2,188	9,653	25,011	48,721
Active contributors[2]	9	212	846	3,228	8,442	16,945
Very active contributors[3]	0	31	190	692	1,637	3,106
No. of English language articles	25	16–000	101–000	190–000	320,000	630,000
No. of articles, all languages	25	19–000	138–000	409–000	862,000	1,600,000

1. Contributed at least 10 times
2. Contributed at least 5 times in last month
3. Contributed more than 100 times in last month

Source: Benkler 2006: 72

Like Castells, Benkler believes that the combination of the Internet and network form marks a seismic shift in the socio-economic order of the 21st century as compared to the 20th. The title of his book, *The Wealth of Networks*, alludes to the foundational text of market economics, Adam Smith's *The Wealth of Nations*, first written in 1776. Smith and other Classical economists identified the expansion of markets and trade as being at the core of new forms of wealth creation (on Smith, see Dobb 1973). In the late 19th and the 20th century, free-market economics was somewhat usurped by the rise of the large corporation, and what James Beniger (1986) termed the 'control revolution' and Alfred Chandler (1977) the 'visible hand', whereby the combination of corporate control over resources on a large scale and scope, the capacity of planning to enable control over the external environment, and the combination of rewards and sanctions over individual employees that ensured loyalty and identification over time made the corporation the superior form of economic organisation. Benkler's argument is not that social production through networks will quickly supplant both markets and corporate hierarchies as other forms of economic organisation. Indeed, he acknowledges that 'the rise of social production does not entail a decline in market-based production' (2006: 122). For many businesses, the principal change is in 'the relationship of firms to individuals outside of them ... [as] consumers are changing into users—more active and productive than the consumers of the industrial information economy' (2006: 126).

Social production will have the most impact in those areas of economic life that lend themselves most readily to its core characteristics, such as those industries connected to information, knowledge, communications, culture, and creativity. At the same time, as the size and significance of these sectors is growing, particularly in advanced capitalist economies, the impact of social production will have a considerably wider resonance over time. As a general rule, the more important non-contractual factors are to an economic relationship—such as gifts, reciprocity, and trust—the more significant models of social production will be. This will in turn generate conflicts and contradictions at the heart of the 'core' sector of the networked information economy, as 'social production in general and peer production in particular present new sources of competition to incumbents that produce information goods for which there are now socially produced substitutes' (Benkler 2006: 122). Copyright law has very often been the flashpoint at which these conflicts have been played out. Chapter 11 will explore in more depth the nature of these conflicts and the role that authors such as Benkler,

Lawrence Lessig and others associated with Creative Commons as a socio-legal response to these debates have played in this intersection of competitive rivalry between incumbents and emergent enterprises and business practices based on proprietary and non-proprietary understandings of knowledge and its relationship to property.

Blogs as social software

Web logs, or *blogs*, are user-generated websites where entries are made either by individuals or by groups, in an informal journal style, and are displayed in reverse chronological order. They are typically interactive in their nature, and networked in their form. They solicit and respond to the commentary of others on the material posted on the blog, they characteristically offer links to the blogs or websites of others with related interests (what is known as a *blogroll*), and—while mainly text-based—they can provide links to other media resources such as video and photos (a video-based blog is called a *vlog*, while a photo-based blog is a *photoblog*). The term 'blog' refers to both the online artefact created—the word is an amalgam of Web and log, or the need to diarise—and to the act of maintaining such an online resource, or blogging. The social network of blogs and bloggers is referred to as the *blogosphere*, and it is through the networks of association that are a feature of individual blogs that it can be argued that 'the social networking of blogs and the potential for collaboration ... [provide] a decidedly human dimension to the publishing and publicising of information', in ways that 'represent for authors an opportunity to reach out and connect with an audience never before accessible to them, while maintaining control over their own personal expressive spaces' (Bruns & Jacobs 2006: 5).

In November 2006, there were 57 million active bloggers worldwide (BBC 2006). The 2006 survey of US bloggers conducted through the Pew Centre's *Internet and American Life* (Lenhart & Fox 2006) project found that about 12 million Americans aged 18 or over, or 8 per cent of that country's Internet-using population, kept a blog, and that blogs were viewed by 57 million Americans aged 18 or over, or about 38 per cent of the US Internet-using population. They found that bloggers are considerably younger than the Internet population overall, with 54 per cent being under 30, compared to 24 per cent of Internet users; indeed, 19 per cent of Internet users aged 12–17 kept a blog. In terms of general online media and communications practices and habits, bloggers overwhelmingly have a home broadband network connection, consume a large amount of other online media content (particularly news), are highly engaged with other forms of technology-based social interaction, and tend to source material more widely than other media users (Lenhart & Fox 2006: 4–6). In terms of what motivates people to establish and maintain a blog, the Pew Internet survey found that making money was the least important reason, and that about a third of bloggers saw the content of their blog as a form of journalism, with creative expression, documenting of personal views and experiences, and keeping in touch with friends and family being the most important motives.

Blogs have been a vitally important component of *social software*, discussed in Chapter 1 in the context of Web 2.0. Social software is software that supports group interaction, and Davies argued that:

> The principle of social software is to break down the distinction between our online computer-mediated experiences and our offline face-to-face experiences. It is software that … seeks to integrate the Internet further into our everyday lives, and our everyday lives further into the Internet. It is software that seeks to eradicate the gulf separating two such separate social networks. (Davies 2003: 7)

Table 5.2 Motives for developing a blog: Pew Internet survey of US bloggers

Reasons for developing a blog: US bloggers survey 2005–06	Major reason %	Minor reason %	Not a reason %
To express yourself creatively	52	25	23
To document your personal experiences or share them with others	50	26	24
To stay in touch with friends and family	37	22	40
To share practical knowledge or skills with others	34	30	35
To motivate other people to action	29	32	38
To entertain people	28	33	39
To store resources or information that is important to you	28	21	52
To influence the way other people think	27	24	49
To network or to meet new people	16	34	50
To make money	7	8	85

Source: Lenhart & Fox 2006: iii

In locating the rise of blogs in Internet history, Clay Shirky has argued that they are part of a 'third age' of social software (GBN 2002; Shirky 2003). The first age was email itself, and particularly the 'cc' tag line, which allowed one-to-one or one-to-few communications to be shared with others that were indirectly related to the communication message but who it was important to keep informed. The second age was the rise of virtual communities, as captured by Rheingold (1994), Turkle (1995), and others. For Shirky, one of the key limitations of both software and how it was used in this period—the mid- to late 1990s—was that both the software and the modes of development of Web content tended to be static, had limited interactivity, possessed a centralised mechanism of content control, and operated on a largely 'broadcast' model, whereas the participation in chat rooms, online discussion forums, and so on was not occurring through the Web but often through conduits such as email. As a result, there was a limited sense of community in the latter (which lent itself to flame wars, discontinuation of subscription, information overload, etc.), and a lack of interactivity surrounding the development of Web pages. By contrast, the 'third age' of social software has evolved around the principles of Web 2.0, which place a particular emphasis on collaboration, community-building, simplification of software and access points for users, 'light touch' regulation of site content, and relative ease in producing, distributing, accessing, and responding to the full range of forms of digital media content. In cases where such principles have been extended to collaborative publishing models, such as the *Wikipedia*, this also extends to collaborative editing (Bruns 2005).

 ## INTERVIEW: MARK BAHNISCH

Mark Bahnisch is a sociologist who established the Lavartus Prodeo (www. lavartusprodeo.net) site in 2005, and who has lectured at the Queensland University of Technology and Griffith University in Brisbane, as well as undertaking consultancy activities for the Australian and Queensland governments and for community organisations. *Lavartus Prodeo* is a collaborative blog site which 'discusses politics, sociology, life, religion and science from a left of centre perspective'. The title of the site was taken from Rene Descartes' account of the 'masked philosopher': 'Like an actor wearing a mask, I come forward, masked, on the stage of the world ... It will be for the masked philosopher to unmask the sciences and to make their continuity and their unity appear with their beauty'.

This interview was conducted in April 2007, prior to the 2007 Australian federal election.

Lavartus Prodeo *is a collaborative blog site. Could you say more about how that* **works?**

[MB:] There's a fair bit of negotiation among the contributors, which seeks to develop protocols for moderation and the direction of the site, as well as day-to-day and longer-term decisions on editorial policy and strategy. We attempt to reach decisions by consensus and we use a Google group to facilitate online decision-making. Generally, we see the process of running and editing the site as a collaborative endeavour, and while different contributors have different interests, we aim to collaborate horizontally without any formal division of labour or hierarchy. Most of the time it works really well—over time we've developed a shared understanding of the culture of the site and worked out a shared view of what role we want the blog to play and where we want to take it.

The site describes itself as 'discussing politics, sociology, culture, life, religion, and science from a left of centre perspective'. Can you say more about what that means? Do you view the site as being politically partisan towards political parties of the Left, for example?

[MB:] Only in the sense that we're partisan against parties of the Right. For instance, in 2007 we'll be campaigning on a platform to reclaim the Senate from a government majority. That implies an anti-government campaign, but not one explicitly supporting Senate candidates of any of the Left or left of centre parties. We have a variety of political views represented among contributors, including one member of the Greens and one member of the ALP. But most of us don't have strong party loyalties, and we see our role as offering (sometimes very) critical support to Left parties within the political process and strongly opposing the Coalition government. Our position is made more explicit in a statement on the blog about how we've decided to handle election year commentary. Basically (unlike some American blogs) we don't want to be a blog that acts to mobilise and cheer on supporters of any particular party.

In terms of other issues that we cover, we believe that the personal is the political, and we're the only large Australian political blog with substantial commentary on issues from feminist and queer viewpoints, and we also believe that we have a role to play in airing perspectives on a whole gamut of issues that are rarely represented or presented in the commercial media.

What do you know about your readership, both in terms of site statistics, and their more general characteristics (e.g. age, level of education, interests)? What do you think attracts people to the site?

[MB:] From our site statistics, we know that our readership has steadily been growing since about August 2006. It's difficult to know exactly who is reading, because we haven't attempted to do any market research on our readers and it would be difficult to get a representative sample. However, based on impressions from the minority of readers who are also regular commenters, I'd say we have a younger demographic than some of the other Oz political blogs, and more women. My impression is that our audience is largely university-educated, many being current postgrad students and academics, which may be a reflection of the position within academia that I occupy and the backgrounds of our bloggers.

One interesting thing you can derive from the stats is that we get frequent hits from domains internal to media organisations such as Fairfax, News Limited and the ABC and from Parliament.

Lavartus Prodeo *is significant in the Australian blogosphere, but the Australian political blogosphere seems to have less traction in wider public debates than, say, equivalent sites in the USA. Do you think this is a characteristic of the sites themselves, the political system, Australian political culture, or what else?*

[MB:] I think it's a mixture of both. There are some obvious differences between the two countries which affect all media, the size and scale of the audiences being the most important one. Therefore there's been less professionalisation of Australian blogging, and less of a sense that the blogosphere presents a broad-ranging alternative to the mainstream media. But I think Australian political culture is also an important variable—the absence of primaries and much stronger party discipline has led to less of a tradition of civic involvement in debate. Of course, to some degree, political blogs are deliberately designed to shake up that culture.

It is now the case that all major Australian news media outlets have online sites, and these have blogs attached to them. What can independent blog sites do that these cannot?

[MB:] If we confine ourselves to political blogs in the mainstream media, they're few and far between, in large part because the ABC has reservations about control of content and balance and because Fairfax has a hit-driven celebrity/dating/trash blogging strategy. Tim Dunlop's *Blogocracy* is the most interesting, because it's a blog written by an independent blogger who has been tapped on the shoulder by News Limited. In many cases the blogs are more interesting as a phenomenon because of the amount of discussion they generate, and the degree to which it's largely hostile and critical of the established lines and talking points of the punditariat. Few of the so-called 'bloggers' on the News platforms are really that, with a few exceptions such as Andrew Bolt, who, had he not been a journo, would have been a prominent blogger!

Independent blogs are able to provide a much more diverse range of views, to report and analyse from positions different to those in which the punditariat are embedded, and often to escape the dominance of the news cycle through writing about other issues than those currently prominent, and campaigning over a sustained period of time on particular issues.

How do blogs interact with the established news media around political and other issues? Do they have an impact on government decision-making?

[MB:] There are probably two things here. The first is that bloggers feed into the news conversation, particularly those bloggers who have a foot in both camps. The second is that op/edders and journos regularly pick up themes and perspectives from blogs (almost always without attribution). Strategically, that can be quite useful to bloggers.

I don't think there's much scope for impacts on public policy at the moment as most blogs tend more to be concerned with the dynamics of politics than the substance of policy. But I think that might change, particularly with issues such as climate change where there are bloggers who are both expert and passionate.

What developments do you see as likely in this area over the next five to ten years?

[MB:] I think that local blogging will become much more important. Bloggers will tend to have more of an impact where they have genuine knowledge and 'live' the issues they write about—that might mean local or state politics or it might be an issue or perspective. I think there will be a continued blurring of the lines between the independent blogosphere and the mainstream media, and I think that one development worth watching would be the degree to which aggregator sites emerge which provide a genuine alternative to news sites for the sort of demographic who regularly access news and views via the Net.

Blogs, social software, and social capital

One question that arises from the development of blogs and other forms of social software is whether their development contributes to the growth of *social capital*, and in particular to new forms such as virtual social capital. In his well-known work on the significance of social capital, Putnam (1995: 665) defined social capital as 'features of social life—networks, norms, and trust—that enable participants to act together more effectively to pursue shared interests ... Social capital, in short, refers to social connections and the attendant norms and trust'. Woolcock (2001: 13) defined it as 'the norms and networks that facilitate collective action', while Davies (2003: 11) defined it as the 'value of social networks' and as 'a resource which we can invest time and money in, and which pays returns'.

The promotion, nurturing, and maintenance of forms of social capital has been identified as being critical to overall economic performance, the avoidance of adverse social consequences (crime, drug abuse, adverse public health outcomes), and to the emergence of new forms of social entrepreneurship that fill gaps between market-led solutions and government-driven reform programs (Putnam 1995; Leadbeater 2000; Woolcock 2001; Davies 2003; World Bank 2003). In addressing such questions, Aldridge and colleagues (2002) distinguish between three main types of social capital:

1 *bonding social capital*, characterised by strong social bonds between individuals, for example members of a family, a local community, or an ethnic community
2 *bridging social capital*, characterised by weaker, less dense but more cross-cutting ties, for example with business associates, links across ethnic groups, links between families and communities
3 *linking social capital*, characterised by connections between those with differing levels of power or social status, for example between political elites and the general public, policy-makers and local communities, and individuals from different social classes.

Early commentaries on the relationship between the Internet and social capital saw a naturally positive correlation between the decentralised and inclusive nature of the Internet and the revivification of civic engagement and a sense of community (e.g. Rheingold 1994; Sclove 1995; Schuler 1996). Nonetheless, Putnam himself (2000: 177) was cool on the idea that Internet users would be more civically engaged, and expressed concerns about unequal access to the new technology and 'cyber-balkanisation'. There were related concerns about the adverse impact of Internet use on family life and engagement in other 'offline' activities (Nie & Erbring 2000), and the tendency towards group polarisation and heightened political conflict in environments that heightened interaction between those with divergent points of view (Sunstein 2002). Empirical work that emerged during this period found that the Internet acted, on balance, as a positive stimulus to community engagement and civic and political participation, but that it needed to be recognised that the nature of the Internet itself was changing such forms of engagement and participation, and that new metrics were needed for new media (Wellman et al. 2001). In a similar vein, Aldridge and colleagues (2002: 48–9) concluded that the Internet was promoting a transformation of forms of civic engagement, particularly among younger users, where sustained engagement with globally networked organisations was becoming more important than traditional locality-based forms of participation in community organisations such as sporting teams, local churches, or Rotary clubs.

The question that remains is whether social software and its facilitation and promotion of large-scale public online participation is changing the nature of engagement and participation and their relationship to social capital. If we use the definitions of social capital provided above, blogs are clearly a use of social software to develop new forms of social capital that are bridging and, to varying degrees, bonding and linking. The function of *permalinks* within blogs, which enable a permanent link to be established to other blogs and the documents posted on them even as they change (and the URL changes with them), is one of the many indicators of the desire of bloggers to maintain an ongoing sense of community, not only with their readers, but with the wider community of bloggers with whom they coexist. On a variety of indicators, it would seem that we should regard the rise of blogging and other forms of social software as having a positive impact on the development and maintenance of social capital, even if they may also represent to their critics (e.g. Keen 2007) a new form of narcissism on a global scale.

The other issue with blogs is whether their moment has peaked. While the number of daily blog posts grew from 500,000 at the time of the US presidential election (October 2004) to 2.5 million at the time of the Israel–Hezbollah conflict in southern Lebanon (June 2006), it was notable that growth subsequently plateaued (Doctorow 2006). The Gartner Group estimated that the number of blogs worldwide would level off at about 100 million, and there are also about 200 million abandoned blogs, or blogs that were started but whose creators have long since ceased to post on the site, including celebrities such as Lindsay Lohan, Melanie Griffith and Barbra Streisand (*Australian* 2007). Even if this is true, it may well be the case that some have ceased to blog because they have moved to other forms of social software, and it is also the case—as often occurs in the age of the global Internet—that the fastest rates of growth are outside the English-speaking world. For example, as tensions escalated in the Middle East, the Farsi or Persian language—the majority language of Iran and Afghanistan, and a significant language through Central Asia and the Middle East—became one of the top ten languages of the blogosphere (Doctorow 2006).

Downsides of networks

It is important to conclude this chapter, which has emphasised the positive and transformative capacities of networks to social, economic, cultural, and political relationships, with some consideration of the potential downsides to the network form, both in terms of its internal logic and its wider socio-economic impacts. The first is that, at a purely technical level, networks frequently fail. Servers crash, infrastructural systems fail, website access becomes overloaded and hence unavailable, and acts of what contract lawyers term *force majeure* occur, which can range from power blackouts on a particular location because of an overloaded electricity grid, to acts of war or terrorism that decimate core communications infrastructures almost instantaneously, as happened in the Downtown Manhattan district of New York in the immediate aftermath of 9/11.

Second, we always need to be conscious of the insider/outsider dimensions of networks. At a global level, Castells has drawn attention to the inclusion/exclusion dimensions of access, involvement, and participation that arise in a networked global economy that are based on geographical location and the geopolitical significance of that location in the global space of flows (see e.g. Castells 2000: 70–165). In relation to the creative industries, McRobbie (2005) has argued that a form of 'network sociality' in these sectors has generated a form of 'PR meritocracy', whereby familiar patterns of social exclusion on the basis of gender, race, ethnicity, social location, and other factors continue to occur, but they are based less upon overt discrimination than upon the question of who has the time and capacity for after-hours social networking. Gill's work (2002) on participation in project-based new media work, and the very significant barriers faced by women and by people with young children (again, mostly women) is pertinent in this context.

Finally, networks have historically been associated with corruption specifically, and inequalities of access more generally. Al Qa'eda and its offshoots presents an example of a network that is innovative in its organisational form but massively damaging to populations worldwide in terms of its wider geopolitical implications and how these impact on populations at a very local level (e.g. shopkeepers, tourism service operators, and restaurateurs in Bali seeking to maintain tourist-related trade after the 2002 and 2005 bombings). The example of *The Sopranos* provides a very clear instance in popular media of how bonding social capital can work to anti-social purposes (Lavery 2002), and comparable cases can be identified with, among others, the family-based and ethnically structured nature of criminal organisations such as the Sicilian mafia, the Colombian drug cartels, the Russian *mafiyas*, the Chinese Triads, and the Japanese *Yakuza*.

In a different way, high levels of bonding social capital in particular have been associated with racial intolerance and conflict between communities. One example includes the Catholic/Protestant divide in Northern Ireland, where there is a great deal of bonding social capital within the sectarian communities, but what is missing are those forms of social capital that bridge these sectarian community divides. Whether the rise of the Internet, ICTs, and social networking media provide new forms of virtual social capital that can effectively work across such divides remains a question with an unknown answer.

 ## USEFUL WEBSITES

BoingBoing: A Directory of Wonderful Things <http://boingboing.net>. A lively online site committed to aggregating and publicising the most interesting things to come from blogs and other forms of social networking software.

International Network for Social Network Analysis <www.insna.org>. A site dedicated to gathering and distributing academic research on social networks. The INSNA was founded by Barry Wellman in 1978, and the professional society has over 1000 members worldwide.

Technorati <http://technorati.com>. A site that aggregates blog contributions and provides data on hit rates for blogs and other forms of social software, and also provides analysis and commentary on developments in the blogosphere.

06

participatory
media cultures

A more participatory media culture has always been one of the great promises of new media. Early writers such as Rheingold (1994) envisaged the rise of a virtual public sphere, while Turkle (1995) saw identity as being able to become much more fluid and changeable in the virtual world of cyberspace. The scope for new media to be more participatory arose from its apparent structural differences from the forms of *mass communication* that had been predominant media models in 20th-century societies. Authors such as Thompson (1995) and McQuail (2005) have identified some of the key features of mass communication:

1 the use of media technologies which enable large-scale *production* and *distribution* of informational and symbolic content to reach the largest audience possible, who in turn possess technological devices for *reception* of such content
2 *institutional separation* of the producers/distributors and receivers of media content, arising from both the costs of access to technologies of production and distribution, and the role played by various media gatekeepers as determinants of what constituted 'professional' media content

3 an *asymmetrical power relationship* between producers/distributors and
   receivers of media, with the latter having little scope to respond to a
   largely *one-way communications flow*

4 relations between producers/distributors and receivers/consumers of
   media that were largely *impersonal, anonymous* and, in most instances,
   commodified through the reliance of large-scale commercial media
   industries upon advertising revenue (i.e. the audience was viewed as a
   'target market')

5 tendencies towards *standardisation of content*, as the desire to maximise
   aggregate audiences (market share) created dynamics that promoted
   media content with the broadest possible appeal (i.e. limited scope
   for market segmentation through product differentiation).

The mass communication paradigm in turn rested on the *transmission
model of communication* which—allowing for factors such as feedback, noise,
and signal failure—saw communications as primarily a one-way flow of
messages from senders (typically few) to receivers (typically many). While
this model was certainly being challenged conceptually from the 1970s
through cultural studies and its focus on the complexities of decoding and
the activity of audiences (Hall 1982; cf. Bassett 2007 for a recent evaluation),
and was eroding as a model for an understanding of media industries from
the 1980s, it was the rise of the Internet and networked ICTs in the 1990s
that heralded claims that we were experiencing a decisive break from mass
communications as we went into the 21st century. This argument typically
had two components, one relating to the capacity of new media to enable
greater participation in politics and political communication, the other
relating to new media's potential to enable more and more people to become
media producers and distributors as well as consumers.

Many have identified the possibility of new media and ICTs enabling
greater democratic political participation, and fostering a new, more egalitarian and participatory form of citizenship and political engagement. The
factors commonly cited as enabling ICTs to be a force for broadening and
deepening democracy have been identified by several authors (Tsagarousianou
et al. 1998; Hague & Loader 1999; Clift 2000; Blumler & Coleman 2001),
and include:

1 the scope for horizontal or peer-to-peer communication, as distinct
   from vertical or top-down communication

2 the capacity for users to access, share, and verify information from a wide range of global sources

3 the lack of government controls over the Internet as a global communications medium, as compared to more territorially based media

4 the ability to form virtual communities, or online communities of interest, that are unconstrained by geography

5 the capacity to disseminate, debate, and deliberate on current issues, and to challenge professional and official positions

6 the potential for *political disintermediation*, or communication that is not filtered by political organisations, 'spin doctors', or the established news media.

The second, related conception of this rise of participatory media through the Internet and networked ICTs is their capacity to promote do-it-yourself (DIY) media production. Blogs, and other Web 2.0 technologies, are substantive manifestations in a digital environment of what McKay (1998) termed—in the context of protest activities in 1990s Britain—*DIY culture*. McKay defined DIY culture as 'a combination of inspiring action, narcissism, youthful arrogance, principle, ahistoricism, idealism, indulgence, creativity, plagiarism, as well as the rejection and embracing alike of technical innovation' (1998: 2). Picking up on McKay's suggestive proposition, Hartley (1999a) developed the concept of *DIY citizenship*, which related the decline of deference and a growing reluctance to accept the authority of established institutions of the media as well as government, and a demand for speaking rights, meaningful interaction with authority figures, and what Hartley (1999a: 186–7) termed *semiotic self-determination*, or the right to determine one's own identity. Although new media is not at the centre of either McKay's or Hartley's analysis of DIY culture and citizenship, it certainly has fed into and amplified tendencies in the wider media and public culture where, as Deuze has argued, 'people not only have come to expect participation from the media [but] they increasingly have found ways to enact this participation in the multiple ways they use and make media ... the Internet can be seen as an amplifier of this trend' (2006: 68).

Participatory media

The concept of participatory media predates the rise of the Internet and networked ICTs. The Hutchins Commission on Freedom of the Press, set up in the USA in 1942, argued in its final report in 1947 that a responsible press needed not only to have full, truthful, and comprehensive reporting of events, but should also 'serve as a forum for the exchange of comment and criticism', as well as providing 'a representative picture of constituent groups in society' (quoted in McQuail 2005: 171). The sense that mainstream commercial media have failed to meet such objectives acted as a stimulus to the development of various forms of *community media* or *alternative media* in the second half of the 20th century. These ranged from party-political or openly partisan forms of media (print media examples from the United Kingdom have included *New Statesman*, *Marxism Today*, *Tribune*, and *Morning Star*), very locally based newspapers and monographs, and the community broadcasting sector. The latter often had an explicit remit to promote access, participation, and openness to perspectives not covered in mainstream media, and such activity was at the cornerstone of the PBS in the USA and the organisations associated with the Community Broadcasting Association of Australia (CBAA), to take two examples (see Rennie 2006 for an overview). The Community Broadcasting Foundation (CBF) defines the Australian community media sector in the following terms:

> Community media distinguishes itself from other media by actively promoting access and participation in the processes of media operations, administration and production. Community broadcasting is volunteer driven with over 20,000 volunteer broadcasters and support staff helping to deliver media 'for the people by the people'. The sector provides invaluable opportunities for community access, participation, training, experimentation and innovation in radio and television production. (CBF 2007)

Atton (2001, 2002, 2004) has drawn attention to the extent to which definitional confusion about what constitutes 'community', 'alternative', and 'radical' media may have historically understated the significance of these forms of media to the contemporary media landscape. For Atton, the assumption that such media need to be in direct opposition to existing sites of media-political power has constituted an important limitation to understanding the role and significance of the community sector since, as Couldry (2003) has also noted, it fails to register innovation within the media system itself, which has no *prima facie* connection to the politics of the content that is distributed. This leads Atton to define alternative media as being characterised by:

1 *de-professionalisation*: the capacity to write, publish, and distribute news, ideas, and comment that is not contingent upon the acquisition of a set of

professional skills, values, and norms that render a potential contributor 'qualified' to disseminate such material;

2 *de-institutionalisation*: the ability to get such material into the public domain, which is not contingent upon the decision-making practices of large-scale media institutions, whether in the commercial or public sectors;

3 *de-capitalisation*: the willingness to distribute media in all forms that can occur through mechanisms that require low up-front investments and low recurrent costs, so that the capacity to distribute and disseminate media content is not thwarted by the prior need for market viability of the distributing venture. (2002: 25)

A different way of understanding participatory media emerged from cultural studies and the observations made from within this theoretical framework about how the circuit of mass communication was never complete and always contested, since the personal, political, and emotional meanings and investments that audiences made in the mass-distributed products of popular culture were frequently at odds with the intended meanings of their producers. Cultural studies theorists (e.g. Hall 1986; Fiske 1987, 1992; Turner 1990) questioned the claim that the dominant meanings of popular media reflected the class interests of those who own and control the institutions that control the means of production and distribution. They drew attention to the complex and contested nature of the politics of meaning through use of the Italian Marxist Antonio Gramsci's concept of *hegemony* (1971). This work drew attention to the extent to which readings of popular cultural texts rarely duplicate the 'preferred reading' of their producers, but are instead commonly characterised by 'negotiated' or even 'oppositional' readings; and *textual polysemy*, or the ways in which the meaning of a text is never simply given by the intentions of its author, but is rather subject to a wider social negotiation through structures and systems of interpretation. One important implication of such work, made most explicit in the work of John Fiske (1987, 1992), was that there were 'two economies' in mass media: a *financial economy*, driven by the profit maximisation strategies of commercial media institutions, and a *cultural economy*, where the popularity of media texts is determined through 'the exchange and circulation of ... meanings, pleasures and social identities' (Fiske 1987: 311). Since success in the former is contingent upon success in the latter, it followed that popular media needed to be open to multiple interpretations by a socially diverse and mixed population, in order to be both popular and commercially successful.

This brief detour through *active audience theories* in cultural studies is relevant to debates about participatory media in the new media context as it draws attention to arguments that have been catalysts to the nature of participatory media in what Jenkins (2006a) terms convergence culture. For Jenkins, contemporary phenomena associated with Web 2.0 activities such as blogging, and sites such as *YouTube, MySpace*, and *Flickr* need to be understood in the context of the history of fan cultures that have developed around popular media over a number of years, which include fanzine reinscriptions of the *Star Trek* series, engagement with the *Twin Peaks* television scripts through alt.tv virtual community sites, and the engagement of games developers as well as the developers of reality TV programs such as *Survivor* with their online user communities (Jenkins 2006a,b). Following on from earlier insights from cultural studies, Jenkins proposes that convergence is, by its nature as a cultural as well as a technological phenomenon, both a top-down and a bottom-up process:

> Media companies are learning how to accelerate the flow of media content across delivery channels to expand revenue opportunities, broaden markets, and reinforce viewer commitments. Consumers are learning how to use these different media technologies to bring the flow of media more fully under their control and to interact with other consumers. The promises of this new media environment raise expectations of a freer flow of ideas and content. Inspired by those ideals, consumers are fighting for the right to participate more fully in their culture. Sometimes, corporate and grassroots convergence reinforce each other, creating closer, more rewarding relations between media producers and consumers. Sometimes, the two forces are at war and those struggles will redefine the face of ... popular culture. (2006a: 18)

Web 2.0 and everyday creativity

One of the issues opened up by second-generation new media technologies, referred to under the general rubric of Web 2.0, is whether they have opened up significantly more opportunities for people to produce and disseminate creative work, and whether they can demonstrate their creativity to a much wider community of people. In noting the growing capacity of new media technologies to enable the 'capturing and sharing' of digital content in its various forms, Lawrence Lessig observes:

This digital 'capturing and sharing' is in part an extension of the capturing and sharing that has always been integral to our culture, and in part it is something new. It is continuous with the Kodak model, but it explodes the boundaries of Kodak-like technologies. The technology of digital 'capturing and sharing' promises a world of extraordinarily diverse creativity that can be easily and broadly shared ... Technology has thus given us an opportunity to do something with culture that has only ever been possible for individuals in small groups, isolated from others. Think about an old man telling a story to a collection of neighbours in a small town. Now imagine that same story-telling extended across the globe. (2004: 184–5)

In the context of Web 2.0 and the websites and technologies associated with it, this has of course become a reality. Lessig's example of photography draws attention to the shift from what he refers to as the 'Kodak model', where photos become easy for all to take, but where their processing remains reliant on specialists, and distribution and is largely contingent on the ability of the photo-taker to show people their photos in face-to-face situations (e.g. the photo album or slide night), to the model now provided by online sites such as *Flickr* (www.flickr.com). Digital cameras (including those embedded in mobile phones) and their link to computers make it easy for photographers of all levels of skill to take pictures and upload them onto their personal computers. What sites such as *Flickr* enable are different levels of distribution of such content. If you have a series of cute baby photos that you would like to share with your extended family, but that family is geographically dispersed, you can use *Flickr* site capabilities to regulate access to those photos. If, however, you are a budding professional photographer, and wish to have your work available to a wider community of users (including potential clients and buyers of your work), the *Flickr* site enables your work to be subject to peer ranking systems that provide ongoing feedback about your work and expose it to very wide communities of interest.

Burgess (2006) has linked this growing capacity for 'ordinary' cultural participation—across the amateur/professional divide—with the democratising and participatory potential of new media technologies through the concept of *vernacular creativity*. She defines vernacular creativity as 'both an ideal and a heuristic device, to describe and illuminate creative practices that emerge from highly particular and non-elite social contexts and communicative conventions' (2006: 206). The concept of the 'vernacular' is used 'to distinguish "everyday" language from institutional or official modes of expression', while Burgess defines creativity as 'the process by which available cultural resources (including both "material" resources—content, and immaterial resources—genre conventions, shared knowledges) are recombined in novel ways, so that they are both recognisable because of their familiar elements, and create affective impact through the innovative process of this recombination' (2006: 206). In developing a definition of vernacular creativity as 'a productive articulation of consumer practices and knowledges … with older popular traditions and communicative practices' (2006: 207), Burgess draws upon the work of Atton (2002) and Couldry (2003) on media democratisation, which identifies the capacity of 'hybrid forms of media *consumption-production* … [to] challenge the entrenched division of labour … that is the essence of media power' (Couldry 2003: 45).

Leadbeater and Miller (2004) refer to this as the *Pro-Am Revolution*. Defining 'Pro-Ams' as 'innovative, committed and networked amateurs working to professional standards' (2004: 9), they identify activities as diverse as rap music and music sampling, the Linux open source software program, the Jubilee 2000 campaign around Third World debt, user modifications of *The Sims* online computer game, and the activities of Muhummad Yunnus in alleviating poverty in Bangladesh through micro-credit schemes, as examples of how 'when Pro-Ams are networked together, they can have a huge impact on politics and culture, economics and development' (2004: 12). Arguing that 'Pro-Ams work at their leisure, regard consumption as a productive activity, and set professional standards to judge their amateur efforts', Leadbeater and Miller (2004: 23) distinguish the 'Pro-Am' from both the casual leisure enthusiast and the accredited professional through the following typology:

Figure 6.1 Pro-Ams in the wider participatory community

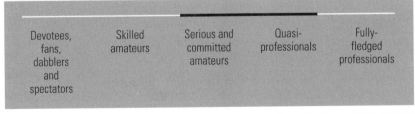

| Devotees, fans, dabblers and spectators | Skilled amateurs | Serious and committed amateurs | Quasi-professionals | Fully-fledged professionals |

Source: Leadbeater & Miller 2004: 23

Leadbeater (2007) has extended this argument to propose that the 21st-century social-economic system is one that will be based on *mass creativity*. He proposes that modern capitalism is, as Benkler (2006) also argues, based on systems of social production that blur historical lines of demarcation between commercial production, public sector provision, and the community/non-profit sector. The rise of 'Pro-Am' production models, and the scope for mass distribution with continuous feedback through networked new media technologies, generates 'a huge challenge to the established organisational order and the professions who design, control and lead them':

> Consumers turn out to be producers. Demand breeds its own supply. Leisure becomes a form of work. A huge amount of creative work is done in spite of, or perhaps because, of people not being paid ... They embody a new ethic of collaborative, shared effort, not often motivated by money ... The truth is that most traditional commercial organisations do not want their consumers to become collaborators. They quite like them passive and so dependent ... The idea that you might be able to lead more effectively in a far more open, transparent and conversational way ruins all the fun. *The irresistible force of collaborative mass innovation is about to meet the immovable force of entrenched corporate organisation.* (Leadbeater 2007; emphasis added)

CASE STUDY: DIGITAL STORYTELLING

Digital storytelling has emerged since the mid-1990s as an important set of initiatives to use new media technologies to enable ordinary people to tell their own stories in a compelling format that can be readily available to others. It frequently involves autobiographical films of eight minutes or less in length, with an interactive element, that can be distributed through the Web or television. Importantly, it is not simply about enabling access, as we find with Web pages, Web cams, social networking sites, and so on, but involves a facilitated process whereby those who have specialised knowledge in the use of these digital technologies provide training to relatively new users, not only in how to use the technologies, but to tell stories in ways that have strong underlying narratives and are emotionally compelling for an audience (Lambert 2002; Burgess et al. 2006). This commitment to community engagement and empowerment differentiates it from related new media forms such as interactive journalism, narrative-based games, or personal blogs or home pages.

Two broad developments mark out the conceptual as well as practical origins of digital storytelling. First, a production workshop was developed in 1993 by the American artist and media producer Dana Atchley at the American Film Institute. This served as a catalyst for Joe Lambert and others to develop training workshops in the San Francisco Bay Area, which constituted the basis for the Centre for Digital Storytelling (CDS), established in 1994. Inspired by a vision of cultural democracy and community arts activism, the centre's focus is on grassroots initiatives, personal narratives, and the empowering of those unfamiliar with the use of digital technologies. The CDS is a 'non-profit training, project development, and research organization dedicated to assisting people in using digital media to tell meaningful stories from their lives', with a focus on personal voice, thoughtful and emotionally direct stories, and facilitative teaching methods which enable knowledge-sharing and knowledge transfer (CDS 2007).

The second major initiative has come from the BBC, and its decision in 2001 to commission the *Capture Wales* project, led by Daniel Meadows from Cardiff University's School of Journalism, Media, and Cultural Studies (Meadows 2003). In 2002, a comparable initiative was undertaken by the BBC in England, titled *Telling Lives*. Digital stories produced with the assistance of the BBC are distributed across many BBC sites, including dedicated websites (www.bbc.co.uk/wales/capturewales/; www.bbc.co.uk/tellinglives/), and through BBC television, BBCi satellite television, and BBC Radio in the case of audio stories. The BBC has further developed its resources for online DIY storytelling and media participation through its *Create* site (www.bbc.co.uk/create/), which offers a plethora of tools and sites from which to develop digital content in the form of films, stories, music, artworks, reviews, journalism, and family histories. There is also the BBC *Action Network* (formerly *iCan*) which has promoted grassroots community political activism (www.bbc.co.uk/dna/actionnetwork/).

While the BBC initiative shares obvious features with the approach of the USA's CDS, it is also overlaid by elements of the BBC's remit to promote citizenship and to tell stories and represent experiences from across the United Kingdom. In the BBC Charter Review process that commenced in 2004 and was completed in 2007, the six core principles for the BBC in the 21st century were identified as sustaining citizenship and civil society; promoting education and learning; stimulating creativity and cultural excellence; reflecting the United Kingdom's nations, regions, and communities; bringing the world to the United Kingdom and the United

> ## CASE STUDY (*cont.*)
>
> Kingdom to the world; and Building Digital Britain (DCMS 1998). Digital initiatives such as digital storytelling serve this new active citizenship agenda in the digital age by creating opportunities for people to become more active citizens, particularly at the local and regional levels, and stimulating the creativity of audiences by giving them a chance to tell their own stories and make their own programs (BBC 2005). Initiatives in digital storytelling and related manifestations of everyday creativity support the proposition of Burgess and colleagues (2006: 13) that:
>
> > Communication policy around networked media should not only be concerned with ownership, content regulation and controls, but should also try to 'do no harm' to, and even support, platforms, technologies and practices that enable the flowering of the unpredictable forms of everyday and ephemeral creativity and engagement that make up active participation in the networked cultural public sphere.
>
> **Further reading**
> Meadows 2003; Burgess et al. 2006; BBC 2007; CDS 2007

Debating creativity

The first decade of the 21st century has seen a surge of interest in creativity that shows few signs of abating. The popular business literature has been full of work that exhorts corporate managers to unlock the creative potential of their staff, while there is also an extensive self-help literature on how to realise personal creativity (see de Bono 1995; Gary 1999; Nussbaum 2005 for examples; cf. Osborne 2003; Flew 2004a for discussion). Tim Berners-Lee, a key figure in the development of the World Wide Web, identified a critical flaw in its commercially driven evolution since the mid-1990s as being that interactivity was promoted ahead of intercreativity (Berners-Lee 2000). The legal scholar Lawrence Lessig (2004) has identified the suppression of creativity as being a critical flaw of current intellectual property regimes. In his highly influential *The Rise of the Creative Class*, Richard Florida (2002: 5) identified creativity as '*the* decisive source of competitive advantage' in the 21st-century global economy.

Creativity is, however, a famously slippery conceptual category. In one highly influential understanding, which has its origins with Plato and the 19th-century Romantics, any harnessing of creativity to organisations or to policy agendas is anathema, as creativity arises from the 'free, wakeful play of the imagination' (Negus & Pickering 2004: 7). In this discourse, creativity possesses the following characteristics: it views creative people as 'special' people (the 'troubled genius' persona); it closely links creativity to the arts and not to business, science, or technology; the creative process is understood as being essentially spontaneous; and it has the implicit assumption that creativity cannot be formally taught, since it is a 'gift' that some have and others don't.

Bilton has observed that whereas arts practitioners have come to be somewhat more circumspect about such understandings of creativity, and increasingly interpret their activities through frameworks such as performative research or *practice-led research* (Gray 2006; Haseman 2006), the notion of creativity as the wild play of imagination has found new champions in the business community. This leads to assumptions that 'creative people need to be protected from commercial realities, that budgets and deadlines might interfere with the eccentric, child-like world of pure inventiveness … [and] managers are warned from "meddling" in the creative process because their rules and rationality have no validity in the world of art and innovation' (Bilton 2007: 8).

Such discourses in turn invoke scepticism about the value of the whole notion of creativity. In the context of debates about the creative industries (see Chapter 9), Donald (2004: 236) remains unconvinced that creativity is 'anything other than a conceptual black hole', and that trying to teach creativity is 'absurd and self-defeating' since demonstrated creativity is 'invariably a by-product of learning to do other, more concrete … things'. In a similar vein, Osborne (2003: 510) declares himself to be *against* creativity, in so far as it has become an omnibus, feel-good term that 'as a combination of doctrine and morality … can be captured by business gurus and management writers, Californian lifestyle sects, new age groups, post-identitarian philosophers, literary critics turned cultural theorists, intellectuals, postmodern geographers, anti-globalisation protestors, whoever'.

Authors such as Robinson (2001), Bilton and Leary (2002), Negus and Pickering (2004), and Bilton (2007) provide ways of addressing some of this conceptual vagueness that has surrounded the concept of creativity, moving the debate beyond the Platonic conception of creativity as a unique individual gift. Robinson (2001: 116, 118) defines creativity as '*imaginative processes with outcomes that are original and of value*', which requires that 'creative ideas are more than novel; they are valuable'. Bilton and Leary (2002) argue that the criterion of value is as central as that of newness or innovation, even if it is recognised that the value of a new idea, concept, or product may not be appreciated at the time and place in which it is presented to the world. Negus and Pickering (2004) draw attention to the need not only for creative activities to demonstrate extrinsic value, but for creative acts to be not only expressed but effectively communicated, and to draw upon symbolic and representational systems that can be understood and appreciated by a wider audience, whether a relatively discrete community of scholars or practitioners, or audiences in the wider sense of the general public. This parallels the notion of a *field* of creativity, to be discussed below.

One study that illustrates how conceptual understandings of creativity have been usefully extended into the policy realm is the *Beyond Productivity: Information Technology, Innovation, and Creativity* report for the US National Research Council of the National Academies (Mitchell et al. 2003). *Beyond Productivity* makes much of the importance of *domains* of creativity, recognising that 'no intellectual domain or economic sector has a monopoly on creativity' (2003: 18). It acknowledges that creativity manifests itself differently across the scientific, technological, economic, and cultural domains, in diverse forms such as patents and designs, entrepreneurship, and artistic product. Identifying information technologies as a 'glue' that can bring these domains of creative practice into a closer collaborative set of relationships, they map these interconnections in the manner set out in Figure 6.2.

Figure 6.2 Domains of creative practice and the role of information technology

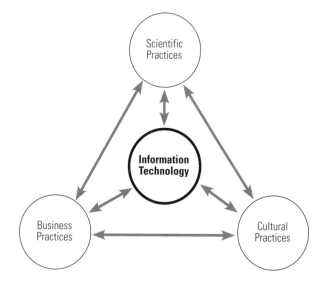

Source: Mitchell et al. 2003: 25

The specific focus of *Beyond Productivity* was the extent to which developments in information technology and creative practice can be mutually reinforcing, generating dynamic forms of IT-related creative practice (ITCP), and new modes of research, collaboration, education, and wealth creation that bring together the fields of art, design, and information technology. Arguing that 'to work within the realm of information technology and creative practice … individuals or groups need to be fluent in multiple disciplines' (Mitchell et al. 2003: 30), *Beyond Productivity* goes on to identify the institutional and policy challenge as being how to better facilitate such cross-disciplinary interaction.

In the education context, Seltzer and Bentley (2000) sought to identify the implications of a growing stress on creativity in the knowledge economy for learning and for educational institutions. They reject claims that creativity is primarily associated with brilliance, a unique artistic sensibility, innate talents, or even acquired skills, arguing instead that:

> [creativity] requires the ability to solve problems progressively over time and apply previous knowledge to new situations. Creativity is also bound up with context—it can only be defined and assessed in relation to the context in which it is achieved. It must be developed through the interaction of the learner, her underlying goals and motivations, and the resources and context in which she operates. (2000: 19)

They identify the four core characteristics of creativity, which they associate with creative problem-solving:

· the ability to formulate new problems, rather than depending on others to define them
· the ability to transfer what one learns across different contexts
· the ability to recognise that learning is incremental and involves making mistakes
· the capacity to focus one's attention in pursuit of a goal. (2000: 19)

For these writers, the paradox of the creative age for education is that the rapidly changing socio-economic environment requires individuals to be increasingly adaptive, but the wrong way in which to train people for this environment is to cram more content into course curricula so that people can formally learn more and more skills. This would fall into the fallacy that creativity is the unique property of the individual. In practice, creativity is deeply shaped by both the domains in which it is applied (the arts, sciences, business, policy-making, community sector organisations, schools, etc.), and by those who validate creativity by making judgments on it, or what they term a *field*. The nature of a field may vary from the judgments of teachers, professors, assessors, judges, or peers, to the purchasing decisions made by consumers. Given that the realisation of creativity necessarily entails an interaction between the person, activity, and task, the domains in which it is applied, and the fields through which it is validated, creative outcomes can never be guaranteed by a school curriculum, a government policy, or any single institutional instrument or form. Seltzer and Bentley (2000: ix) argue that it is best promoted in environments characterised by trust, freedom of action, application across a variety of contexts, the balance between skills and challenges, interactive exchange of knowledge and ideas, and the experience of achieving concrete, real-world outcomes.

In his review of literature on management and creativity in the creative industries, Bilton (2007) draws attention to the phenomenon of 'the genius and the water-carrier'. Drawing on a comment by the former French international footballer Eric Cantona that his team-mate Didier Deschamps was 'merely a water-carrier', Bilton argues that it is precisely the existence of 'workhorse' players whose play is characterised by hard work and unspectacular endeavour that allows the brilliant but sometimes undisciplined players such as Cantona (and others such as Diego Maradona in the Argentinian side) to flourish, even if it is those who are perceived to be 'creative geniuses' who attract the most attention and, no less significantly, sponsorship. But flamboyant creative individual talents such as Cantona, Maradona, David Beckham and others are only as good as the teams around them. Bilton identifies in this a wider metaphor for the organisation of creativity in the media entertainment industries, where creative teams and projects depend on uncreative people and activities:

> Creativity in the commercial creative industries is represented through the branding and packaging of individual talent and the personality cult fostered around stars and celebrities. Yet behind the scenes, a more realistic unit of analysis for creative processes and products is the team of partnership. At the core of this creative team is the double-act of the genius and the water-carrier. Creative thinking, like football, depends upon a union of contrasting abilities and styles of thinking or playing. (2007: 19)

CASE STUDY: KEY THEORIES OF CREATIVITY AND THEIR RELEVANCE TO BUSINESS

As we have noted, thinking about creativity has become increasingly important in the 21st-century corporate world, even if there is some debate about how effectively the issues it raises are engaged with in practice. The turn to *creativity as an economic asset* arises from both 'push' and 'pull' factors in the business world. The primary *push* factor has been the growing recognition that it is the ability to generate new ideas, concepts, products, and services that is the key to competitiveness in a knowledge economy, rather than deriving greater efficiencies of use from existing production processes that was central to industrial economies. This is clearly the sine qua non of new media and creative industries, but increasingly characterises industry overall, and the service industries in particular (Giarini 2002; Flew 2004b). The key *pull* factor has been the growing realisation that in the context of globalisation, production activities that are reproducible in multiple locations (i.e. not dependent on location-specific clusters of personal skills, knowledge, and entrepreneurship) are shifting to lower-wage economies, as costs associated with transport and communication fall dramatically (Storper 1997; Flew 2007). While it has long been recognised that manufacturing based on semi-skilled labour has been moving inexorably towards China as the 'world's factory', the surprise of the early 21st century was that more 'hi-tech' knowledge-based jobs in service-related industries are no less geographically mobile, with India in particular emerging as the nation with large numbers of skilled, tertiary-trained, and comparatively low-cost workers.

Putting aside a variety of management 'fads' around creativity in the workplace, such as brainstorming, role-playing, or the 'chicken cheer' (Gary 1999; Bilton 2007), the major influences on contemporary thinking about creativity in business and elsewhere derive from the work of three key authors. The first is Teresa Amabile, the Edsel Bryant Ford Professor of Business Administration at the Harvard Business School. In her pioneering work on the social psychology of creativity, *Creativity in Context*, Amabile argued that 'a product or response will be judged as creative to the extent that (a) it is both a novel and appropriate, useful, correct or valuable response to the task at hand, and (b) the task is heuristic rather than algorithmic' (1996: 35). By heuristic, Amabile refers

CASE STUDY (cont.)

to tasks that 'do not have a clear and identifiable path to solution', meaning that problem-finding is as important a creative task as problem-solving.

Margaret Boden is a second key theorist of creativity, whose work has been most influential in information technology-related fields. In *The Creative Mind* (1990), an important distinction is made between creativity in a psychological sense (*P-creativity*) and creativity in a historical sense (*H-creativity*). P-creativity refers to ideas that are fundamentally novel with respect to the individual mind that had the idea, while H-creativity refers to ideas being fundamentally novel with respect to human history more generally. Boden argues that while much of the history of ideas and creativity focuses on 'H-creative' individuals, such approaches are rendered problematic by the obvious counterpoint that discovery is by its nature a social process. By contrast, Boden's interest is in P-creativity, and she argues that it provides not only some coordinates for understanding how originality is possible and not contingent on other social and historical factors, but also a basis for understanding how the creativity of individual human beings can be sustained over time. P-creativity is also a benchmark for understanding a creative idea as one that is not simply new or novel, but one that is difficult to understand or interpret within the existing set of generative rules that we use to understand and interpret other, more familiar ideas (1990: 35–40). Boden's interest in this question relates to a specific question she has posed in relation to computers and information technology more generally, which is whether they can be creative, and not simply innovative in recoding and reorganising existing products of the human mind. Boden's answer to this is complex and not easily summarised, but she does conclude that up to a point, it is possible for computational programs to model the generation of creative ideas. The idea that the creative process is something uniquely human that cannot be replicated through computational devices rests for Boden on a misunderstanding of creativity as the unique by-product of certain types of human experience (Boden 1990).

The final key theorist of creativity to be considered is Mihaly Csikszentmihalyi. Again rejecting definitions of creativity that derive from the characteristics of certain types of people—noting in this case the overlaps that exist between being talented, creative, and a genius—

Csikszentmihalyi instead proposes a *systems model of creativity* that identifies it as arising from the interaction of three elements:

1   a *domain* for creativity, consisting of a discrete set of symbolic rules and procedures (e.g. mathematics, music, and cognitive science are domains, but humanity, culture, and the human condition are not)
2   a *field* into which new ideas are received, which includes all of those individuals who act as gatekeepers to the domain, which may include academics, critics, and curators in the arts, managers, investors, and venture capitalists in business, or designers, programmers, and product developers in information technology fields
3   an *individual person* who, 'using the symbols of a given domain … has a new idea or sees a new pattern' (Csikszentmihalyi 1996: 28), and this is incorporated into the relevant domain through adoption within the relevant field.

From this, Csikszentmihalyi defines creativity as 'any act, idea or product that changes an existing domain, or that transforms an existing domain into a new one', and he defines a creative person as 'someone whose thoughts or actions change a domain, or establish a new one'.

Of these three theorists of creativity, Amabile most directly relates her work to the issues facing business. She has identified six counter-propositions that challenge some of the prevailing myths of creativity that are commonly found in the corporate world:

1   Creativity comes primarily from the intrinsic motivations of all people, rather than from the 'creative types' within the organisation.
2   It is supportive yet challenging work environments, rather than money, that motivates people to be creative at work.
3   Time to think about problems, rather than time pressure, best promotes creativity.
4   Joy and happiness, rather than fear, best drive people towards creative solutions.
5   Collaboration rather than competition leads to better creative solutions.
6   Corporate downsizing damages the potential for creativity in organisations, rather than promoting it. (Amabile 2004)

CASE STUDY (*cont.*)

Boden's work has been very important in thinking about computers and artificial intelligence because, while her argument ultimately points to the limits of computers in generating creative ideas, it also points to the extent to which creative ideas draw upon generative rules and systems that computational programs are extremely good at modelling and replicating. It took human minds, for instance, to develop the Google search algorithm, but the nature of search algorithms is that, once developed, they can become very sophisticated in dealing with a multiplicity of forms of data in systematised ways that are creative in how they organise information, even if the original algorithmic capability could not be developed from the computational devices themselves.

Csikszentmihalyi's work is important in drawing our attention to the ways in which creative ideas arise in relation to particular domains of application, and that new ideas require some form of acceptance in a wider field through which they are evaluated and applied. These arguments indicate that creative ideas will be of little value to organisations that have neither the competence nor the resources to apply and absorb them. Many of the failures of the dot.com boom of the late 1990s arose from uncritical acceptance of a cult of 'learn from Amazon' or 'learn from eBay', whereby insights generated in very specific contexts were seen as generally applicable to everything from broadcast television to university education. It also alerts us to the dangers of too much innovation, which runs ahead of the markets and communities it is intended to serve. This is explored in relation to the 'innovator's dilemma', discussed in Chapter 10.

Further reading

Boden 1990; Amabile 1996; Csikszentmihalyi 1996; Sternberg 1999; Robinson 2001; Bilton 2007

USEFUL WEBSITES

BBC Create <www.bbc.co.uk/create>. A comprehensive do-it-yourself media tool-kit, with over 50 sites from which users can access tools to assist in producing and distributing everything from music and short films to news stories and family histories. Designed for users of all ages, it also enables children to create ringtones, become sports reporters, and send in pictures of the *Teletubbies*.

Centre for Digital Storytelling <www.storycenter.org>. Established in the San Francisco Bay Area in the mid-1990s, the CDS has been a pioneer in enabling people without digital media skills to develop online stories that reflect on their life experience.

Confessions of an Aca-Fan: The Official Weblog of Henry Jenkins <www.henryjenkins.org>. Professor Henry Jenkins practises what he preaches concerning participatory media, with a lively blog where he posts daily, with the aim of bridging the gap between academic media research and a general public which is grappling with trying to make sense of these emerging forms. Jenkins covers everything from computer games to censorship to professional wrestling.

games:
technology, industry,
culture

TERRY FLEW and SAL HUMPHREYS

The global interactive games industry is large and growing, and is at the forefront of many of the most significant innovations in new media. While measures of industry size vary, it was estimated that global revenues in the games sector were at least $US30 billion in 2006; in the USA, the Entertainment Software Alliance, which represents the major players in the games industry, found that sales of computer and video game software were $7.4 billion in 2006 (ESA 2006). The two major games forms are games purchased as a stand-alone package and played on games consoles commonly attached to the television (video games), and online multiplayer games (sometimes also called massive multiplayer online games or MMOGs), which are played on personal computers that have broadband connectivity and are accessed on a subscription basis. In 2005, video games accounted for over 85 per cent of the total games market (ESA 2006: 10). There is also growth in gaming undertaken through handheld mobile devices such as mobile phones and personal digital assistants (PDAs), and this will develop further with advances in wireless telecommunications.

The significance of interactive games to new media development extends substantially beyond their economic role. *The Economist* (2005) observed:

> Games are widely used as educational tools, not just for pilots, soldiers and surgeons, but also in schools and businesses ... Anyone who has learned to play a handful of games can generally figure out how to operate almost any high-tech device. Games require players to construct hypotheses, solve problems, develop strategies, and learn the rules of the in-game world through trial and error. Gamers must also be able to juggle several different tasks, evaluate risks and make quick decisions ... Playing games is, thus, an ideal form of preparation for the workplace of the 21st century, as some forward-thinking firms are already starting to realise.

Kline and colleagues (2003: 24) have identified interactive games as 'the "ideal commodity" of a post-Fordist/postmodern/promotional capitalism—an artefact within which converge a series of the most important production techniques, marketing strategies, and cultural practices of an era'. The games industry itself identifies direct spin-offs for technological innovation and consumer demand relating to computer processing, demand for broadband services, mobile telecommunications, and digital content, and indirect spin-offs and technology transfer to sectors as diverse as real estate and travel, military training, health care, intelligence testing, and corporate training (Crandall & Sidak 2006).

The convergence of continuous technological innovation, dynamic corporate marketing and branding practices, and the intensity of immersive play and interactive experiences place this sector at the leading edge of new media innovation and debates associated with the cultural appropriateness of digital content, gender identities, the experience of childhood, and intellectual property regimes. Moreover, the rise of games and gaming culture, and particularly the development of MMOGs, where the players are increasingly the creators of the game's content and form themselves into online virtual communities, brings to the fore a series of debates about participatory media culture and user-led innovation, as users increasingly become the creators, and not simply the consumers, of their own media. At the same time, as critical work by authors such as Kline and colleagues (2003) and Terranova (2004) reminds us, all is not necessarily rosy in the games garden. There are significant disputes about issues ranging from the ownership and control of user-generated content in proprietary online games to poor working conditions and burn-out among those working in games production.

This chapter will examine the history of games and the games industry, with particular reference to the transformations of the industry value chain that have occurred over time in what has been a highly volatile sector, strongly subject to boom-and-bust economic cycles. It will critically evaluate the significance of the move from console-based or 'shrink-wrap' gaming to online games and the emergence of MMOGs, and how they have transformed both the games industry and games culture. It will conclude with a consideration of possible future trends in the games industry, and the new issues being presented by the emergence of games with player-created content, virtual communities based around games, and the diverse forms of labour—well paid, badly paid, and unpaid—that keep the global interactive games industry moving.

Games history

Early computer games were developed by the military-industrial-academic complex that also spawned the Internet, with researchers involved with the US nuclear program at MIT's 'Artifical Intelligence' unit generating games in their spare time such as the joystick-based *Spacewar* (completed in 1962) and the paddle-and-ball game *Tennis for Two* (first created in 1958, but patented in 1968 by Ralph Baer). These would be prototypes for the games that would take off into mass-market success in the 1970s, such as *Pong*, released by Atari in 1972, and *Space Invaders*, released by Midway in 1978. These games, and later games such as *Monaco GP* and *Pac-Man*, were primarily arcade-based games, played on coin-operated machines in public places, although console-based games systems, played at home through the television, were becoming increasingly significant. In 1982, worldwide home sales of video games were about $US3 billion, and arcade games grossed $US8 billion in revenue; this compared to international sales of popular music of $US4 billion at this time (Kline et al. 2003: 103–4). But the industry experienced a bust in the mid-1980s, partly triggered by the development of too many titles of poor quality, and Atari—the giant of the industry at this time—had massive losses for its parent company, Time-Warner.

The second half of the 1980s was dominated by Nintendo, as the crash of the North American video game market coincided with its launch of the Nintendo Entertainment System (NES) in 1985, accompanied by the phenomenally successful *Super Mario Bros.* game, whose sales by 1990 had grossed $500 million. Learning from the Atari experience that quality of titles, and not simply volume, was the key to success, its games were marked by dramatically improved pacing, visuals, sound, and dynamism, thus greatly enhancing the experience of play. Nintendo also developed a way to outsource the development of games content to third parties, while retaining quality control over the games through strict licensing procedures, and commenced the process of separating the game engine from the game content. Importantly, Nintendo developed a sophisticated marketing culture, which gave information and support to players and thereby nurtured a gaming subculture, while also using this infrastructure to gain player feedback about the games. *Mario* also provided the basis for spin-offs into other media, with *Super Mario Bros.* providing the basis for a successful children's TV cartoon show and a less successful Hollywood film, as well as lots of spin-offs in the form of T-shirts, comic books, removable tattoos, lunch boxes, etc.[1]

The 1990s were marked by the entry of Sega into the games environment with the 16-bit Genesis console, which used its superior micro-processing capability to generate bigger animated characters, better backgrounds, faster play, and better sound. While not initially successful against Nintendo, Sega's strength lay in its ability to attract games developers to produce for Sega, particularly the giant Electronic Arts gaming company. Sega worked on the proposition, identified by economists Carl Shapiro and Hal Varian (1999: 196), that to develop new markets 'you need to offer performance "ten times better" than the established technology', in order to overcome concerns about switching costs among existing consumers. *Sonic the Hedgehog*, introduced in 1991, was Sega's flagship game. Sega also developed 'riskier' content such as *Street Fighter* and *Mortal Kombat*, marketed strongly at the teenage boy market, which was criticised at the time for being excessively violent (Kline et al. 2003: 132–5). While Sega made significant market inroads, particularly in Europe, Nintendo responded by developing the GameBoy, a miniature, portable, handheld console that would, among other things, genetically transform the thumbs of a generation of users (it also prepared them for mobile phones!). The nature of the console wars changed again in 1994, when the giant media conglomerate Sony launched the PlayStation, which capitalised on both Sony's high-profile brand identity and the shift in games storage devices from cartridges to CD-ROMs, which were much cheaper to produce and distribute. This period also saw computer-based gaming, long the sleeping giant of the sector, rise in prominence with the development of *Wolfenstein* (1991), *Myst* (1993), *Doom* (1994), and *Quake* (1995). These games were much more 'adult' than standard gaming fare and, importantly, exploited the possibilities presented by the Internet to generate player-developed content. The makers of *Doom*—id Software—released their source code online, thereby allowing players to develop their own levels of the game, and thus extend and modify the game itself.

By the early 2000s, the console-based games industry was divided along the familiar post-Fordist business paradigm of a large number of games producers, a smaller group of games distributors or publishers, and a very small group of games hardware producers. The games hardware industry was dominated by Sony, which released PlayStation 2 in 1999, Nintendo, which produced GameCube in 2001, and Microsoft, which launched its Xbox amid much fanfare in late 2001. For companies such as Sony and Microsoft in particular, involvement in the games industry was at the forefront of their endeavours to establish their media content platforms at the centre of future consumer access to all forms of information and entertainment in the emerging broadband Internet environment. Key players in games distribution, or games publishing, include Acclaim Entertainment, Atari, Capcom, Eidos, Electronic Arts, LucasArts, Midway, Namco, and Take-Two Interactive Entertainment. Sony, Sega, Nintendo, and Microsoft are also very significant games publishers as well as platform distributors. Games development occurs through a bewildering and changing array of digital software production houses, which maintain a range of subcontracting, licensing, and fee-for-service arrangements with the games publishing houses. As an industry characterised by inherent risk, where 5 per cent of successful titles effectively cross-subsidise the 95 per cent that do not achieve 'break even' sales, the sector exhibits the classic risk profile of the creative industries, where 'hits' are greatly outnumbered by 'misses' (Cutler & Company 2002: 18). Games distributors nonetheless seek out a range of titles in order to ensure a diverse portfolio of creative product in the market or under development, and games developers learn to live with chronic insecurity, high upfront costs, and the need to develop market savvy in dealing with games publishers/distributors.

The 2000s have been dominated by the growth of online games, or MMOGs. *Ultima Online* was launched in October 1997, and by early 2001 had almost 250,000 subscribers. Its success would in turn be overtaken by the phenomenal rise of the online role-playing game *EverQuest*, released in July 1999 by Verant Interactive, a division of Sony Entertainment Online. *EverQuest* is an online role-playing game, or what Castronova (2005) termed a massively populated persistent world (MPPW), where players adopt avatars (online 'personas') and undertake a range of activities such as trading, exploring, producing items, and engaging in combat, on the fantasy world of Norrath.

The growth in MMOGs has been further stimulated by the emergence of games such as *Dark Age of Camelot*, *The Sims Online*, and *Star Wars: Galaxies*. In Asia the game *Lineage* had attracted over 4 million subscribers by 2002, and it is estimated that 17 million South Koreans are regularly gaming in PC *Baangs*, with up to 17 million engaged in 'e-sports' more generally, particularly around games such as *StarCraft* (Herz 2002; Cho 2006; Rossignol 2006). But the real impact in the MMOG market has been Blizzard's *World of Warcraft*, launched in 2004, which by January 2007 claimed 8 million subscribers worldwide. It has successfully entered the Asian market with over 3.5 million subscribers in China, and has over 2 million US subscribers.

Consoles have moved to capitalise on online environments with both Microsoft's Xbox live and Sony's Playstation3, each having online connectivity and networked gameplay. Voicechat is also available, meaning players in disparate locations can communicate with each other by talking rather than typing. This move away from keyboard controls is extended even further by Sony's Playstation Portable (PSP) and Nintendo's Wii. The Wii has introduced game controllers that incorporate motion sensors and integrate players' movements with on-screen action, and the console itself is particularly targeted at those who are new to gaming.

Games industry: Integrating and disintegrating the value chain

The games industry has thus evolved a multi-layered structure over its more than 30-year history, where games development, distribution, platforms, and users have found themselves in shifting and interconnected arrangements. What is important to players is of course access to the gaming experience, and industry profitability is typically tied to the software (i.e. the games), with hardware sold at minimal sustainable costs, and often at a loss.[2] More recently, games development has been dominated by the rise of *middleware*, which straddles the games hardware/software divide. Middleware involves the development of games engines, including physics engines that can be repurposed for different games, renderware, and other software tools that assist with the production of the games software. These middleware tools reduce the amount of time that developers need to spend programming for each game, and represent a move towards some standardisation within the industry.

What is most highly valued in the games industry is the creative abilities or intellectual capital of those involved in the development of games, in areas such as creative design and scripting, software programming, project management and production, and systems development. Yet this can in turn generate familiar tensions in the digital creative industries between the creative people, the technology developers, and the 'suits', or those responsible for the mass marketing of commercial games product. The video games industry crash of the mid-1980s, and the meltdown of Atari in particular, was triggered in part by the incompatibility of the creative ethos of games designers and the corporate environment and expectations of traditional media giants such as Time-Warner, as well as the pressure to rush poorly designed titles to market in order to meet marketing deadlines. This in turn generated a consumer backlash to what Kline and colleagues (2003: 105) referred to as the 'suck factor', or 'software pumped out without quality control [which] failed because the experiences it offered were simply not worth the investment of time or money'.

More recently, Electronic Arts (EA) has been criticised for rushing products to market that still contained significant 'bugs', and for overworking its employees. In 2004, it paid $30 million to settle class action suits undertaken by both game artists and programmers for alleged non-payment of overtime and other benefits, after it was claimed on sites such as the 'EA Spouse' blog that it had become mandatory for staff to work 80 hours a week at all times (Feldman & Thorsen 2004). There is widespread criticism from within the games industry of its reliance on *crunch time*, where staff are expected to work 80+ hours a week in the period leading up to the launch of a game, as it leads to sleep deprivation, poor productivity, high levels of staff turnover (also known as 'churn'), bugs and other errors in the games product, employee burn-out, and an adverse impact on not only the employees themselves, but on their spouses and families (Robinson 2005). The head of Gas Powered Games and head designer of the PC-based real-time strategy (RTS) game *Supreme Commander*, Chris Taylor, drew attention to this when he argued at the 2007 Game Developers' Conference that staff who worked regular hours produced considerably better games than those subject to 'crunch time' regimes:

> You make better games when you work regular hours. You're more creative—when you go home at night you're still thinking, because you're creative people. So when you get back at the computer, you have all these ideas and you get them down anyway ... We don't want people to live in the office at Gas Powered Games. (Quoted in Ramsay 2007)

It has been argued that the creative industries have long exemplified a post-Fordist business model, where the generation of creative content is structurally separated from its distribution and marketing (Christopherson & Storper 1986; Garnham 1987; Aksoy & Robins 1992; Caves 2000), and this certainly characterises the games industry. Just as the 1980s industry fallout marked the realisation that games hardware should be developed separately from games software, the 1990s marked a further break-up between games development and games publishing or distribution. The games industry today is characterised by a complex and recursive game development value chain. Sawyer (2002) has argued that the game industry value chain can be seen as having six distinct but connected layers:

1   *capital and publishing layer*, involved in investing in new titles, and seeking returns through licensing for those investments
2   *product and talent layer*, which includes developers, designers, and artists, who may be working under individual contracts or as part of in-house development teams
3   *production and tools layer*, which generates content production tools, game development middleware, customisable game engines, and production management tools
4   *distribution layer*, or the 'publishing' industry, involved in generating and marketing catalogues of games for retail and online distribution
5   *hardware layer*, or the providers of the underlying platform, which may be console-based, personal computer-based, or accessed through new generation mobile devices
6   *end-users layer*, or the users/players of the games.

Among the significant trends that Sawyer identifies in the games industry in the first decade of the 21st century are:

· a shift from 'shrink-wrap'-based distribution, marketing, and purchasing of games, by cartridge or CD-ROM, to online distribution, which will make it much easier to upgrade games through online 'expansion packs'
· increasingly simultaneous releases of games and associated products, such as music or movies, enabling greater marketing coordination in multiple markets
· the global growth of pervasive gaming experiences, as games products increasingly span platforms (console, computer, television,

handheld device) and use mobile and wireless technologies to reach people wherever they are, and whenever they want

- the rise of game players as *fourth-party developers* of game content, which will accompany more open source models of game design, development, and engineering.

It is the last of these that is of particular interest, since it places the games industry at the centre of the shift from mass media models based on producer-defined content where users constitute consumers of the already defined product, to the possibility of an endlessly recursive loop between producers and consumers. Sawyer observed that the modification of game content by online user communities has been a characteristic of computer-based games since the mid-1990s. Games such as *Counter-Strike*, for instance, are a user modification, or 'Mod', of an earlier computer-based game, *Half-Life*. While this 'community of modifiers' may be about 1 per cent of a particular game's user base, the number of those involved will clearly grow as both the international community of gamers grow, and as more games offer modifying opportunities. Sawyer (2002) estimated that this could generate as many as 600,000 established online game community developers by 2012, and that 'for the industry value chain, this foretells the rise of an entirely new component to the gaming industry. If user-led development continues to mature, it will begin to integrate itself into the overall industry, but it will also seek tools and services specific to its role in the development process'.

The emergence of user-led games development has been associated, particularly in the online games environment, with a new dialogue between the games industry and game players, where the latter increasingly constitute a community that is in an ongoing interactive dialogue with games developers about the nature of the game. Modding is a particularly prevalent example of this, common in most first-party shooter (FPS) and RTS games. The example of *Counter-Strike* emerging out of modifications of the *Half-Life* game is an example of a *total conversion*, or the creation of a whole new game out of the features of another. As this is commonly in breach of the original developer's copyright, it is uncommon; more common are what are known as *partial conversions*, or the addition of new items, weapons, characters, enemies, models, modes, textures, levels, story lines, and game modes by players themselves (Wikipedia Contributors 2007). Very popular games such as *World of Warcraft*, the *Star Wars* games, the *Doom* series, *Command & Conquer*, and *Battlefield 1942* actively promote and assist user modification, and very lively online user communities exist to provide tools and software to assist. This of course draws attention to the question of who owns the subsequently modified content, as most games also have End-User Licensing Agreements (EULAs) that assign the ownership of that content to the game's creators. A key issue arising from game players becoming content co-creators is therefore that of control over the game itself, and associated ownership of the player-created intellectual property that resides both within the game and in associated fan-based media such as websites, blogs, and other forms of online user community formation.

Game cultures

One thing that differentiates games from other media forms is that games make people play. Playing can be a solitary pastime, but is more often something done with other people. Digital games are proving to be increasingly social—a trend that works against the mainstream media's portrayal of players as isolated, usually adolescent, boys, hidden away in darkened bedrooms, failing to engage with the social world. Recent statistics show that between 40 and 50 per cent of computer game players are women, and that the average age of players is increasing, and is now between the late twenties and early thirties (ESA 2006; Brand 2007). Digital games are played in many different, often very social and public, settings. Consoles and computers may be located in the living areas of domestic homes, where people often play with friends and family. LAN parties, where people get together in larger public spaces and create networks of computers to play with each other, have been held for many years now. Large gatherings of dedicated game fans occur at events like the 'EverQuest Fan Faires', where several thousand players of EverQuest come together for weekends of socialising and playing. In these ways people create communities around their game-playing activities, much as they have done around sports, hobbies, and other pastimes.

In South Korea, the phenomenon of 'PC Baangs' is widespread. South Korea has one of the highest rates of broadband penetration in the world and apart from connecting domestic spaces this has enabled many Internet café-style online game rooms to be set up. Here people play online games together. The main game played is the strategy game StarCraft, which is 'not just a game in South Korea, it is a national sport ... Five million people ... play. And three cable stations broadcast competitive gaming full-time to a TV audience' (Herz 2002). South Korea also had the largest online role-playing game for many years, *Lineage*, which has over 3 million subscribers (*World of Warcraft* has exceeded this figure in the past couple of years). Players of *Lineage* often play together in PC Baangs, talking to each other across the room as they play together in the virtual space.

The PC Baangs are a very explicit example of the ways in which online and offline spaces can be seen as 'merged' rather than separate. The high rate of broadband connectivity and the specific cultural mores of Korean society may mean that other countries don't develop public games cultures in the same way, but the potential is there (Rossignol 2006). Even when players aren't physically located in the same space, they are often involved in socialising together. This is particularly so with the online gaming communities. In many of the online games, whether they are FPS games like *Quake*, action games like *Counter-Strike* or role-playing games (RPG) such as *World of Warcraft* and *EverQuest*, play is organised around clans or guilds. Players will form or join groups that persist over many sessions of play, sometimes for years. Clans and guilds can be made up of people who know each other offline (friends and families often play together), people who have never met in person, or a combination of these. Clans and guilds vary in their styles and functions. Some exist in order to fight or raid together, others exist for more social purposes, providing an online 'family' for players. Like sports teams, clans and guilds can create an experience of belonging, and of cooperative teamwork as well as competition. People learn to carry out particular roles within groups, and organise themselves into joint projects (slaying dragons, completing quests, fighting other clans, raiding, building cities or empires ... whatever the game environment enables).

Like any other social formation, these groups are both self-regulating, creating their own social norms, and subject to regulation and constraint through the code of the game and sometimes through the policing of the game by owners/administrators/publishers who run the game. The values that are policed vary from game to game. Many of the values encoded into game cultures reflect offline cultural values, but games also offer a chance to emphasise alternative or subjugated values in the name of fantasy and play. Real-world law also comes into play in the regulation of games spaces. Players and publishers enter into EULAs or Terms of Service agreements and this is where some of the terms of game-play are encoded.

It is often argued, particularly in the mainstream media, that digital games cause violence. The 'effects-based' research which gives rise to the 'computer games cause violence' discourse is mostly psychology-based research, often linked to 'moral panic' discourses, particularly after horrific events such as the shooting of schoolchildren at Columbine High School in Littleton, Colorado in 1999.[3] The assumption behind such research—cause-effect behaviouralist models of communication—is a flawed one. Evidence that games cause violent behaviour is thin and highly contestable (Vastag 2004). Differing contexts of consumption will always mean we need to take account of the particularities of players and how and why they play. Behaviouralist, cause-and-effect models often take insufficient account of the relevance of cultural contexts and the ways in which media are actually implicated in the circulation of meanings in our cultures.

Questions of identity often arise in relation to digital games. Key debates have focused on the representations offered to players (in the forms of avatars), the question of how players identify with or relate to their avatars, and the styles of play suggested and enabled by games and whether they are gender-biased. Representations of gender in digital games are often sexist, with hard-bodied muscled men and soft-bodied nearly naked women being common. Bryce and Rutter (2002: 246) found in their research that 'female game characters are routinely represented ... as princesses or wise old women in fantasy games, as objects waiting on male rescue, or as fetishised subjects of male gaze in first person shooters'. These roles emphasise female passivity and highlight a dominance of masculine themes. Not all games are like this, but enough are to make it notable as a general trait.

Representations need to be considered in the light of consumption. Players use games and their enabling representations in many ways. For instance, a player's response to playing as a stereotypical female avatar may range between a number of possibilities. Some women enjoy adopting what they feel to be an image of femininity more acceptable or desirable than their real-world body. Some women may feel completely alienated by what they see as an offensive or unreal representation of femininity. Some women may choose to play as male characters instead. Some men play as women characters because they perceive they will be given more gifts by the male characters. Some men will play a female avatar for quite instrumental reasons—if the female character has different abilities to the male, what it looks like doesn't matter; what it can do, does (Newman 2002). Some people like to experiment with cross-gendered play out of their own curiosity. Identity tourism, as Nakamura (2000) notes, tends to perpetuate and accentuate existing stereotypes, as people perform alternative identities based on understandings gleaned from other media representations.

The context of play is one of the more important factors in determining the gendering of games. Thus access to the machines to play the games on may be gendered. The game-world, rather than being completely separate from the 'real world', is embedded in a real-world context that determines game experience. A final argument on gender and games is that different genders have different gaming styles or preferences and that these differences are not catered to by the market (Cassell & Jenkins 1998). However, this is a much disputed idea with limited currency.[4]

Games and the academy: Game cultures and games studies

As the computer games industry grows and employs more and more people in various industry capacities, and games engage more of the leisure time of a growing number of users, they have become an increasingly significant object of academic research. There has been significant growth in games studies, through centres such as the Experimental Game Lab at Georgia Tech in the USA (http://egl.gatech.edu), the Centre for Computer Games Research at the IT University of Copenhagen (http://game.itu.dk), academic journals such as *Game Studies* (www.gamestudies.org) and *Games and Culture* (gac.sagepub.com), and texts such as *Digital Play* (Kline et al. 2003), *Game Cultures* (Dovey & Kennedy 2006), *The Business and Culture of Games* (Kerr 2006), *Computer Games: Text, Narrative and Play* (Carr et al. 2006), and *Understanding Digital Games* (Rutter & Bryce 2006), in what is a fast-growing literature. While computer games have been studied from computer science perspectives, or their impact on players from medical and psychological perspectives, the game studies literature is distinctive in aiming to bring insights from critical humanities traditions to the study of computer games, without subsuming their distinctive forms and properties into existing film, media, or cultural studies paradigms.

Some of the distinctive features of digital games are user interactivity, immersion in a virtual environment, social interaction within the game, and the capacity of players to become co-creators of content, especially in multi-player games. While none of these are unique to games, they do point to a more productive relationship between the players and the game text than has characterised other media. This relationship involves more than active interpretation of the text or identity construction through consumption: it is a form of engagement that serves to *create* the text each time it is engaged with. Early game studies debates revolved around the ways games texts 'work', with a particularly intensive debate between those who hold that narrative is the key organising structure of a game (the *narratologists*) and those who subscribe to play theory (the *ludologists*). Computer games employ aspects of narrative, and authors such as Murray (1997) and Bolter and Grusin (2000) identified games as emergent forms of story-telling, or 'cyber-dramas', that would evolve greater narrative complexity over time. By contrast, *ludologists* such as Aarseth (2001) and Juul (2003) argued that there was a quite different relationship of the player to the game, since the goal-driven nature of games means that the emotional engagement with the text comes, not from the engagement with characters and events such as occurs in conventional narratives, but because the player is an actor themselves. The engagement thus comes because the player is the performer, and the game evaluates the performance and adapts to it. As a result, these authors argued the need to incorporate elements of *play theory*, as an alternative to traditional models derived from literary theory and the applied humanities (Juul 2003; Liestøl 2003).

Two further developments can be noted in this fast-changing field. One has been the growing awareness that games studies needs to engage more systematically with the political economy of the games industry. Kline et al. (2003) and Kerr (2006) in particular give close attention to the changing economic dynamics of the global games industry, and it is also discussed in detail in Dovey and Kennedy (2006). Four features of the political economy of games stand out from this literature. First, the sector is subject to strong dynamics of concentration and consolidation, despite the plethora of games titles available. This is most apparent in the console-based games market, where the big three console providers—Sony, Microsoft, and Nintendo—can exert substantial control over games publishers and developers, but it is also a characteristic of the PC-based and multiplayer online games markets (Kerr 2006: 54–61). Second, games production increasingly occurs through global production networks, although production in emergent countries remains very much tied to the distributional relations controlled by the big console and publishing companies based in the USA, Japan, and, to a lesser extent, Europe (Kerr 2006: 76–9). Third, workplace relations in the games industry are notoriously harsh, with long hours, extended 'crunch times', job insecurity, and a sense of 'forced workaholism' leading to high rates of labour turnover and burn-out among those employed in the sector (IGDA 2004). Kline and colleagues (2003: 200) argued that 'management harnesses youthful technophilia to a compulsive-obsessive work ethic, one-dimensional character formation, and a high rate of burnout'. Gill (2002, 2006) has identified how this work environment is particularly incompatible with family or parental responsibilities, and how many women in new media sectors intensely dislike this combination of 'laddish' culture and a lack of interest in social skills or self-care; employment rates for women in the games industry are well below those of most other sectors (Dovey & Kennedy 2006: 61–2). Fourth, as the sector seems to clone a certain type of worker—young, male, and with limited responsibilities outside work—and since the market best understood in the sector is males aged 13–25, it is highly likely that 'the prospects for widespread innovation become very limited … [as] a minority of gamers with a particular set of tastes command a large cultural space which is disproportionate to their actual numbers' (Dovey & Kennedy 2006: 62).

Emergent games are becoming increasingly popular. Rather than dictating the direction of play, emergent games offer environments, and sets of rules, but not a hard-and-fast direction in which play must proceed. What results is an endless variety of unexpected play directions emerging from players' own decisions about what to do within that environment. Many multiplayer online games take this form, to a greater or lesser extent. A role-playing game like *EverQuest* or *World of Warcraft* provides a world for players to log into, and they play with each other within that world. There is a system of 'levelling up' that gives a sense of progress to players, but the particular ways in which they achieve that progress are not set, and some may choose not to progress and to do other things instead, such as focusing on more social aspects of the game. Structurally, the 'text' is added to and changed by the player, rather than being finished by the developer. The publishers rely on the players to continue the cycle of development. Thus we could see the game as a result of a combination of paid and unpaid labour whose features arise in a variety of new media contexts, but are particularly marked in relation to games. It is clear that player creativity is part of the game production cycle in a number of ways. Emergent games are based on a *recursive* model of production, whereby players create various iterations of the 'text'. They can also become part of the production cycle as 'modders'—people who make new objects for games, new levels or artificial intelligence for games, or even whole new games (like *Counter-Strike*, mentioned earlier, which is a player-developed game that uses the *Half-Life* game engine). Industry is currently faced with choices about how much they embrace the player creators or mod-communities as part of their structure. Some are openly encouraging of such communities, releasing the source code and tools for creating content. Others have chosen instead to enclose their games in heavily policed copyright or intellectual property regimes which preclude the creation of derivative works by fans. As models, the former seeks to leverage the R&D capacities of the player communities and harness the creativity of players, the latter hold to more conventional models of production and IPR management.

These choices in licensing in the new production models hold opportunities for really innovative new industry structures—structures that fully embrace the recursive and fluid features of the networked, interactive technology and the passion of the gamers. It is here, too, that work must be done to determine what the rights of this passionate productive community might be. Who should own the intellectual property rights of player-created content? How can IPR be micromanaged such that these practices don't become exploitative? Is property even the most appropriate model to be using? Intellectual property is much better suited to conventional 'texts' that are fixed or 'finished', rather than ongoing collaborative creations like games made through the joint effort between developers and players.

We should understand games as an exemplar application for online interactive environments. The networked nature of the production cycle is one that will become more prevalent with time. These issues are not restricted to games, but are indicators of structural changes that give rise to broad-scale challenges to existing regimes of the management and regulation of media. The more interactive applications are created and used in our increasingly connected and networked environments, the more issues of regulation, ownership, and service will arise and need to be looked at in light of the different nature of interactive texts.

Online social environments such as multiplayer online games hold the challenges not only of resolving issues of IPR management, but of community management. What governance regimes are instituted by media corporations who have as their main goal the generation of profit rather than social equity? Should there be any checks and balances on corporate behaviour in this respect or should it be left to the marketplace to regulate? These are questions that will rise in importance as more and more people live parts of their lives inside proprietary spaces and contribute to the economic well-being of media corporations. Although the media publishers may not have financial obligations to the player creators, they may instead incur social obligations. Issues such as the terms of access to environments, freedom of speech, and privacy are all currently determined through EULAs or Terms of Service Agreements, which in most cases are heavily weighted in favour of the publishers. Such imbalances may come to be the subject of struggle and negotiation in the same way as the ownership of player-created intellectual property.

Computer games were successful interactive entertainment applications long before other applications. They have shown the way forward—with structural design and technological innovation generating engaging and often profitable environments. Their position at the forefront of innovation in the digital world has meant they often indicate where change, negotiation, and controversy will arise in much broader arenas. It is well worth attending to the issues that arise from computer games: the structural changes to the nature of the 'text'; the reorganisation of the relations of production and the impacts on industry; the reshaping of the role of consumers and the impacts on social relations; and the new configurations of 'authorship' and the impact on intellectual property are just some of the areas that have wide significance and justify academic attention.

 USEFUL WEBSITES

Game Studies <www.gamestudies.org>. An online academic journal dedicated to developing cross-disciplinary research into games. It has been the leader in developing the 'play'-based approach to studying games.

International Game Developers Association <www.igda.org>. Website of the peak international game developers' association. It includes particularly interesting resources on Quality of Life issues for those working in the games industry.

WomenGamers.com <www.womengamers.com>. A site for women who play computer games, who work in the games industry, and for anyone interested in questions around gender and gaming.

citizen journalism

What is citizen journalism?

Citizen journalism can in one sense be defined by some of its more conspicuous examples. The South Korean *OhMyNews* site (http://english.ohmynews.com/), established in 2000, has as its slogan 'every citizen is a reporter', and accesses only 20 per cent of the content for its online site from its employed staff, with the balance coming from the estimated 50,000 South Koreans who post news stories onto the site. The *malaysiakini.com* site (www.malaysiakini.com) was established in 1999 by two young journalists, Steven Gan and Premesh Chandran, who had become disaffected with the degree of state control and self-censorship within Malaysia's print and broadcast media, and saw an opportunity to 'use the Internet to provide free and fair news to the Malaysian public and to set new standards in journalism as well as to support the development of freedom of speech, social justice, and democracy in Malaysia' (Malaysiakini 2007; cf. George 2006). In the USA, bloggers are variously credited with the political demise of the Senate Majority Leader Trent Lott for remarks he made supporting racial segregation, and revealing that a story run by CBS news anchor Dan Rather claiming that George W. Bush avoided the draft was based on forged documents. In

Britain, the BBC has been promoting a citizen journalism model linked to community activism from within its own portal, through its *Action Network* initiative (www.bbc.co.uk/dna/actionnetwor). In Australia sites such as *Crikey* (www.crikey.com.au), *New Matilda* (www.newmatilda.com.au), and *On Line Opinion* (www.onlineopinion.com.au) seek to both promote new stories and to generate alternative means of gathering and aggregating news and opinion online. Internationally, the *Indymedia* network (www.indymedia.org), founded in the USA in the context of the 1999 'Battle of Seattle' protests against the inaugural meeting of the WTO, is a global, activist-based network of print, satellite TV, video, and radio that is all user-generated, and has over 150 independent media centres worldwide, across more than 30 countries.

Is there then a new model of citizen journalism emerging around these various new media initiatives? There are a number of influential voices who think so. Dan Gillmor, founder of the Centre for Citizen Media, argues in *We the Media* that whereas conventional 'Big Media … treated the news as a lecture', the new models of citizen journalism enabled by Web 2.0 technologies will see an evolution towards 'journalism as a conversation or seminar'.

> The lines will blur between producers and consumers, changing the role of both in ways we're only beginning to grasp now. The communication network itself will become a medium for everyone's voice, not just the few who can afford to buy multimillion-dollar printing presses, launch satellites or win the government's permission to squat on the public's airwaves. (Gillmor 2006: xxiv)

Bowman and Willis (2003: 9) refer to the rise of *participatory journalism* as 'the result of many simultaneous, distributed conversations that either blossom or quickly atrophy in the Web's social network'. They define participatory journalism as 'the act of a citizen, or group of citizens, playing an active role in the process of collecting, reporting, analysing and disseminating news and information. The intent of this participation is to provide independent, reliable, accurate, wide-ranging and relevant information that a democracy requires'.

Couldry (2003) has explored the wider implications of the relationship between participatory media, alternative forms of journalism, and questions of media power. Arguing that media power is best understood as a form of *symbolic power*, or the power to construct and communicate dominant ideas, Couldry finds the potential significance of user-generated media as lying in its capacity to accumulate organisational and economic resources that can be used to tell different stories, and generate alternative sources of influence.

To achieve substantive changes in the concentration, organisation, and uses of media, what needs to be looked for are:

1 *New ways of consuming media*, which explicitly contest the social legitimacy of media power;

2 *New infrastructures of production*, which have an impact upon who can produce media and in what circumstances;

3 *New infrastructures of distribution*, which change the scale and terms on which media and other forms of symbolic production in one place can reach other places. (2003: 44)

For Couldry, the potential arises for new forms of media production and consumption associated with the Internet and user-generated content to generate 'new hybrid forms of media *consumption-production* … [that] would challenge precisely the entrenched division of labour (producers of stories versus consumers of stories) that is the essence of media power' (2003: 45).

Three elements are critical to the rise of citizen journalism and citizen media. The first is *open publishing*. The development of an open publishing architecture by Matthew Arnison and others involved in the 'Active Sydney' group in 1999, and the adoption of such open source models by the Independent Media Centres (*Indymedia*) that year, was a landmark development in enabling new forms of news production. Arnison (2003) drew parallels between open publishing and the free software movement, arguing that the key to open publishing, as with open source software, was that the process of production was open and transparent. Second, *collaborative editing* is vital to citizen journalism. In his taxonomy of peer-to-peer (P2P) publishing, and the extent to which a site and a news practice can be deemed to be open and participatory, Bruns (2005) differentiates such sites on the basis of the scope for user participation at the input stage (contributing stories), output stage (ability to edit or shape final content), response stage (ability to comment on, extend, filter, or edit already published content), and the extent to which specific roles (editor, journalist, user, reader) are fixed in the production process. This generates a continuum of openness across online news sites, from mainstream online news sites where a division between the producers and users of news remains even if there is scope to comment on stories, through to 'gatekeeping lite' sites that promote user contributions and some collaborative editing, through to the editor-assisted open news model of South Korea's *OhMyNews* and *Media Channel* in the USA, and the completely open and decentralised *Indymedia* models (Figure 8.1).

Figure 8.1 A continuum of openness for online news models

Traditional, 'top-down'

Emergent, 'bottom-up'

| Mainstream/ online news sites | Supervised gatewatching ('gatekeeping lite') | Editor-assisted open news (e.g. *OhMyNews*) | Open news |

A third factor promoting citizen journalism is *distributed content* through RSS (Rich Site Summary or Really Simple Syndication) feeds. The great virtue of RSS is that it can take the work out of accessing new and interesting information, as users can establish an ongoing link with the sites that generate content that is of interest to them, and link to it on their own sites as they see fit. While RSS development has occurred at some distance from the concerns of citizen journalism, it greatly assists it by reducing the search costs associated with accessing valuable information and insight from trusted sources, as well as building user communities, thereby transforming news and information distribution from a hierarchical, top-down model with high barriers to entry to a more decentralised and networked model.

Deuze (2003) has proposed that the diversity of forms of Web-based journalism can be conceived of as operating across two axes of control and connectivity. One relates to *content*, and the extent to which the content that appears on an online news site is primarily or exclusively sourced from an existing news organisation's staff of employed journalists, with the content that is published subject to established editorial protocols, as compared to sites that source content widely and emphasise the forms of network *connectivity* that arise from diverse sources participating in providing content to the site. The second relates to the *cultures* in which content is generated, and the extent to which participatory communication is either nonexistent or highly moderated, as compared to sites where comment and participation are open and largely unmoderated. For Deuze, this generated the following differentiation between the online news sites of mainstream news organisations such as CNN, BBC, and MSNBC, index and category sites such as the *Drudge Report* or *Crikey*, meta-comment sites such as *MediaChannel*, and share and discussion sites such as *Slashdot* (Figure 8.2).

For Deuze, this in turn raises the question of what it means to transfer news production and distribution to the online environment. He suggests a fourfold typology of ways in which online news media is related to the content-connectivity access on the one hand, and the extent to which journalistic culture is open or closed on the other. To take the four types outlined in

Figure 8.3, (1) *orienting* online journalism is largely a repurposing of pre-existing media content; (2) *monitorial* online journalism is principally driven by news organisations seeking better user demographic data; (3) *instrumental* online journalism is useful for the journalist involved, as it enables him or her to understand their audience better, but it does not generate new models for how news and information content is developed into the future; and (4) *dialogic* online journalism begins to take journalism in quite new directions, by opening up new models for news production, collaborative editing and filtering, and user participation in site development.

Figure 8.2 Categorising online news sites by content generation and participatory communication

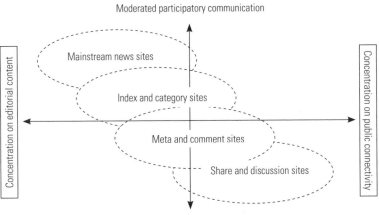

Source: Deuze 2003: 205

Figure 8.3 Types of online journalism

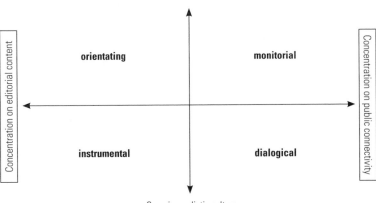

Source: Deuze 2003: 218

CASE STUDY: CITIZEN JOURNALISM FROM A NEWS EDITOR'S PERSPECTIVE

One response to the developments outlined above could be that this is all well and good for the cyber-boffins and the digital counter-culture, but it is not really what journalism is about, or what the public expect from journalists. There are journalists who argue that established norms and practices of professional journalism continue to work well in the online environment, and do not require Web 2.0 or blog-type 'solutions' grafted onto them. The *Los Angeles Times* columnist Joel Stein (2007) published a particularly pointed piece (possibly tongue-in-cheek) where he advised his readers not to bother sending him an email of their opinions about his column, as he was not interested in their opinions or in having conversations with his readers. Blogging for *The Age* in Australia, James Farmer (2006) argued that the citizen journalism concept confused citizen media, or a person's capacity to put up anything they want onto the Web, with journalism, which 'is a profession … [that] provides the quality and breadth of content that keeps an enormous number of readers coming back for more'.

In his work on citizen journalism with the Poynter Institute (www.poynter.org) in the USA, the journalist and editor Steve Outing (2005) identifies confusion and scepticism as two common responses among news editors to the concept of citizen journalism. In order to address this through a form of checklist for established news organisations, Outing identified a series of layers of opening up a newsroom to citizen journalism, from those that have few implications for how the organisation is run to those that are genuinely transformative in their impact:

1   *Opening up online articles and columns to user comment and feedback.* While this does require some degree of site moderation in order to filter objectionable or potentially defamatory material, it clearly adds insight for both journalists and readers to know what other readers are thinking about the topic or issue discussed, and is used in most online news publications today.
2   *The citizen add-on reporter.* Comments and further information on stories of ongoing interest can be solicited from interested members of the community as additions to the material published by the employed journalists.

3 *Open source or participatory reporting.* This involves collaboration between journalists and their readers on the development of news stories and opinion pieces that indicates the building of a wider community of interest around the topic. An example of this was Margo Kingston's *WebDiary* that ran off the *Sydney Morning Herald* website (www.smh.com.au) as a blog adjunct to her columns from 2000 to 2005 (Kingston 2003).

4 *The citizen bloghouse.* This involves inviting or employing bloggers who can be expected to develop ideas and content that will generate ongoing traffic to your online site. Examples in Australia include John Birmingham's *Blunt Instrument* blog on the *Brisbane Times*, an online-only news site for south-east Queensland published through the Fairfax organisation (www.brisbanetimes.com.au), and Tim Dunlop's *Blogocracy* site on the News Limited website (http://blogs. news.com.au/news/blogocracy/index.php/news).

5 *Stand-alone citizen journalism sites.* Examples of these include *hyper-local* news sites in the USA such as *MyMissourian* (www. mymissourian.com), *WestportNow* (www.westportnow.com), and *Bluffton Today* (www.blufftontoday.com), which are driven by news and blog contributions from their local communities (Schaffer 2007).

6 *The Pro-Am Hybrid.* This is the model that *OhMyNews*'s founder and CEO Oh Yeon-Ho has adopted since the site's establishment in 2000, which it is now seeking to refine further as it becomes an international news service. It mixes a full-time news staff with a rolling roster of 'citizen journalists', whose number has grown from 727 in 2000 to over 50,000 worldwide today, with news staff acting as coaches to citizen journalists in how to develop and refine journalistic skills (Yeon-Ho 2007).

7 *Integrating citizen and professional journalism 'under one roof'.* Outing observed that this is the point at which established news media organisations become particularly skittish about citizen journalism, as it entails removing the by-line distinction between types of journalist and types of content. The 'professional ideologies' of journalism that underpin concerns about such developments are discussed below, but Outing's conclusion is that the tendency to 'wall off' citizen journalism will diminish over time, and that a more

Contextual factors behind the rise of citizen journalism

From CAR and public journalism to Web 2.0 and the public's journalism

Media theorists such as Ithiel de Sola Pool (1983) correctly anticipated that journalists would quickly identify the potential of the Internet to enhance their professional capacities, because it gave them vastly expanded access to information and new channels for distribution. The Internet emerged at a time of perceived crisis for journalism, arising from a sense of growing disconnect between journalism as an organised and institutionalised professional practice and the audiences and communities it intended to serve.

Two key responses in the 1990s to this environment of opportunity and threat were computer-assisted reporting and public journalism. *Computer-assisted reporting* (CAR) enabled a triangulation of reporting, where journalists could cross-check information provided to them by key informants with other sources of information and data that were on the public record and now readily accessible through the Internet. CAR aimed to make journalism a more scientific practice, and its advocates looked for a new era of 'precision journalism', where the truth-claims of journalists would be backed up by thickets of verifiable data (Cox 2000). The second development was the rise of *public journalism*, also known as civic journalism. The core principle underpinning public journalism was that of 'seeing people as citizens rather than as spectators, readers, viewers, listeners, or an undifferentiated mass', in order to act in ways that can 'bring a genuine public alive' (Rosen 2000: 680, 683). Campbell (2000: 693) saw experiments in public journalism as aiming to: '(1) treat citizens as experts in their own lives and aspirations ... (2) treat citizens as political actors who create public knowledge by deliberating together ... [and] (3) create new forms of story-telling and reporting to enrich information'. Public journalism had the aim of reinvigorating the democratic and participatory nature of democratic society by emphasising journalism's social responsibility remit of 'encouraging citizens to engage each other in a search for shared values' (Glasser 2000: 683).

Despite their differences, both nonetheless rested on a common assumption that there exists a unique and powerful professional grouping—journalists—who may or may not choose to use new media to serve better another constituency—audiences, or the general public—and that the choice to do so essentially rested with the profession itself. It is this dynamic that has been eroding quickly with the rise of Web 2.0 and social software, to the point where advocates of public journalism, such as Witt (2004), have observed that 'public journalism', where journalists, academics, and news editors could meet and discuss what to do next, has advanced to 'the public's journalism', where a new generation of new media users were taking matters into their own hands.

Questioning journalism as a professional ideology

The technological developments associated with the rise of citizen journalism have occurred at a time when claims to the uniqueness of journalism as a profession have been contested. Zelizer (2004, 2005) has argued that journalism has to be ultimately understood as a culture, and those who self-define as journalists 'employ collective, often tacit knowledge to become members of the group and maintain their membership over time' (2005: 200). Other definitions of what constitutes journalism and journalists—as a profession, an industry, an institution, or a craft—are, for Zelizer, inadequate, as they always present boundary issues as to who is included and excluded. By contrast, the cultural definition clarifies why, how, and by whom these boundaries about what is journalism and who is a journalist emerge, linking them back to the culture of journalism itself, and the 'connections [that] are made that link internal mind-sets about how the world works with the external arrangements by which social life is set in place' (2005: 201).

Deuze (2005) has argued that journalism is ultimately an occupational ideology shared among those who self-classify as journalists. Ideology is understood here in the dual sense of being 'a system of beliefs characteristic of a particular group, including—but not limited to—the general process of the production of meanings and ideas within that group', and as a process whereby 'the sum of ideas and views—notably on social and political issues—of a particular group is shaped over time, but also as a process by which other ideas and views are excluded or marginalised' (2005: 445). Deuze tests this hypothesis by identifying five common claims that are made about journalism by journalists themselves and by those who research journalism as a profession, and testing these against two potentially disruptive influences on journalism: the impact of new media technologies, and multiculturalism, or the implications of greater cultural diversity in modern societies (see Table 8.1).

The end of the 'journalist as hero'

Hallin (1994) has argued that the period from the 1960s to the late 1980s was one of 'high modernism' in American journalism, 'an era when the historically troubled role of the journalist seemed fully rationalised, when it seemed possible for the journalist to be powerful and prosperous and at the same time independent, disinterested, public-spirited, and trusted and beloved by everyone, from the corridors of power around the world to the ordinary citizen and consumer' (1994: 172). The 'journalist as hero' had a clear image in the popular consciousness, as Dustin Hoffman and Robert Redford portrayed the *Washington Post* journalists Carl Bernstein and Bob Woodward in the 1976 film *All the President's Men*, about the reporting of the Watergate scandal and the resignation of Richard Nixon. The image was that of young investigative journalists with a commitment to late nights at the office, checking their facts and sources closely, and linking up with well-connected insiders, who could bring down the US President. Through the 1970s and 1980s, the wages of high-profile journalists continued to rise,

Table 8.1 Journalism as a professional ideology: Deuze's analysis of change factors

Core elements of journalists' professional self-definition	Underlying concepts and applications in practice	Impact of new media technologies	Impact of multiculturalism
Public service	Acting as 'watch-dogs' or 'alert services' to the wider public	'The public' is increasingly using new media to tell its own stories	Need to actively seek new angles and voices from undiscovered communities
Objectivity	Need for neutrality, fairness, impartiality, and 'professional distance' from sources	Interactivity presents the journalist with multiple and conflicting points of view	Need to move from binary ('both sides of the story') to multiperspectival approaches
Autonomy	Freedom from censorship, whether by governments, companies, or colleagues	Collaborative production models increasingly becoming the norm	Need for more community-based reporting and awareness of entrenched social inequalities
Immediacy	Information needs to be produced and disseminated quickly in order to have value and currency	Reflection, complexity, and ongoing editing and updating of news becomes possible, involving users in the process	Speed tends to negate recognition of diversity, in terms of newsroom cultures, sourcing, and how news is distributed
Ethics	Need to be guided by a formal code of ethics as collectively agreed to by one's peers in the organisation and/or relevant professional body	New media tend to evoke an 'ethics on the run', as online site moderation cannot mirror an internally derived organisational ethic/culture	Issues about what is/is not 'suitable' content become more complex as societies become more diverse, and mechanisms for dialogue need to be established

Source: Deuze 2005

particularly in television, as the cult of the 'journalist as hero' was embraced through programs such as *60 Minutes*.

Hallin noted that there were inherent problems with journalists seeking to fill a vacuum in political institutions and public debate. One reason was that journalists are often 'too close to the powerful institutions whose actions need to be discussed' (1994: 175). Another problem is that the commercial nature of news makes it difficult for journalists in large, mainstream organisations to veer too far from what they perceive to be 'public sentiment', or to get too far offside with any major political entity, for fear of losing audience or market share. Hallin also argued that the journalistic ideal of objectivity tended to generate a focus on 'attributions, passive voice constructions, and the substitution of technical for moral or political judgements [that] is largely designed to conceal the voice of the journalist' (1994: 176). He argued for new forms of journalism that aimed to be in dialogue with the wider public rather than 'mediating between political institutions and the mass public', and where 'the voice and judgement of the journalist ... [are] more honestly acknowledged' (1994: 176). He wrote *We Keep America on Top of the World* before the rise of the Internet and blogging; many advocates of blogging would argue that it has sought to fill the vacuum in 'high modern' journalism that Hallin identified.

Journalism and its sources—from contact to capture

Access to quality information sources has long been at the heart of quality journalism, but this reliance on contacts generates its own problems. It is no coincidence that Woodward and Bernstein worked at the *Washington Post*, and not in Montana or Arkansas; being located in the heart of the American political beast—Washington, DC—and with a well-resourced newspaper behind them, they could successfully pursue source-led investigative journalism. But this insider access generates its own forms of capture. At its most overt, as with the concept of 'embedded journalists' developed during the 2003 US-led invasion of Iraq, journalists stood accused of essentially reporting the US military point of view as the condition of access to combat zones (Schechter 2003).[1] More generally, one can simply count the number of phrases such as 'Sources close to the Prime Minister/President say', 'Government officials say', or 'Well-placed insiders say' in the stories of many feature writers, columnists, political correspondents, and front-page newspaper stories to get a sense of the extent of the reliance of much mainstream journalism upon official sources, and the relations of dependence this generates. This has become increasingly sophisticated in recent years with the rise of what Ward (2003) terms the 'PR state', where government management of media through public relations moves beyond issue-based 'spin' to highly coordinated information management strategies, and where large-scale government advertising aimed at 'selling' new policies becomes a vital part of the revenue stream of commercial media organisations (Young 2006).[2] Indeed, some have noted that it is increasingly political satire, as seen in US programs such as Jon Stewart's *The Daily Show* and *The Colbert Report*, and Australia's *The Chaser's War on Everything*, to comment irreverently on developments in politics, that one would expect leading political journalists to be more attuned to.

Implications of eroding revenue bases for traditional media

The media business has traditionally been a highly profitable one, with major media outlets realising rates of profit well above industry averages. But there are several signs that the business models that served media so well in the second half of the 20th century are less robust in the early 21st century, and this has implications for how news production is to be financed. In the case of newspapers, classified advertising has traditionally provided the 'rivers of gold' that cross-subsidised other activities within the organisation, but this is now seriously challenged by the rise of sophisticated search engines such as Google that can be both global and hyper-local, and by direct selling of products and services through sites such as eBay. Broadcast television has lost significant market share to cable and satellite-based subscription services throughout the world, and there are fewer and fewer opportunities to reach the mass audiences that were once the lifeblood of commercial television. More generally, television is now in serious competition with other media for audience attention, not only with the personal computer and Web-based services such as *YouTube* and *Joost* (www.joost.com), but with the other ways in which the television itself can be used, including console-based gaming and DVD viewing.

This is not to proclaim the end of mass media, as a number of high-profile analysts wrongly prophesied in the 1990s (e.g. Gilder 1994; Negroponte 1995). Such an analysis overestimates the significance of changing media consumption patterns for particular demographics in countries where media such as television is long established, and underestimates the significance of the growth of access to television and other mass media on a global scale. Moreover, it conflates the media as distribution conduits with media as program content; theorists of 'TV III' (Rogers et al. 2002; Creeber & Hills 2007) point out that successful TV content, whether it be *The Sopranos*, *Big Brother* or live feeds of World Cup soccer, are now accessed across multiple platforms, ranging from TV to DVDs, networked personal computers, mobile phones, and other wireless and handheld devices, and is repurposed in multiple formats to best 'fit' the relevant media form. The issue is rather with advertiser spending, and the extent to which it is migrating from mass media forms to technologically driven niches, and the implications of this for cross-subsidy of various forms of journalism within organisations that produce news. One feature of blogs and citizen journalism is that they are typically a lower-cost means of generating content than traditional news practices (such as hiring feature writers, high-profile on-air presenters, and opinion journalists), and this is certainly attracting the attention of established news media outlets.

Lifestyle, entertainment, and celebrity journalism

The space that is increasingly occupied in media of all forms by lifestyle, entertainment, and celebrity journalism is clearly observable, from the plethora of new magazine titles devoted to these topics, to their prominence in the online environment, although we currently lack an authoritative academic analysis of these forms (on celebrity and journalism, see Turner 2004; Hermes 2005; Marshall 2006). Many accounts of these developments tend to reflect critically on how the rise of this space is 'eroding' journalism, rather than on these forms of journalism themselves, they now dominate the magazine industry, are increasingly central to television, and occupy a growing space within the print media industries, particularly in their online versions (see Turner 1999, 2005 on 'tabloidisation' debates in relation to journalism). Bloggers are of course well represented in these fields, as seen with widely accessed sites such as *Welcome to Perez Hilton* (http://perezhilton.com). At the same time, it is notable how prominent the celebrity, entertainment, and lifestyle formats are on the online versions of the established news media sites. There is a study yet to be done about whether the prevalence of this content is greater on these sites than it is in the print and broadcast equivalents, and what should be made of it. Related to this is the need for more detailed information about how news and information is consumed online. One theory is that online news is frequently consumed in small chunks by office workers, and this fits well with the format that has evolved with celebrity magazines, which get through a lot of stories very quickly, and which typically require little background or context, as readers typically know who the celebrities are (Newson 2006).

The crisis of democracy and the decline of deference

It has been argued that, in the established democratic nations, there is increasingly a *crisis of democracy*, where 'old styles of representation have come under pressure to change ... [because] traditional structures and cultures of policy formation and decision-making are perceived as being remote from ordinary citizens' (Coleman & Gøtze 2001: 4; cf. Castells 1998; Giddens 1998). Coleman and Gøtze have observed that:

> As citizens have become less deferential and dependent, and more consumerist and volatile, old styles of representation have come under pressure to change. There is a pervasive contemporary estrangement between representative and those they represent, manifested in almost every western country by falling voter turnout; lower levels of public participation in civic life; public cynicism towards political institutions and parties; and a collapse in once-strong political loyalties and attachments. (2001: 4)

It was argued in Chapter 5 that, overall, blogs are a positive factor in the development of social capital, with their mix of subjectivity, interactivity, and connectivity (McNair 2006: 122–4). Similarly, since more active participation by citizens in the policy process is believed to lead to both better public policy and greater public trust in its implementation (OECD 2003; Coleman 2006), it can be argued that citizen journalism formats that are widely accessible, independent of powerful vested interests, and can have wider public influence will have a positive impact on reinvigorating the democratic public sphere. This is even acknowledging that they are often more partisan and feisty, reflecting a wider decline in deference to established forms of elite authority, from political leadership to opinion-leading journalism. As McNair (2006: 73) observes, 'If one function of the public sphere is to render power transparent before the people ... it is better from the democratic perspective to have an excess of critical media scrutiny ... than a deficit'.

New opportunities to express alternative views in countries with state-controlled media

The significance of the Internet as an alternative source of news and information is even starker in those countries that are not democracies, or are recent democracies, and where there is a history of state control (direct or indirect) over official media sources. The relationship between the rise in Internet use in Indonesia and the gradual, complex democratisation of Indonesian society and politics in the period following President Soeharto's 'New Order' provides a fascinating case study of this. One consequence of the fall of the Soeharto government in 1998 was an explosion in independent journalism during the subsequent period of *reformasi* (Romano 2003). The Internet has been quickly embraced as a tool by political activists and reformers, and has been a vital element of scrutiny and commentary on elections and political affairs generally since the first free elections in Indonesia in 1999 (Hill & Sen 2005).

George (2006: 43–54) has discussed the role played by the Internet in enabling *contentious journalism* in Malaysia and Singapore. Both Malaysia and Singapore are countries that have held formal democratic elections, but where the same political organisations—the United Malaysian National Organisation (UMNO) in Malaysia and the People's Action Party (PAP) in Singapore—have held power continuously since independence. A variety of controls over the media have been important components of this continuous rule, including Internal Security and Official Secrets Acts, defamation laws, the allocation of print and broadcast media licences, close personal connections between media owners and government officials, and controls over media access and sources. The Internet has opened up a space for dissenting points of view and what George terms contentious journalism, in countries where dissenting journalists 'have enough space to practice their craft openly on the Internet ... but not constitutional protection from political censorship or politically motivated reprisal' (2006: 3). The ability to do this has been driven in part by the commitment of governments in both countries to rapid development of the Internet and a leading position in the global information economy, through Singapore's *Intelligent Island* policies and Malaysia's *Vision 2020*, but George documents the continuing precariousness of websites dedicated to alternative points of view, with *Malaysiakini.com* being the most notable survivor over time, while *Sintercom.org* was ultimately forced to operate outside Singapore (George 2006; cf. Lee 2006 on Singapore).

We need to be careful about easily equating the rise of the Internet with moves towards greater democratisation, media freedom, and citizen journalism. Kalathil and Boas (2003) have discussed how governments can widen the population's access to the Internet while simultaneously maintaining political and media control, citing China and Singapore as case studies. Even without the elaborate network of controls and filters that has developed in China, which critics have dubbed the 'Great Firewall of China' (Human Rights Watch 2006), Kalathil and Boas note that the Internet need not constitute a wedge that threatens dominant political forces since (1) most Internet traffic does not have an ostensibly political purpose; (2) there are periodic crackdowns by governments on some forms of Internet use; (3) mechanisms for content control and filtering can be developed for online content akin to those of other media within a national information infrastructure; and (4) state authorities can use the Internet to deliver their own messages more effectively and to enhance their own legitimacy. Indeed, in the case of both China and Singapore, Internet censorship has occurred alongside measures to improve citizen access to government services online and some citizen–government direct interaction. Nonetheless, when crises of control do emerge, as occurred in China and Hong Kong SAR during the 2003 SARS outbreak, the Internet emerges as a vitally important source of alternative information (Nip 2006).

CASE STUDY: OHMYNEWS

The South Korean online newspaper *OhMyNews* was established in 2000, with the guiding principle that 'Every citizen is a reporter'. It was unique in encouraging its readers to submit, edit, and publish stories, establishing an open source model of news reporting. Only about 20 per cent of the site's content is written by the 55-person staff, with the majority of articles written by an estimated 50,000 Korean citizens, and it has an ongoing readership of about 2 million and an estimated 15 million hits a day (Wagstaff 2004). Non-employed contributors get paid about $US16 for stories that are accepted, so one would not go into this field for the money. *OhMyNews* generates about 70 per cent of its revenues from advertising, with the balance from story syndication and reader donations.

Its influence in Korea became apparent in 2002 when the newly elected President Roh Moo Hyun gave his first interview to *OhMyNews*. In 2006, an English-language version, *OhMyNews International*, was launched, with citizen reporters in over a hundred countries, and all of its content being sourced from citizen reporters. A version of *OhMyNews* was also launched in Japan in 2006. *OhMyNews* has been identified as an element of what has been referred to as the 'Korean wave' (*hallyu*) of digital media and popular culture that has had a major impact internationally, and particularly in Asia, during the 2000s.

Its founder and CEO, Oh Yeon-Ho, is passionate about his belief in citizen journalism. He has argued that *OhMyNews* marks a 'complete departure from the media culture of the 20th century ... [that will] change the culture of how news is produced, distributed, and consumed, all at one

CRSE STUDY (*cont.*)

time' (Yeon-Ho 2004). Arguing that every citizen is a reporter, he proposes that 'journalists aren't some exotic species; they're everyone who seeks to take new developments, put them into writing, and share them with others'. To that end, three guiding principles of what he terms the *news guerrilla* approach are:

1 Abolish thresholds to being a reporter;
2 Break down set formulas for news articles;
3 Demolish the walls that separate media, and separate journalists from citizens. (Yeon-Ho 2004)

Oh Yeon-Ho (2007) has also identified 10 preconditions for user-generated news content to be of value, based on the principles of credibility, responsibility, influence, and sustainability:

1 Be sure that material is factually correct.
2 Avoid copyright infringements.
3 Create content that aims to meet the needs of audiences, rather than the wishes of the reporters.
4 Make the most effective use of the media platform being used to deliver content.
5 Produce stories that will be shared with others.
6 Aim for critical mass in audiences and reach key decision-makers.
7 Seek to have impact in the 'real world'.
8 Aim to make a positive contribution on issues, and avoid simply being negative or critical.
9 Encourage contributors to make ongoing contributions to the site.
10 Develop a sustainable business model and understand your market.

The Korean context is a significant factor in *OhMyNews*'s success. South Korea is a country that is large in terms of population (41 million), but relatively small geographically, with much of the population clustered into a small number of urban centres. It also has arguably the world's highest take-up of broadband technologies, with at least 70 per cent of the population having high-speed broadband access. It also has a volatile political history, and an established media that have been unashamedly partisan and conservative (Park et al. 2000). As we have noted in this chapter, however, the challenges that *OhMyNews* presents as a commercially successful alternative model for news media production and distribution, and its championing of citizen journalism as the future of news, present important issues for news media globally.

 ## INTERVIEW: GRAHAM YOUNG, EDITOR, *ON LINE OPINION* AND FOUNDER, *NATIONAL FORUM*

On Line Opinion is a not-for-profit e-journal that provides a forum for public social and political debate about current Australian issues. First published in 1999, it has become one of Australia's leading independent online journals dealing with news, politics, and current affairs.

Its founder, Graham Young, established *On Line Opinion* after having worked in the Queensland Liberal Party, where he was state vice-president and campaign chairman. The latter role gave him insight into the potential for the Internet in political affairs.

Can you tell us what On Line Opinion *is, and why it was initially developed?*

[GY:] *On Line Opinion* is a blog written by people who are too busy and too well informed to find the time to blog. We conceived of it before the term blog was invented. We thought there were a lot of people with good ideas and expertise who wouldn't have the time to maintain a personal Web page and, even if they could, wouldn't have the time or expertise to generate large amounts of traffic.

The idea was that if we could centralise the best of this material onto a central site, we could handle traffic and publishing issues, and you'd get higher quality ideas out there than in most other publications. This was a multi-author blog before people had gone through the blogging craze and realised that a single-author blog was hard to maintain.

What do you know about On Line Opinion*'s readership?*

[GY:] Statistics are always a bit difficult. According to Nielsen Net Ratings we get around 125,000–150,000 unique browsers a month. That doesn't mean it's a different person each time—it might be, it might not. Server logs say we get around 350,000 unique browsers a month. The real figure is probably somewhere in the middle.

We've also surveyed our users. We used an opt-in survey, so there are methodological issues, but it seems to be consistent with surveys that other online journals like *Open Democracy* (www.opendemocracy.net) have done.

What we know is that about 25 per cent of the readership are in education as a teacher or a student. We also have higher than average levels of people in government departments, politicians, and staff reading. The media's pretty well represented as well.

How does On Line Opinion *differ from other mainstream media that deal with politics and opinion?*

[GY:] First, it's conceived of as more of a forum than a traditional journalistic enterprise. We don't try to provide balanced articles. We try to provide a context where you get balance over time between articles.

We don't have the journalistic idea of balance—we think point of view is the most important thing a writer brings to the article. Readers are capable of discerning between two arguments and coming to their own conclusions. So it has a more literary, postmodern view of the world than most current affairs publications have.

How has On Line Opinion *changed since it was first published and what relationship does this have to other developments in new media?*

[GY:] It was first published in April 1999. The first big change was frequency; it was originally going to be monthly, as a specialist journal covering politics and current affairs. Then we started getting more material, and publishing more regularly but the same sort of material.

The really big change was in November 2004 when we put a forum into place. The forum now contributes 38 per cent of total site visits. It's entirely user-generated content and when we introduced the forum it was for comments on articles—we were actually following the blog phenomenon there. Blogs have been allowing people to comment since almost the beginning but we did it as a second move.

Then we introduced a general forum—effectively a bulletin board where any-one can start a thread. We see that as being to a certain extent a sub-genre of blogging. While they're not running their own blog, in a sense they're doing a blog post that readers can comment on. To ensure quality, fresh threads are subject to moderation. Anyone can post, but they have to meet a standard.

While we've been behind blogs at times we've always been ahead of the mainstream media, which are now getting into blogs and commenting on articles.

We also introduced a stand-alone blog ourselves (*Ambit Gambit*) to see how the phenomenon worked.

The other thing we've done is use the site for qualitative polling. That's the other big innovation—we haven't seen anyone else follow us there. Even though AC Nielsen does online panels they don't use them in the same way and they're not a media organisation.

In what way does your approach to soliciting material differ from mainstream media?

[GY:] I've never worked in the mainstream media, so I don't know how they do it, but I can guess. We get a lot of unsolicited material, which I assume is normal. For certain issues we approach people, so some articles are commissioned. We can't afford to pay, but then, much of the opinion in the mainstream media is unpaid as well. I don't think it differs much at all.

How do you think the Internet has changed politics in Australia and elsewhere?

[GY:] I don't think it has in Australia, which is really disappointing. That was one of the reasons why I set up *On Line Opinion*—I thought this medium was going to totally revolutionise politics. It facilitates a conversation. Electors can speak back to the parliament and the government as well as chatting to each other. But Australian politicians have been slow to take it up. I suspect we lack the depth of social and entrepreneurial capital that makes these things possible.

You've really got to look to the USA for innovation in politics and the Net, and there it's driven by an entirely different dynamic. In the USA you've got much more of a franchise system where an individual candidate in a sense wins a franchise when they win a primary. They don't have strong central organisations so they need to do a lot more for themselves. They need to relate pretty closely to the electorate, which forces them to innovate. Here, the most critical relationship is with party preselectors who they all know personally.

A key difference between 1999 and 2007 is that now nearly all media organisations have an online presence. Is there still a role for independent online publishing?

[GY:] Most journalists are pretty uniform in their viewpoint. You've theoretically got two competing major publishing houses, News Corp and Fairfax. You do get a bit more right-wing opinion in the News Limited papers and a bit more left-wing in the Fairfax papers, but I don't think anyone's particularly hungry or driven by news values any more. The journalist's main purpose is to create content to hold the advertisements apart. Non-mainstream media have the potential to re-energise the hunger and the passion for news and ideas by enlisting gifted and driven amateurs. In so much as its overheads are much lower than the mainstream media, and it's not so commercially oriented, this model works as an alternative media form.

Citizen journalism, a new public sphere, and journalism as a human right

In Jürgen Habermas's classic account of the public sphere (1995), journalism is envisaged as a domain of our social life through which public opinion can be formed out of rational public debate, which in turn can lead to democratic decision-making arising out of an informed public consensus. Authors such as Carey (1995) have argued that the commercial imperatives of news media and the need for 'instant news' have undercut journalism's claims to be contributing to Habermas's modernist vision of a rational public sphere. But it has been asked whether new media developments can generate a new public sphere. The example of South Korea's *OhMyNews* demonstrates one possibility that it might. In a similar vein, the Qatar-based media service *Al Jazeera* has been identified as contributing to an Arab and Muslim public sphere. This is because of its presence as a clear alternative to highly censored Middle East media, its willingness to address controversial issues, its positioning as an outlet for dissenting and oppositional voices, and its capacity to give voice to those elements of civil society and popular opinion not represented by the governments or the state-controlled media outlets of the region (El-Nawawy & Iskandar 2002; El Oifi 2005).

In considering whether the Internet can constitute a public sphere, Papacharissi (2002) makes the important qualifying point that 'a new public space is not synonymous with a new public sphere', since 'as public space, the Internet provides yet another forum for political deliberation. As a public sphere, the Internet could facilitate discussion that promotes a democratic exchange of ideas and opinions. A virtual public space enhances discussion; a virtual public sphere enhances democracy' (2002: 11).

With this qualification in mind, Papacharissi concludes that the Internet could not yet be considered a virtual public sphere because of inequalities of access, difficulties in bringing together conflicting points of view, and some of the limiting imperatives of reliance upon commercial funding models from large-scale distribution, but that it certainly advances the possibility for such a public sphere to emerge. Importantly, she emphasises that the nature of the medium itself, and the relationship between interconnectedness, real-time discussion, and communication at a distance make it unlikely that the Internet would ever conform to the Habermasian ideal of a public sphere. She instead speculates that 'the Internet will not become the new public sphere, but rather something radically different [that] will enhance democracy and dialogue, but not in a way that we would expect it to, or in a way that we have experienced in the past' (2002: 18). It is far more likely to be, as Brian McNair (2006) has argued, a more crowded, noisy, chaotic, competitive, and rancorous communications space than was envisaged for the modernist public sphere, but that does not in turn dismiss the potential to generate something more akin to a globalised and democratising public sphere.

The British journalist and editor Ian Hargreaves has argued that 'in a democracy, everyone is a journalist. This is because, in a democracy, everyone has the right to *communicate* a fact or a point of view, however trivial, however hideous' (Hargreaves 1999: 4). In a similar vein, Article 19 of the UN Universal Declaration of Human Rights asserts that everyone has 'the right to freedom of opinion and expression', and the right to 'seek, receive and *impart* information and ideas through any media and regardless of frontiers' (United Nations 1948; emphasis added). Hartley (2008) has drawn on these arguments to propose that the right to practise journalism is a human right, and that user-generated content, participatory media, and the turn from 'read-only' mass communications to 'read-write' citizen media is accelerating this possibility. Hartley also proposes that contemporary forms of Web-based journalism are increasingly *redactional*, based around editing existing materials into new forms. Hartley argues that a major barrier to the further development of citizen journalism in these forms is in fact professional journalism itself, which has evolved into a representative function, acting on behalf of the public rather than as a part of the public, and becoming increasingly remote from the audiences and readerships they ostensibly serve.

McNair (2003, 2006) has argued that citizen journalism and user-generated news content need to be understood in the context of a wider shift in the underlying paradigm of journalism and news production from what he terms the 'control paradigm' to 'cultural chaos'. Drawing on the rise of 'chaos theory' in the natural sciences, McNair refers to *cultural chaos* in the context of 'a contemporary communications environment in which, as in nature, chaos creates as well as destroys, generating in the process enhanced possibilities for progressive cultural, political, and social evolution, as well as trends towards social entropy and disorder' (2006: xii). McNair argues that we are moving from information scarcity to information abundance and from closed to open information systems, which in turn challenge the entrenched authority of both political institutions and established media organisations. With the capacity to produce and distribute news, and with information and journalism becoming more and more available to more and more people, the sheer proliferation of voices and opinions enabled by new media generates 'a significant augmentation of the degree of diversity of viewpoints available to users of the globalised public sphere' (2006: 201). Even while most media organisations remain hierarchical and centralised, as do many of the political, business, and other institutions they report on, the combination of the networked structure of the Internet and 24-hour, real-time news 'produces an environment where information cascades become more unpredictable, more frequent, and more difficult for elites to contain when they begin' (2006: 202).

Scott (2005) has questioned the salience of the business models underlying much online journalism, noting that online news services can potentially lead to a further 'tightening' of news content in order to meet the demographic targeting of news audiences by advertisers, with online site content increasingly driven by the marketing divisions of news organisations rather than by their journalists. While this is certainly one potential outcome, which will no doubt reveal itself in a number of news media organisations, the argument that has been developed here proposes that if mainstream news media organisations respond to the threat/opportunity matrix that they face by stripping back online news provision to the bare bones in order to cut costs, they will be met by a new generation of competitors for 'access to eyeballs' in a rapidly changing new media environment. What is apparent is that debates about the relationship between democracy, citizenship, news, and journalism have acquired a new intensity in the 21st century, as the impact of new media shifts the underlying paradigms that have informed journalism and news production in the 20th-century age of mass media and mass communication.

USEFUL WEBSITES

Centre for Citizen Media <http://citmedia.org>. This site is aimed to 'enable and encourage grassroots media, especially citizen journalism, at every level'. The centre was established as a joint initiative of the University of California, Berkeley's Graduate School of Journalism and the Berkman Center for Internet and Society at Harvard University Law School. Its founding Director is Dan Gillmor, author of *We the Media: Grassroots Journalism by the People, for the People* (Gillmor 2006).

J-Lab: Institute for Interactive Journalism <www.j-lab.org>. *J-Lab* is an incubator for innovative news experiments that use new technologies to help people engage actively in critical public issues, based at the University of Maryland's Philip Merrill College of Journalism. It supports community news and citizen media initiatives through its *New Voices* program, as well as researching these through the *Knight Citizen News Network*.

OhMyNews (English language version) <http://english.ohmynews.com>. The international site for what has been the world's most significant and influential contribution in the field of citizen journalism.

09

creative
industries

The rise of creative industries

The rise of creative industries is related to the growth in cultural production and consumption, the increasing significance of knowledge and creativity to all aspects of economic production, distribution, and consumption, and the growing importance of the services sector. It is linked to the dynamics of knowledge-based, global, and networked economies (Castells 2000), as well as to the renewed attention being attached to the importance of location and place as drivers of creativity and innovation. This turn to the creative industries arises in part from the scope of ICTs to allow for greater flexibility in production, such as small-batch production rather than long production runs, as well as the increasingly common global separation of research and development activities from commodity production through global production networks (Ernst & Kim 2002). In industries such as film, television, and games, for example, this has been described as the 'Global Hollywood' model, where concept development and content production are increasingly geographically separated (Miller et al. 2001). The rise of creative industries is also reflective of the growing significance attached to design and signification, to everything from urban spaces, offices, retail outlets, cars, mobile phones, and, indeed, corporations and governments themselves in an era of 'promotional culture' and electronic commerce (Graham 2006).

The rise of creative industries is commonly tracked in economic terms. In the earliest work that used the concept, the Department of Culture, Media, and Sport in the United Kingdom identified the creative industries sectors as being worth £112 billion to the UK economy in 1997, accounting for 5 per cent of British GDP (DCMS 1998). Globally, John Howkins (2001) estimated the creative industries to be worth US$2.2 trillion in 1999, and to account for 7.5 per cent of global GNP (Howkins 2001: 114), although it is important to note that this figure has been questioned on the basis of its inclusion of all research and development as well as the software industries into the creative industries (Cunningham 2002). A study from the USA estimated that the copyright industries accounted for 7.75 per cent of US GDP and 5.9 per cent of national employment (2002). In the European Union (EU), where there is certainly no shared definitional understanding among its members as to the nature of the sector, it has nonetheless been observed that employment growth rates in cultural occupations were four times the EU average (4.8 per cent growth between 1995 and 1999, compared to overall employment growth in the EU of 1.2 per cent), and that people working in cultural occupations were almost three times as likely to be self-employed as the EU average (40.4 per cent compared to 14.4 per cent for the EU as a whole), and twice as likely to have a tertiary educational qualification (MKW 2001: 84–6). In a recent international survey of the creative industries and their wider relevance to economic development, UNCTAD proposed that this sector now accounts for 7 per cent of global GDP, with estimates of annual growth of 10 per cent or more per annum, with annual growth in some sectors of 20 per cent or more (UNCTAD 2004).

All these figures on the economic significance of the creative industries pose the prior definitional question of what the creative industries are. In the early approach of the Department of Culture, Media, and Sport (DCMS), there was a dual approach. Creative industries were defined as 'those activities which have their origin in individual creativity, skill and talent and which have the potential for wealth and job creation through the generation and exploitation of intellectual property' (DCMS 1998). More pragmatically, the Creative Industries Task Force identified 13 sectors as constituting the creative industries:

Table 9.1 Creative industries in the United Kingdom (DCMS study)

Advertising	Interactive leisure software
Architecture	Music
Arts and antique markets	Television and radio
Crafts	Performing arts
Design	Publishing
Designer fashion	Software
Film	

Source: DCMS 1998

This list-based approach inherently carried an *ad hoc* and pragmatic element where, in the UK case, the inclusion of sectors such as architecture and antiques was based on the institutional alignment of culture with the heritage sector. Garnham (2005) has argued that the linking of arts, media, and IT sectors has involved an unduly optimistic uptake on more longstanding problems and issues in the arts and cultural sectors, in order to link arts and cultural policy to the 'sexier' domain of information policy. In a different but related vein, Healy (2002: 101) has argued that the evidence for transition towards a new economy that has creativity as its 'axial principle' is at best mixed, and cautions against 'using new economy jargon to give a bullish defence of the arts in economic terms'.

Underpinning these discussions are shifting understandings of culture and its nature, role, and significance. The historically constituted tension between 'culture as aesthetics' and 'culture as everyday life' has been noted in the historical genealogy of the term (Williams 1976; Bocock 1992). What is now apparent is that there are three further overlays on the concept of culture that have significant implications for how we think about the creative industries:

1 *culture as mediated symbolic communication,* or the interaction between systems of mass-mediated representation of social reality and the everyday reality of lived experience, much of which occurs through mediated forms (TV and radio, computers, mobile phones, etc.)

2 *culture as resource,* or the tendency identified by Yúdice (2003: 9) for culture to be 'increasingly wielded as a resource for both socio-political and economic amelioration' across a range of fields, and

his associated concept of the *expediency of culture*, or the growing understanding of its role as being involved in the deployment of specific resources to identifiable ends

3 *culture as policy discourse*, or the role identified by Bennett (1998) for cultural policy as a mechanism for intersecting governmental priorities into everyday conduct, which have historically revolved around citizenship and the cultural sense of belonging to a nation, but are increasingly concerned with the management of culturally diverse populations.

Economic drivers of creative industries

The rise of the creative industries has been driven by a mix of economic and cultural factors, with a very significant public policy overlay. Factors driving the adoption of creative industries policy discourse have included: the 're-branding' of arts industries and arts policy to emphasise their significance as wealth-generating sectors (see e.g. Americans for the Arts 2007); the more general identification of creativity as a key driver of growth and innovation in a knowledge-based economy; the implications of digital convergence for bringing together the media and communications, cultural content, and information technology sectors; and the turn towards user-generated content in the context of Web 2.0. Hartley has argued that 'the idea of the creative industries seeks to describe the *conceptual and practical convergence* of the creative arts (individual talent) with cultural industries (mass scale), in the context of new media technologies ... within a new knowledge economy, for the use of newly interactive consumer-citizens' (2005: 5).

The three key economic drivers of creative industries have been the rise of the service industry sectors, the emergence of the knowledge-based economy, and the 'culturalisation' of the economy as services become increasingly central. Arguably the major trend in advanced capitalist economies since the 1970s has been the rise of the *services industries* as the principal source of employment, wealth generation, and innovation. In terms of both employment and the share of total output, the services industries have grown in significance throughout the 20th century, and especially in the period after 1970. Castells and Aoyama found that in 1990, services accounted for 75 per cent of employment in the USA and 70 per cent of employment in the UK, compared to 52 per cent in the USA and 47 per cent in the UK in 1920 (Castells & Aoyana 1994). Taking even more of a macro-historical perspective, Abramovitz and David (2001) have observed that the growth in the share of *intangible capital* (devoted to knowledge production and dissemination on the one hand, and education, health, and well-being on the other) has been accelerating in the US economy for the whole of the 20th century, and its share of total wealth has exceeded that of tangible capital (physical infrastructure, equipment, inventories, natural resources etc.) since the early 1970s. This trend can only be partly explained by the movement of manufacturing to lower-wage economies in developing countries. It is increasingly true of many developing countries: India has established itself as a global leader in IT-based services, while revisions in 2003 to how GDP was calculated in China found that the services sector was twice the size (40 per cent of the Chinese economy) as was previously thought. Moreover, manufacturers are themselves increasingly engaged in the services industries. Giarini (2002) has observed that the pure cost of production or manufacturing of goods rarely accounts for more than 20 per cent of the final price, and that 70 to 80 per cent of the cost is attributable to service and delivery functions undertaken before manufacturing (R&D, financing), during manufacturing (quality control, safety), selling (logistics, distribution networks), during product and system utilisation (maintenance, leasing), and after product and system utilisation (waste management, recycling).

The relationship between information, knowledge, and creativity, and the ways in which sustained technological and economic innovation are accompanied by social, cultural, and institutional innovation, is strongly connected to the rise of creative industries. The nature of a knowledge-based economy, and the role played in it by networks and clusters, will be explored in more detail in the next chapter. It is nonetheless worth noting four features that are relevant to the rise of the creative industries. The first point is that there is an increasingly significant role for knowledge in all sectors in the 21st-century 'new' economy, as noted by Leadbeater:

> In the new economy more of the value of manufactured products will come from the software and intelligence that they embody, and more of what we consume will be in the form of services. Across all sectors the knowledge content of products and processes is rising … Knowledge push and market pull have made know-how the critical source of competitive advantage in the modern economy. (2000: 39)

The concept of *knowledge push* refers to the growth in outputs in education and scientific research arising from public and private investment, and the ways in which ICTs speed up the production, collection, and dissemination of such research outcomes, enabling more rapid transformation into new products, services, activities, and processes (David & Foray 2002). *Market pull* factors that promote the rise of a knowledge economy include economic globalisation, increased competition, greater sophistication in consumer demand, and the growing importance of intangible assets, such as branding and know-how, to competitive advantage.

The second point is that, as Brown and Duguid (2000) have observed, knowledge is not synonymous with information. At an epistemological level, they distinguish knowledge from information on the basis of the personal dimensions of ownership of knowledge, the difficulties in disembedding knowledge as content from those who possess it, and the need for knowledge transfer to involve a learning process. Arguing that a knowledge economy is different, not only from an industrial economy but also from an information economy, they emphasise how 'the importance of people as creators and carriers of knowledge is forcing organisations to realise that knowledge lies less in its databases than in its people' (2000: 121).

The third point relates to the differentiation within the services sector between forms of employment that are in some sense 'creative' (involving the generation of new ideas, expressive of a personal vision at some level, associated with relatively high degrees of work autonomy), and those service industry jobs that are largely repetitive and quasi-industrialised in their nature (e.g. serving at a McDonald's fast food restaurant, working at a call centre, or operating the checkout at a chain retail store). The work of Richard Florida (2002) makes a number of claims in this area, and these will be considered in the next chapter, but it is important to note the importance attached to a *creative milieu* as a key driver of creative industries development. Brown and Duguid's observations about the embodiment of knowledge and learning in people and communities is supported by Andy Pratt's (1998) observation that knowledge in the new economy is characterised not only by its weightlessness but also by its embeddedness in people, locations, networks, and institutions, and the related point that cultural activity and employment is not only growing, but is becoming more tied to places, especially cities. Justin O'Connor (1999) has connected this to new modes of cultural production and consumption among the young (18–35 years old) in urban centres where:

- making money and making culture are one and the same activity
- there is an antipathy to distinguishing between 'work time' and 'leisure time'

- there is a heavy reliance on informal networks for information and ideas
- there is an emphasis on intuition, emotional involvement, immersion in the field, and an 'enthusiast's' knowledge of the market
- cultural producers desire to 'work for themselves' and outside the nine-to-five routine.

The fourth and final set of issues relate to the *culturalisation of economic activity*. Du Gay and Pryke (2002) and Amin and Thrift (2004) have argued that there has been a growing 'culturalisation of economic life', and that evidence of this can be found in the increasing importance attached to organisational culture as a key to economic performance; the rise of the services sector, where there is a 'more or less direct relationship ... between one or more service provider and one or more service customer' (Du Gay & Pryke 2002: 3); and the growing role played by cultural intermediaries in sectors such as advertising, marketing communication, and public relations. In *The Age of Access*, Jeremy Rifkin (2000) located the rise of services industries in a wider pattern of transformation of the nature of property and markets that includes the following shifts:

- from markets and discrete exchanges between buyers and sellers, to networks based on continuing relationships between suppliers and users
- from wealth based on the ownership of tangible assets (plant, equipment, inventory, etc), to the outsourcing of production, and wealth creation based on access to intangible assets, most notably goodwill, ideas, brand identities, copyrights, patents, talent, and expertise
- from the ownership of goods to the accessing of services
- from production and sales to customer relationship marketing
- from production-line manufacturing and long product cycles to the Hollywood organisational model of project-based collaborative teams brought together for a limited time.

For Rifkin, these changes together marked the rise of *cultural capitalism*, developing out of new forms of linkage between digital communications technologies, culture, and commerce:

> More and more of our daily lives are already mediated by the new digital channels of human expression. And because communication is the means by which human beings find common meaning and share the world they create,

commodifying all forms of digital communications goes hand in hand with commodifying the many relationships that make up the lived experience—the cultural life—of the individual and the community. (2000: 138)

The creative industries also have their own distinctive dynamics as industries, which authors such as Lash and Urry (1994), Rifkin (2000), Lash (2002), and McRobbie (2005) have suggested are increasingly becoming the norm in many sectors in the 21st-century market capitalist economy. The Harvard economist Richard Caves (2000) has drawn attention to core features of these sectors, whether or not they are publicly or privately supported:

1   considerable *uncertainty* about the likely demand for creative product, due to the fact that creative products are 'experience goods', where buyers lack information prior to consumption, and where the satisfaction derived is largely subjective and intangible

2   the ways in which creative producers derive *non-economic* forms of satisfaction from their work and creative activity, but rely on the performance of more 'humdrum' activities (e.g. basic accounting and product marketing) in order for such activities to be economically viable

3   the fact that creative production is frequently *collective* in its nature, which generates a need to develop and maintain creative teams with diverse skills, who often also possess diverse interests and expectations about the final product

4   the almost *infinite variety* of creative products available, both within particular formats (e.g. videos at a rental store), and between formats

5   *vertically differentiated* skills, or what Caves terms the 'A list'/ 'B list' phenomenon, and the ways in which producers or other content aggregators rank and assess creative personnel

6   the need to *coordinate diverse creative activities* within a relatively short and often finite time-frame

7   the *durability* of many cultural products, and the capacity of their producers to continue to extract economic rents (e.g. copyright payments) long after the period of production.

What these characteristics point to, for Caves, is major risk and uncertainty about the economic outcomes of creative activities. This uncertainty and risk, and the need to spread risk and provide insurance to creative producers, is one reason for public funding for some creative activities. In commercial terms, risk and uncertainty are also managed through *contracts*, whereby the various parties involved in the production and distribution of a creative product seek to manage risk and diversify rewards, based on the skills and capacities they bring to the project and the need to ensure mutual obligation to meet commitments. The ongoing management of risks, contracts, and creative production processes is a factor that leads to *industrial organisation* in the creative industries, in forms such as publishing, recording, broadcasting, and film companies commissioning production and managing distribution; guilds, unions, and legal arrangements protecting creative producers; and intermediaries such as agents managing the more commercial elements of a career in creative practice.

Policy drivers of creative industries

Creative industries policy has been taken up enthusiastically in a variety of local, regional, national, and international contexts. The concept as a policy discourse has its origins in the initiatives of the Blair Labour government in the UK shortly after its election in 1997, which led to a variety of national and regional creative industries development strategies as well as some highly influential sectoral mapping documents. Since then, some of the policy initiatives that have been undertaken in different parts of the world include:

- Australia: adoption of a creative industries strategy by the Queensland state government in 2001, and a proposed national strategy for developing the digital content industries, as well as a pioneering national mapping strategy that identified the sectors as being 50 per cent larger than was previously understood (Cunningham 2006)
- New Zealand: identification of creative industries as one of the 'three pillars' of the 2002 Growth and Innovation Framework, with biotechnology and information and communication technology
- Singapore: the *Remaking Singapore* strategy has sought to redefine the economic base of the city-state around creativity and entrepreneurship (Leo & Lee 2004)
- Sweden: the Knowledge Foundation was established by the Swedish government to examine the role and significance of what it terms the *experience industries*, which it identified as constituting 6.5 per cent of the Swedish labour market (Nielsén 2004)

- South Korea: what is known as the 'Korean Wave' (*Hallyu*) or the growing international popularity of film, music, television, games, and entertainment software from South Korea, has been tapped into by the Korean Ministry of Culture and Tourism, which is investing heavily in developing Korea's digital content industries
- Hong Kong: the *Baseline Study of Hong Kong Creative Industries*, undertaken by the Centre for Cultural Policy Research at the University of Hong Kong (CCPR 2003), identified the importance of creative industries to the image or branding of Hong Kong, as well as the opportunities to shift the local economy towards high-value-added services as labour-intensive manufacturing shifted to the Guangzhou (Pearl River Delta) regions of mainland China
- European Union: the MKW study commissioned by the EU (MKW 2001) found that employment growth rates in cultural occupations were four times the EU average, and that people working in cultural occupations were almost three times as likely to be self-employed and twice as likely to have a tertiary qualification as those in other sectors (cf. Flew 2005)
- China: The Eleventh Five-Year Plan, promulgated in 2005, drew attention to the need to develop the creative industries (*chaungyi gongye*) in order to take advantage of opportunities in the digital content sectors, which combine knowledge economy priorities with the need for enhanced creativity. This is part of a wider set of debates about how China can move from being the 'world's factory' ('Made in China'), to a 'Created in China' agenda, which sees China as a leader in intellectual property development (Keane 2004; Hartley & Keane 2006).

Internationally, UNCTAD (2004) has estimated that the creative industries, which it identifies as lying at the crossroads between the arts, business, and technology, are growing at 10–20 per cent annually, or 2–3 times the growth rates of the global economy overall. It has explicitly linked expansion of the creative industries to globalisation, around five trends:

1 deregulation of national cultural and media policy frameworks
2 increasing average global incomes, which allow for more 'discretionary' expenditure on arts, cultural, and entertainment products and services
3 technological changes, particularly the role played by the Internet for the global distribution of digital media content

4   the global rise of service industries, which place a higher premium on intangible forms of knowledge, and are demand sources for creative industries outputs in areas such as design, advertising, and marketing

5   expansion of international trade generally, and trade in services in particular.

Creative policy agendas have been even more marked at the level of cities and regions. Stevenson (2004: 119–20) has described this as the new *civic gold rush* in urban planning and cultural policy alike, where strategies are developed for 'fostering strategically the cultures of cities and regions ... [where] culture and creativity have become ... forms of "capital" that supposedly can be measured, developed, and then traded in an international marketplace comprised of cities eager to compete with each other on the basis of image, amenity, liveability and visitability'. Examples of such strategies can be found throughout Europe, the USA, Canada, Australia, New Zealand, and increasingly throughout Asia. The role played by the European Capital (formerly City) of Culture initiative in developing such 're-branding' of cities has been noted, particularly with the redevelopment of cities such as Barcelona, Glasgow, and Dublin in the 1980s and 1990s (García 2004), and it can also be seen in the competition for cultural leadership between Beijing and Shanghai in China. The boom in public art in the USA has also been linked to such notions of the role of cultural infrastructure as a lever of new forms of place competitiveness (Weiss 2007). In an evaluation of such initiatives in cities in the Netherlands such as Amsterdam, Rotterdam, Tilburg, and Utrecht, Mommaas (2004) observed that such creative city strategies have been driven by a heterogeneous—and sometimes contradictory—mix of policy priorities including:

· attracting globally mobile capital and skilled labour to particular locations

· stimulating a more entrepreneurial and demand-oriented approach to arts and cultural policy

· promoting innovation and creativity more generally, through the perceived interaction between culturally vibrant locales and innovation in other economic sectors

· finding new uses for derelict industrial-era sites in post-industrial economies

- promoting cultural diversity and cultural democratisation, and being more inclusive of the cultural practices of otherwise marginalised social groups.

Two key authors who have influenced these new urban cultural policy agendas have been Charles Landry and Richard Florida. Landry (2000) has drawn attention to the significance of a creative milieu to the development of creativity in modern cities and regions, which he defined as a combination of *hard infrastructure*, or the network of building and institutions that constitute a city or a region, and *soft infrastructure*, defined as 'the system of associative structures and social networks, connections and human interactions, that underpins and encourages the flow of ideas between individuals and institutions' (2000: 133). In outlining the case for considering London to be a creative city, Landry (2005) proposed that culture constituted a valuable resource for cities such as London in the 21st-century global economy in six respects:

1 Both the historical artefacts and the contemporary practices of a city's population generate a sense of local belonging and civic pride.
2 Cultural activities are linked to innovation and creativity, and the capacity of cities to adapt and innovate is the key to their longevity.
3 The cultural sectors are linked to place image and place competitiveness in their ability to attract international capital investment and geographically mobile skilled workers.
4 Culture and tourism are inextricably linked, as tourists seek both the 'high' culture of a city (museums, galleries, historic buildings, etc.) and its popular culture (clubs, bars, restaurants, street festivals, etc.).
5 The growing economic significance of the creative industries in the global economy raises the importance of innovative forms of digital content and of networks that promote innovation and creativity.
6 Culture may be able to promote greater social inclusion and redress economic inequality and social disadvantage, through the ability to provide places where otherwise marginalised groups can engage in collective forms of cultural activity.

Florida (2002) has emphasised *the power of place* for the rise of what he has termed the 'creative class', arguing that creative people attach great importance to being in diverse, culturally vibrant cities with a distinctive identity and a variety of engaging experiences. Florida argued that urban centres with a strong wellspring of cultural creativity will thrive because their economic dynamism is driven, not by government incentives to attract new ICT-related industries, but by what he terms the *Three T's* of *technology*, *talent* and *tolerance*. This is because 'regional economic growth is powered by creative people who prefer places that are diverse, tolerant and open to new ideas. Diversity increases the odds that a place will attract different types of people with different skill sets and ideas' (2002: 249). Florida uses American cities such as San Francisco, Boston, and Austin as examples of 'second-tier' cities that can utilise their embedded reputations for diversity, tolerance, and openness to be dynamic new economy hubs.

Recent work on creative cities has drawn upon some well-established historical lessons. Hall (2000) drew attention to the historic significance of creative cities, in which he includes Athens in the 5th century BC, Florence in the 14th century, London in Shakespeare's time, Vienna in the 19th century, Paris between 1870 and 1910, and Berlin in the 1920s. He argued that what characterised these cities was not simply that they were sites of wealth creation and global trade, but that they were also centres of cultural achievement, large-scale migration, intellectual leadership, creativity, and public dissidence. Jacobs (1994) argued for the centrality of diverse, mixed-use urban centres, and for the contribution of importance of urban villages not only to the quality of life of residents, but also to economic growth, since diverse and concentrated urban zones encouraged the productive cross-pollination of ideas.

Creative industries and the future of arts and cultural policy

Creative industries can be located as the third stage in approaches to public support for the arts, media, and culture. The first stage saw *arts policy* as a distinctive activity, associated with publicly subsidised excellence in the production and exhibition of art forms such as opera, orchestras, live theatre, the visual arts, dance, and literature. Areas that were primarily commercial in their operations, such as the media, were not considered relevant to arts policy, while government-supported activities in these areas—such as public broadcasting and national film production—were understood as being outside the domain of arts policy. Culture in this framework was associated with quality, excellence, national identity, and social improvement: it was by definition outside the domain of the economic. This approach underpinned the development of post-World War II arts policy in many countries until the 1980s.

The second stage was that of *cultural policy*, which brought the media and other forms of popular cultural content production into an expanded policy domain. Cultural policy has been the dominant mode in many European countries, most notably France, since the 1960s, and UNESCO strongly promoted cultural policy development in newly decolonised developing nations (Flew 2005, 2007: 174–8). In those countries where more traditional forms of arts policy had prevailed, such as the UK, cultural policy was seen as a way of moving from an 'idealist' conception of the arts that rejected the commercial market, to one that sought to more actively intervene in the cultural industries and cultural markets (Garnham 1987; Lewis 1990; Mercer 1994). It sought to focus the traditional arts on the challenges presented by establishing greater commercial viability (marketing and audience development, value chain analysis, etc.), new forms of advocacy such as 'arts multiplier' studies,[1] and the opportunities presented by new digital media technologies. In the UK, cultural industries development strategies gained momentum from Labour-controlled local councils in cities that had faced the consequences of deindustrialisation in the 1980s, such as Sheffield and Glasgow.

In Australia, cultural industries research was developed through the Australian Key Centre for Cultural and Media Policy (for example Bennett 1994, 1998), and informed the Keating Labor government's *Creative Nation* cultural policy statement, released in 1994 (Department of Communications and the Arts 1994). Such approaches understood cultural industries as being important in terms of their contribution to national economic development, and pointed to the value-adding possibilities arising from effective policy development, particularly in relation to developing the cultural industries value chain, or ensuring that the products and outputs of artistic creativity were better distributed and marketed to audiences and consumers.

While cultural policy was broader in its remit than traditional arts policy, and identified the economic contribution of the arts and cultural industries, it nonetheless retained a certain 'arts-centredness'. To take one example, cultural economist David Throsby proposed a model of creativity that is 'centred around the locus of origin of creative ideas, and radiating outwards as those ideas become combined with more and more other inputs to produce a wider and wider range of products' (2001: 112). Arguing that 'cultural goods and services involve creativity in their production, embody some degree of intellectual property and convey symbolic meaning' (2001: 112), Throsby proposed a 'concentric-circles' model of the cultural and creative industries based on their level of cultural and non-cultural inputs and outputs 'with the arts lying at the centre, and with other industries forming layers or circles located around the core, extending further outwards as the use of creative ideas is taken into a wider production context' (2001: 113).

Figure 9.1 Throsby's 'concentric circles' model of creative industries

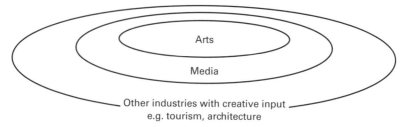

Arts

Media

Other industries with creative input
e.g. tourism, architecture

From this perspective, the differences between a creative industries policy and a cultural policy can be drawn out more clearly (cf. Cunningham 2005). First, as was noted in Chapter 6, it is difficult to sustain the argument that creativity is the exclusive provenance of the arts; in a knowledge economy context it is increasingly seen as integral to sustainability and competitive advantage across a range of sectors (a corollary is that entrepreneurship is no longer seen as the exclusive domain of business, but also exists in the policy, social, arts, and cultural sectors [cf. Leadbeater 2000]). Second, drawing on Howkins' (2001) calculation of the value-adding sectors of the creative economy, it is apparent that the significance of the creative and performing arts is dwarfed by that of highly capitalised and globalised sectors such as publishing, software, design, and the audiovisual industries. Howkins argued that, in 1999, the creative and performing arts accounted for only 2 per cent of the market value of the creative industries overall (2001: 114). Third, creative industries policies tend to work around the relationship between local initiatives and the global cultural economy, whereas the focus of cultural policy has tended to be resolutely national and relatively autonomous from wider economic policy concerns (cf. Flew 2005). Finally, creative industries policy draws on the impact of digitisation and convergence to argue that such policies should enter into the mainstream of national innovation policies, linking the cultural sectors to the knowledge and service industries, present- ing the promotion of creative innovation and the digital content industries as a central part of innovation strategies in the 21st-century knowledge-based economy (Cunningham et al. 2004; PMSEIC 2005).

In his review of the literature, Healy (2002: 101) has argued that evidence for creativity being a new *axial principle* is mixed, and he cautions against 'using new economy jargon to give a bullish defence of the arts in economic terms'. Others have expressed disquiet with the tendency to simply fold arts policy and arts practice into a creative industries policy template. McQuire (2001) has expressed a concern that the creative industries model runs the risk of blurring 'the slender but significant difference between being market-savvy and being market driven', running the risk of losing sight of 'the important role that art has assumed in generating a critical space within contemporary culture' (2001: 209, 210). McNamara (2002) has expressed concern that the creative industries model may generate an unduly narrow definition of creativity as that which acquires commercial value, arguing instead for 'an expansive rather than a narrowly functionalist approach' (2002: 73). In a more policy-related context, O'Regan (2002) has wondered whether the rise of creative industries policy models means that 'even in the domain of "creativity", the close attribute of "the arts", policy-making is no longer being carried out by arts-based cultural policy institutions but by other actors and agents. Even "creativity" seemed too important to be left up to cultural policy institutions and frameworks' (2002: 23). Finally, Rossiter (2006) has questioned the linkage of creative industries to intellectual property, arguing that it may too readily have attached these sectors to intellectual property regimes that are 'reactionary', and can act to inhibit new forms of creativity (2006: 108–11). The issue of intellectual property laws in the digital environment will be returned to in Chapter 11.

The model of creative cities championed by authors such as Landry and Florida has also been challenged. Peck (2005: 763) has argued that Florida's creative cities solutions have the potential to destroy what they aim to celebrate, which is culture, uniqueness, and authenticity. He argues that 'rather than "civilizing" urban economic development by "bringing in culture", creativity strategies do the opposite: they commodify the arts and cultural resources, even social tolerance itself, suturing them as putative economic assets to evolving regimes of urban competition'. Kotkin (2006) has argued against urban development strategies aimed at attracting a mobile and footloose creative class, observing that cities where the creative economy is strongest—such as Los Angeles, New York, and London—are also those where urban inequality is highest. Kotkin has also questioned the claims that the most 'creative' US cities, such as San Francisco and Boston, are more economically vibrant than cities such as Phoenix and Denver, or that the case has been convincingly made that creativity needs cosmopolitan urban milieux and cannot happen in new suburban communities. In an astute insider's account, Oakley (2004: 72–3) has identified problems with such generic, cookie-cutter models of creative industries strategies in the UK context: 'Rather than trying to understand the difference between the creative economy of Glasgow and that of Cornwall, we currently seem hell bent on trying to replicate a single creative industries model across the country. It appears that everywhere needs a university, some incubators and a "creative hub", with or without a café, galleries and fancy shops.'

In *The Flight of the Creative Class* (2007), Florida concedes some of these points. He acknowledges that some of the most creative city-regions of the USA are also among the most unequal, with San Jose, Washington DC, Raleigh-Durham, Austin, and San Francisco being in the top ten in both the creativity and inequality rankings (2007: 190). He also addresses the criticism that the Creativity Index as developed in *The Rise of the Creative Class* may have been overly focused on gays and bohemians, and insufficiently focused on other indices of tolerance, such as tolerance of recent migrants, and that the question of 'openness' relates more simply to '"low barriers to entry" for talent … from across the entire demographic spectrum' (2007: 53). In doing so, Florida proposes the need to move from thinking about a creative economy to that of building a *creative society*, and proposes the need for reform to social institutions that harnesses and extends the benefits of the creative economy to those who may otherwise be excluded, in order to overcome the emergent class divide between those in creative sector and service industry jobs, in a manner that is parallel to the 'New Deal' that Franklin Roosevelt proposed in the 1930s as a response to the Great Depression in industrial America:

> The creative economy is the Schumpeterian growth engine of our age, and the socio-economic dynamic that it sets in motion is the modern-day equivalent of the divide Roosevelt faced—the growth of two divergent classes; the creative and service sectors … We need a strategy that is the modern-day equivalent of the New Deal—one that stimulates the creative economic engine while at the same time extending its benefits to a broad base of people … To be effective, a fuller, more creative society will require that a large number of individuals feel they have a real stake in its emergence and expansion. (Florida 2007: 243–4)

Is 'creative industries' still a useful organising concept?

In light of these various critiques of the creative industries idea, associated policy developments, and related concepts, is it still a conceptually useful organising category? One influential line of thinking, emanating primarily from the United Kingdom, questions this. Linking the shift from 'cultural industries' to 'creative industries' to the shift towards a 'Third Way' for the British Labour Party under Tony Blair, Garnham (2005: 20) has argued that this discursive shift constituted 'an attempt by the cultural sector and the cultural policy community to share in its relations with the government, and in policy presentation in the media, the unquestioned prestige that now attaches to the information society and to any policy that supposedly favours its development'. Hesmondhalgh and Pratt (2005: 5) proposed that creative industries policy discourse constituted a pragmatic turn for cultural policy advocates:

> Cultural policy, previously on the margins in many areas of government, could be seen to be economically relevant in an era when policy was judged primarily in terms of its fiscal rewards ... The popularity of such policies was underpinned by an increasing acceptance amongst both neo-liberal conservatives and the postmodernist left that the commodification of culture was not something that could any longer be 'resisted' through arts subsidies and other traditional forms of cultural policy. Moreover, creative industries policy could be portrayed as democratising and anti-elitist, as opposed to the supposed elitism of arts policy aimed at subsidising cultural production that could not meet its costs through the market.

Hesmondhalgh (2007) has argued against the term 'creative industries', in favour of the concept of 'cultural industries', on the grounds that the concept of creativity is definitionally vague, creative industries policy discourse is too imbued with 'hype' about the 'creative' or 'new' economy, and that strategies to promote 'creative' urban spaces may reproduce established inequalities of access and class-based social hierarchies (Hesmondhalgh 2007: 144–9).

Whether we refer to 'creative' or 'cultural' industries may be in part a matter of preferred nomenclature. Within the United Nations, for instance, UNESCO (2003) refers to the cultural industries, while UNCTAD (2004) refers to the creative industries, yet both are referring to a broadly similar set of arts, media, and digital content industries. Definitional issues plague the creative industries debate, in spite of the eminently pragmatic solution offered by the Singaporean Ministry of Trade and Industry, which proposed that cultural industries were engaged in the 'upstream' activity of content creation, and the creative industries in the 'downstream' activities of distribution and commercialisation (MTI 2003). Both definitions and underlying assumptions about these terms exist within European Union member states, ranging from the view from Germany that 'culture' and 'industry' remain antithetical since aesthetic excellence cannot be mass-produced, to the more pragmatic Finnish position that mobile phones can be a part of the nation's cultural output. Longstanding differences can also be identified between the French perspective on the arts and culture as part of the nation's *patrimoine*, as compared to the alleged British tendency to speak of culture only when it is associated with the media and sport (MKW 2001).

The definitional issues, however, run deeper when they are connected to wider debates about the global cultural economy. Authors such as Hesmondhalgh (2007) broadly adhere to an understanding of the global media-cultural system that is identified in the political economy of global media, whereby core–periphery relations continue to operate on a global scale, with 'Global Hollywood' and its adjuncts in other related industries continuing to dominate the flows of capital to creative projects through favourable intellectual property laws, even as they outsource content production to the four corners of the globe (see Miller et al. 2005; Thussu 2006). By contrast, the creative industries perspective has tended to understand the global cultural economy in less zero-sum terms, and to see the globalisation of media and creative industries as leading to a more matrix-like and mosaic structure. In this approach, new media and creative industries production hubs emerge through processes of 'creative destruction', in which some established production sites decline and others emerge, but where the geocultural space of media and cultural flows has nonetheless become far more complex than was the case in the second half of the 20th century (see Scott 2004; Curtin 2007).

I have argued elsewhere (Flew 2007) that the latter tendency predominated in the 21st-century global cultural economy, as it is increasingly infused by the dynamics of the knowledge-based economy, multiculturalism, diasporic media consumption patterns, and global production networks. Cunningham (2007) has undertaken an extensive documentary search of creative industries policy statements outside the UK to argue that, *pace* Garnham, there is much less of a top-down approach, and more of a tentative and explorative approach to identifying both definitions and policy approaches in the creative industries policy literature. The Asian case is instructive in terms of how such discourses do, or do not, travel. In their seven-country Asian study, Kong and colleagues (2006: 191) identify an 'uneven geography of flows of creative economy discourses'. They differentiate between those nations where policy-makers drew upon already established 'Western' notions of the creative industries (Singapore, Hong Kong SAR), to those where more localised understandings of the concept have gained prominence (Korea, Taiwan), to those where the concept either translates into preservation of existing cultural forms (Japan) or has no policy resonance at all (India). They note China as a significantly ambiguous case, where the long-established interest in the cultural industries (*wenhua chanye*) on the part of the state sits alongside a demand for growth and international competitiveness in the cultural sectors, so that there is considerable experimentation at the level of city authorities in how to develop the creative industries (*chaungyi gongwe*). The interview below with Professor Zhang Xiaoming from the Chinese Academy of Social Sciences provides insight into how the concept of creative industries has developed in China over the 2000s, as part of the national innovation policy (*chuangxin*) agenda.

INTERVIEW: PROFESSOR ZHANG XIAOMING, CHINESE ACADEMY OF SOCIAL SCIENCES

Professor Zhang Xiaoming is the Deputy Director of the Chinese Academy of Social Sciences Cultural Research Institute, and is one of the most experienced and respected researchers of China's creative economy. He has been a key policy advisor in the development of the Chinese government's national and municipal Eleventh Five-Year Plans, and is a consultant for Beijing's Chaoyang district government in the development of clusters such as the 798 Contemporary Art Centre at Dashanzi, the Songzhuang Artists' community in east Beijing, and the Panjiayuan antiques market in Chaoyang District, as well as advising the Shanghai municipal government in relation to the National Animation Centre at East China Normal University. He has been an influential figure in the reform of China's cultural industries in his role as lead editor of *The Blue Book of China's Cultural Industries* series, published by the Chinese Academy of Social Sciences (Social Sciences Documentation Publishing House 2001–07). This series provides recommendations and blueprints for economic and social development. It contains key data and critical analysis on China's cultural industries with authors drawn from government, industry, and academia. Prof. Zhang Xiaoming is the author of *Great Collusion: The Study of Interests Relation in Market Economy* (Renmin University Press 2002), and has also co-authored *The Philosophical Foundation of the Reform* (Sichuan People's Press 1997), as well as publishing over 30 peer-reviewed academic articles.

Thanks to Dr Weihong Zhang for organising and translating the interview, and Ms Yang Yang for further assistance with translation.

What is your understanding of the term 'creative industries'?

[ZX:] By integrating various definitions of 'creative industries' at home and abroad and combining development requirements at the present stage of our country, I define 'creative industries' as 'those industries which have their origin in individual creativity, skill and talent through the generation and exploitation of intellectual property, which will provide consumers with experiential cultural products and services, create a value-added culture in all aspects of the national economy, and improve the quality of social life as a whole through large-scale reproduction and spread by economic organisations'.

There are four key points in this definition. First of all, 'those industries which have their origin in individual creativity, skill and talent … through the generation and exploitation of intellectual property' is taken from the classic British definition given in 1998. Second, 'through large-scale reproduction and spread by economic organisations' refers to the current situation of cultural and creative industries in our country. Third, 'provide consumers with experiential cultural products and services' and 'create a value-added culture in all aspects of the national economy' explain how creative industries serve two basic purposes: lifestyle and productivity. Fourth, 'improve the quality of social life as a whole' absorbs Taiwan's definition of creative industries.

Until very recently, the Chinese authorities have spoken only of the 'cultural industries', which were largely understood as being under state control, and whose products were directed towards the morals and the values of the population.

[ZX:] Cultural industries statistics have been published regularly in China every year. Statistics for 2004 published last year show that state-owned cultural enterprises did not hold an advantage any more in terms of quantity. Cultural products for pure entertainment have already achieved a majority in China's cultural industry.

Do you believe that there has been a shift in thinking from 'cultural industries' to the 'creative industries'?

[ZX:] There has been a nationwide call for greater innovation in China, and the slogan 'building an innovative country' has been put forward [in the 11th National

Five-Year Development Plan, 2006–10]. Innovation and creativity are two closely related concepts. Moreover, science and technology innovation is getting closer to the cultural sector. From the policy aspect, the development of creative industries actually 'borrows' a great deal from policies applied in science and technology innovation.

There has also been a shift in thinking, particularly with the rising economic development level in China's eastern regions. For example, an upgrade of the importance of cultural industries development occurred in Beijing and Shanghai. At the same time, national policy discourse has not changed from 'cultural industries' to 'creative industries' or 'cultural creative industries'. Changes have happened only at the municipal and provincial levels.

The 'creative industries' tend to be seen as being driven more by the market than by the state. Drawing on the models developed by the British government in 1998, and adopted in other countries, this would appear obvious in sectors that are clearly commercial in their nature, such as advertising or software development. How does it impact on those sectors that may be in transition in China, such as film, broadcasting, or news media?

[ZX:] At present, creative industries only develop at the front end of the film, broadcasting, and television industry—film and television production. In China, radio and television broadcasting has not been opened up and investors from outside industries or foreign companies are not allowed to enter into the fray. However, the 'separation of production and broadcasting', which has been carried out for many years, has already made production processes market-oriented. Many films and television productions are produced using private capital. New media are still limited to hardware or production services. The broadcasting of news content via new media has not been opened up yet.

It has been observed that while the Chinese economy is in overall international trade surplus, it is in deficit in cultural goods and services, whereas much of the surplus is derived from low-cost manufactured goods. Do you believe that strategies to develop the creative industries can reverse this deficit in the cultural sectors?

[ZX:] I believe that the introduction of a national policy to encourage Chinese culture to 'go abroad' has already played a role in shifting the trade deficit in cultural goods. For example, subsidies for translation services have encouraged publication exports. This policy has partly benefited from the development of creative industries. However, it cannot be totally attributed to the development of creative industries. In the long term, the development of creative industries will definitely play a key role in promoting Chinese culture abroad. Policy changes are necessary in other areas, and education is the most important of them.

Creative industries are sometimes also referred to as the copyright industries. Recent developments in the WTO have indicated that the US media and entertainment industries see China as a place where copyright infringements are occurring, and they want a tightening up of copyright laws and their enforcement in China. Can you discuss how these debates are viewed from a Chinese perspective, and whether China will be a major developer of intellectual property over the next 5–10 years?

[ZX:] China and the USA are at different stages of development. China is in its middle period of industrialisation while the USA has stepped into a post-industrialisation period. Therefore, the benefits of exchange between China and the USA include two types of commodities, industrial manufacturing goods and copyright products. The first type are low value-added and the second type are high value-added, which is an unequal exchange in itself.

China is still a 'transitional economy'. After its implementation of reform for 27 years, China has just enacted its landmark Property Rights Law, which provides legal protection to private property rights in the field of material production. It now faces the issue of 'intellectual property' protection to establish property rights in the field of culture. This is a brand-new system for the Chinese, who need a process to be educated and to learn.

To deal with the trade conflicts between China and the USA, they should be viewed from the perspective of mutual benefit and win-win progress. China's low-cost manufacturing benefits Americans. Americans' intellectual property products should also yield profits for China. For instance, using 'open source' software, developing international cooperation in research etc. are methods to achieve 'win-win' outcomes that deserve to be discussed.

In any case, China will be a strong country in intellectual property rights creation, which can be predicted from its current education scale and increasing scientific research personnel. Besides, cultural industries are developing rapidly in China. Relying upon its cultural heritage of thousands of years, China will no doubt soon be the biggest country exporting cultural products worldwide.

Will the concept of creative industries be of lasting significance in China? Is it seen as a core component of national innovation policy agendas, or will it be a passing fad?

[ZX:] So far, the concept of creative industries is popular in China, but not all government departments and policy-makers agree with it. 'Cultural industries' will not be changed into 'creative industries' at the national policy level.

But 'innovation' and 'creativity' are two concepts closely related to each other. The increasing confluence of information and cultural industries has led to overlapping policies between a national innovative system and the cultural industries, which results in policy-makers in other fields actively adopting the term of 'creative industries'. Therefore, the term 'creative industries' will not be out of circulation soon.

In the eastern parts of China, cities such as Beijing, Shanghai, and Shenzhen are developing cultural creative industries as an established development strategy, a policy choice that resulted from the development requirements at local municipality levels.

Further reading
Wang 2004; O'Connor & Gu 2006; Zhang, X 2006; Keane 2007

A new way of approaching these questions has recently been proposed by Cunningham and Potts (2007). They propose four models of the creative industries:

1   the *welfare* model, where the creative industries are a net drain on the economy (i.e. they consume more resources than they produce), but they receive public subsidy on the basis of their non-economic 'public good' benefits
2   the *competitive* model, where the creative industries are like other industries and have a neutral effect on the overall economy, albeit with different industry dynamics to other sectors
3   the *growth* model, where the creative industries are experiencing above-average growth to the economy, and are growth 'drivers' in the way that manufacturing was in the 1950s and 1960s and ICTs were in the 1980s and 1990s
4   the *creative economy* model, where complex 'new economy' dynamics are evolving in the creative industries that have wider resonance

throughout the economy, so that they not only evidence above-average growth (as in point 3), but prefigure wider changes in national and international innovation systems.

They argue that while the evidence is not fully conclusive—due in part to the difficulties of measuring the creative industries that accompany the definitional issues—it tends to strongly support points 3 and 4 over 1 and 2, as measured by indicators such as comparative growth rates, proportionate expansion of the number of firms involved in the creative industries sectors, and average incomes of those working in the creative industries sectors. If this is the case, Cunningham and Potts (2007: 17) argue that 'creative industries are a source of economic growth by their ability to generate and process change in the economic system. Irrespective of the social or cultural value of the creative industries, their economic value properly includes their role in the economic coordination in the face of uncertainty'. An implication of this finding is that 'cultural policy, traditionally based on model 1, may require some critical retooling to adapt to what appears to be a model 4 world [and] cultural and arts policy may work best as an adjunct to innovation policy'.

 ## USEFUL WEBSITES

Americans for the Arts Policy Research Centre: Creative Industries <www.artsusa.org/information_resources/research_information/services/creative_industries>. National mapping of the creative industries in the United States, with a strong focus on the creative and performing arts.

Creative Clusters <www.creativeclusters.com>. UK-based national creative economy network.

Creative Economy Online <www.creative.org.au>. An online news and research site on the creative industries, innovation and society. It is hosted by the *ARC Centre of Excellence for Creative Industries and Innovation* <www.cci.edu.au> which is a federally funded Australian university centre for research in the creative industries, with participants from six universities and extensive international collaborative networks.

UNESCO Culture Sector <http://portal.unesco.org/culture/en>. Vast database on global resources on arts, culture and creative industries developed by UNESCO.

10

the global
knowledge economy

The global knowledge economy can be understood as arising from the confluence of three developments. The first is the increasingly ubiquitous nature of new media and globally networked ICTs worldwide. New media are central to globalisation because they constitute the technological and service delivery platforms through which international flows of images, information, finance, communication, and all other digitally based forms are transacted. The media industries are also leaders in the push towards global expansion and integration. Moreover, the media provide informational content and images of the world through which people make sense of events in distant places. The centrality of media to globalisation derives not only from their role as communications technologies that enable the international distribution of messages and meanings, but also from their perceived role in weakening the cultural bonds that tie people to nation-states and national communities (see Flew 2007 for an extended discussion).

The second development is that of globalisation. Globalisation is a term used to describe, and make sense of, a series of interrelated processes including:

- internationalisation of production, trade, and finance, with the rise of multinational corporations, reductions in cross-border tariffs on flows of goods and services, the deregulation of financial markets, and the rise of Internet-based electronic commerce;

- international movements of people (as immigrants, guest workers, refugees, tourists, students, and expert advisers), the development of diasporic and emigrant communities, and the increasingly multicultural nature of national societies;
- international communications flows, delivered through telecommunications, information, and media technologies such as broadband cable, satellite, and the Internet, which facilitate transnational circulation of cultural commodities, texts, images, and artefacts;
- global circulation of ideas, ideologies, and 'keywords', such as the export of 'Western values', democratic aspirations, and environmental consciousness, as well as counter-discourses such as anti-modern fundamentalist movements;
- the establishment of international regimes in intellectual property, which entrench the enforceability of ownership of knowledge and information;
- the emergence of local resistance to globalisation for domestic political and cultural objectives, by both nationalist movements of the political Right, and progressive and anti-colonialist movements of the Left;
- the development of international organisations, including regional trading blocs such as the European Union, the North American Free Trade Agreement (NAFTA), the Association of South East Asian Nations (ASEAN), and the Asia Pacific Economic Co-operation grouping (APEC);
- cultural, professional, and standards bodies such as UNESCO, the World Trade Organization, the World Intellectual Property Organization (WIPO), the European Broadcasting Union, the Asian Broadcasting Union, and the International Telecommunications Union;
- the increasingly significant role played by global non-government organisations (NGOs) such as Amnesty International, Greenpeace, Médecins Sans Frontières, and the Red Cross in domestic and international politics;
- the growing significance of international law to national policies, such as the United Nations Convention on Human Rights, the 'Millennium Round' of the World Trade Organization, and the Kyoto Convention on greenhouse gas emissions;
- the globalisation of the 'war on terror' after September 11, 2001, which has had many implications for global foreign policy, including

its connection to the war in Iraq, the monitoring of citizens within nation-states, the treatment of those seeking asylum from global conflict zones, and the movement of people to and from countries more generally.

Debates about the extent to which globalisation has become the central feature of our times are extensive, with positions ranging from those who may be described as globalisation enthusiasts (e.g. Friedman 2005) to those who are more sceptical of the extent and significance of trends associated with globalisation (e.g. Hirst & Thompson 1996). Overlaid on these analyses of the empirical evidence for globalisation are debates between those who believe that globalisation should be welcomed (Legrain 2002) and those who fear the ways in which it erodes local communications and identities (Barber 2000). Among critical theorists and activists, there are those who argue that the rise of global capitalism has reconfigured the entire terrain of political struggle (Hardt & Negri 2000, 2005), and those who argue that globalisation is not something qualitatively new, but is rather the latest stage in the development of capitalism as a world system (Curran & Park 2000; Callinicos 2001).

As a general point, it can be argued that economic globalisation is more established than political, legal, and cultural globalisation. In saying this, however, I would nonetheless share the conclusions reached by Held and colleagues (1999) and Held and McGrew (2002, 2003) that while globalisation is not completely new, and has not eliminated the significance of nation-states and national sovereignty, there have been real and substantive changes in the relationship between political globalisation and modern nation-states over the last three decades. This has meant that effective political power is increasingly 'shared and bartered' across agencies at local, national, regional, and international levels, particularly with the emergence of supra-national legal frameworks and authority structures (discussed in Chapter 11). As a result, citizens of all nation-states increasingly find themselves enmeshed within 'overlapping communities of fate' (Held et al. 1999: 81). Examples of the latter relate to matters as diverse as the impact of environmental degradation on climates, drug trafficking, global terrorism, immigration controls, arms trading, and non-renewable resource use. In the cultural sphere, one of the complicating factors in these debates relates to the duality of culture as both forms of lived and shared experience and as mediated symbolic communication. Much of the discussion of cultural globalisation relates to the latter, and the implications of common access to global media systems is not the emergence of a single world culture, as Anthony Smith has observed:

> If by 'culture' is meant a collective mode of life, or a repertoire of beliefs, styles, values and symbols, then we can only speak of culture*s*, never just culture; for a collective mode of life, or a repertoire of beliefs, etc. presupposes different modes and repertoires in a universe of modes and repertoires. Hence, the idea of a 'global culture' is a practical impossibility ... the differences between segments of humanity in terms of lifestyle and belief-repertoire are too great, and the common elements too generalized, to permit us to even conceive of a globalised culture. (1991: 171)

The final element of the global knowledge economy is the idea of a knowledge economy. A knowledge economy is one where ideas and intangible assets rather than tangible physical assets are increasingly the central sources of new wealth creation, where 'the economy is more strongly and more directly rooted in the production, distribution, and use of knowledge than ever before' (Howells 2000: 51). Such a transition has occurred not only in the so-called 'post-industrial' economies, as the 'information society' theories of the 1960s and 1970s held (see Castells 1999 for a critique), but has been a global phenomenon, particularly driven by the intersection of international economic competitiveness with foreign direct investment and the use of globally networked ICTs. David and Foray (2002: 9) have argued that the global nature of the knowledge economy is indicated by the extent to which 'disparities in the productivity and growth of different countries have far less to do with their abundance (or lack) of natural resources than with the capacity to improve the quality of human capital and factors of production: in other words, to create new knowledge and ideas and incorporate them into equipment and people'.

David and Foray observed that the rise of a knowledge economy is both a historical trend of the last hundred years, and a process that has accelerated since the early 1990s. In a historical sense, the growth in the share of intangible capital (devoted to knowledge production and dissemination on the one hand, and education, health, and well-being on the other) has been accelerating in the US economy for the whole of the 20th century, and its share has exceeded that of tangible capital (physical infrastructure, equipment, inventories, natural resources, etc.) since the early 1970s (cf. Abramovitz &

David 2001). They attributed the more recent acceleration of knowledge production to:

- the growing diversity of sources from which new knowledge is accessed (e.g. users as a source of innovation)
- the role played by networked ICTs in accelerating the diffusion of new knowledge and the possibilities for collaboration
- the ways in which ICTs enable new forms of codification of once-tacit knowledge through *knowledge management* systems
- the importance of knowledge-sharing through cross-institutional and cross-sectoral *knowledge communities*, of which the open source software movement (discussed in Chapter 11) may represent one of the most globally significant.

Australia's Chief Scientist, Dr Robin Batterham, identified the differences between the 'old paradigm' of economic development, based on the more efficient use of existing physical resources, and the 'new paradigm', based on continuous innovation and the more effective deployment of intangible ('weightless') capital in the new, knowledge-based economy in the terms set out in Table 10.1.

Table 10.1 The 'old' and 'new' paradigms of economic development

Old paradigm	New paradigm
1 Key factors capital, resources, and labour	1 Rising importance of knowledge and creativity
2 More efficient application of existing resources	2 Addition of knowledge-based industry and knowledge-based parts of resource activity
3 Predominant focus on national markets	3 Firms going global and subject to global competition
4 Primary focus on cost competitiveness	4 The imperative to deliver superior value to customers through innovation
5 Relatively long product cycles	5 Trend to shorter product cycles
6 Getting more out of existing businesses	6 Creating new businesses and a new premium on risk-taking and entrepreneurship
7 Reliance on traditional capital sources, such as loans and stock market equity	7 Venture capital as central to new business development
8 Focus on individual achievement	8 Shift to strategic alliances and other forms of collaboration, such as networks and clusters

Source: Adapted from Batterham 2000: 10

Hodgson (2000: 93) has argued that the shift from a manufacturing economy to a knowledge economy, or one that is 'relatively less "machine-intensive", and more and more "knowledge-intensive"', has the following features:

· Both production and consumption processes are becoming increasingly complex and sophisticated.
· Increasingly advanced knowledge and skills are being required in many processes of production.
· Consumers also face increasingly complex decisions about evaluating the quality of goods and services on offer.
· There is an increasing reliance on specialist or idiosyncratic skills.
· The use and transfer of information is becoming increasingly important in economic and social activities.
· Uncertainty is increasingly central to all aspects of economic and social life.

Hodgson ultimately prefers the concept of a *learning economy* to that of a knowledge economy, since the latter implies a fixed stock of knowledge to be distributed throughout a society, whereas 'in a complex and evolving, knowledge-intensive system, agents not only have to learn, they have to learn how to learn, and to adapt and create anew' (2000: 93).

Electronic commerce

One important element of how new media have impacted on ways of doing business has been through electronic commerce. While electronic transactions preceded the rise of the Internet, it dramatically broadened the scope for electronic transactions due to features such as:

· its open, non-proprietary access protocols based on TCP/IP
· the development of the World Wide Web and its standard coding system based on HTML
· ease of access to a diverse range of WWW sites using Web browsers and search engines
· falling costs of personal computing and the growing ease of Internet access from the workplace or home
· the ways in which new media technologies based on the Internet allow for both one-to-many communication and direct one-to-one interaction (OECD 1999: 28–9).

Electronic commerce can take a variety of forms, depending on the degree of digitisation of (1) the product or service sold; (2) the transaction process; and (3) the nature of the delivery agent or intermediary. There are varying degrees of physical or electronic commerce in transactions. For example, buying a book through Amazon.com is not pure e-commerce unless one purchases an e-book, for whereas the agent and the process are both digital, the final product is delivered through physical transportation systems. By contrast, buying software online, acquiring a song from the Apple iTunes site, or purchasing an airline ticket online may constitute pure e-commerce, as the product, process, and agent all exist in digital form. It is also important to distinguish between business-to-business electronic commerce (B2B), which has been estimated to account for 80–90 per cent of all electronic commerce transactions (OECD 1999; Lovelock & Ure 2002), and business-to-consumer electronic commerce (B2C), to which the bulk of the discussion below is devoted, but which is not necessarily at the core of e-commerce transactions (see Figure 10.1).

Figure 10.1 Dimensions of e-commerce

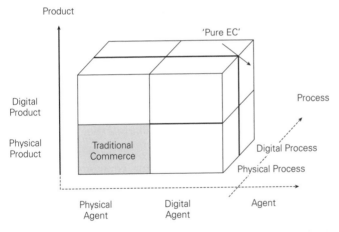

Source: Turban et al. 2000: 5

For businesses, it is argued that they have no choice but to develop an e-commerce strategy. Andy Grove, the former chair of Intel, said that by the mid-2000s all companies will be Internet companies, or they won't be companies at all (*Economist* 1999). Grove's point was that the competitive advantages that accrue to companies from harnessing the Internet were of such significance that neglecting this aspect of their operations would leave them highly vulnerable to losing market share in an increasingly volatile and changing market. The benefits to business of developing an e-commerce strategy have been identified as being:

- expansion of the available marketplace from geographically defined, local markets to national and international markets
- reduction of the costs of creating, processing, distributing, storing, and retrieving information, both within the organisation and between the organisation and its clients (both suppliers and consumers)
- ability to develop highly specialised businesses, able to target particular 'niche' consumer groups
- reduction of inventory and overhead costs, through a move to towards 'pull-type' supply chain management, where processes begin with customer orders and enable just-in-time production
- ability to better customise products and services to client and consumer needs, providing competitive advantages based on 'first-mover' advantages and brand loyalty (Turban et al. 2000: 15).

For consumers, the advantages of e-commerce are:

- ability to undertake transactions 24 hours a day, all year round, from any networked location
- a vastly increased range of products and services
- ability to compare prices online, and find the lowest-cost provider with minimal search cost
- quick delivery of products and services, particularly if they are in digitised form
- ability to interact with other consumers in virtual communities, and exchange ideas and experiences
- ability to participate in virtual auctions (Turban et al. 2000: 15–16).

One of the most important implications of electronic commerce for distribution has been the processes of disintermediation and reintermediation (see Figure 10.2). In the manufacturing sector, the relationship between producers and consumers has traditionally been mediated through a supply chain that includes wholesalers, distributors, and retailers. Similarly, in the creative industries, the relationship between the creators and consumers of content has been mediated through those responsible for aggregating, promoting, marketing, and distributing content for final reception by consumers, giving these sectors their characteristic 'hourglass' structure of many producers, many consumers, but a distributional filter that operates through a small and concentrated number of distributors (Hesmondhalgh 2007: 18–24). One consequence of the rise of the Internet and new media has been *disintermediation*, where a more direct relationship emerges between the creators/producers of content/products/services and their consumers. Another outcome has been *reintermediation*, where intermediary functions remain, but are conducted by organisations whose operations are driven by the new e-commerce marketing logics, such as a shift towards partnership with consumers, 'permission' advertising, product and service customisation, and multiple modes of communication with consumers (Shenton & McNeeley 1997; Turban et al. 2000).

Figure 10.2 Disintermediation and reintermediation

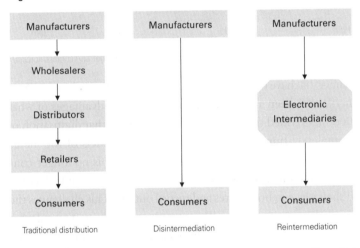

Source: Turban et al. 2000: 64

The whole concept of e-commerce suffered a significant setback with the collapse of the NASDAQ share price index in 2001, and the sense that both e-commerce and dot.com enterprises had been seriously oversold, and most lacked a credible business plan to match their widely hyped ambitions. The rise and fall of the NASDAQ, the USA-based index for high-technology shares, provides an illustration of the dramatic reversal of fortunes for companies operating in this environment within a relatively short period of time, as shown in Figure 10.3. It is notable that, with the more general share market boom of the 2000s, the NASDAQ has been one of the few global share market indexes to reflect that boom.

Figure 10.3 Rise and fall of the NASDAQ, 1998–2001

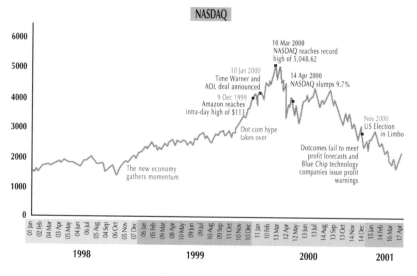

Source: ABC *Four Corners* 2001 <http://abc.net.au/4corners/dotcom/>

The companies that have been most successful in the 2000s, such as Amazon, eBay and Yahoo!, have been able to successfully lever the advantages of what Anderson (2006) has termed the *long tail*. Anderson argues that digitisation of content has completely transformed the distributional models of the media and entertainment industries, as the availability of content is no longer constrained by the distributional bottlenecks such as theatres, radio, and television channels, and shelf space in bookstores and record outlets. This challenges the assumption that only 'mass appeal' media content is profitable, as it reveals that when a wider range of content is made more easily available through online distribution and retail, consumer tastes and preferences for books, movies, music, etc. are far more diverse and niche-oriented than the media and entertainment industries have traditionally assumed. With traditional constraints of geography and scale being eliminated, it is niche content that accounts for a rapidly growing proportion of total online sales, meaning that 'popularity no longer has a monopoly on profitability' (Anderson 2006: 24).

Information and knowledge

The nature and significance of information and knowledge has long been a problematic question in economics. Mainstream economic theories of perfect competition have assumed as a simplifying device that both producers and consumers have perfect information, and behave accordingly in economic markets. Since this is obviously not the case, an extensive literature has emerged on the economics of imperfect information and related questions, such as information assymetries (i.e. when sellers know more than buyers or when some agents have privileged access to information that gives participants market advantage [Akerlof 1970]). But there is also a tradition of information economics, associated with writers such as the Australian economist Don Lamberton, which has asked what it means when information is considered, not simply as a component of how markets operate, but as a form of capital that 'structures the knowledge base of the economic system' (Potts 2003: 477). As Lamberton noted in an early essay, 'identifying information with the cost or time of transmission, and not with the value of a message, may be misleading' (1971: 10).

The concerns of Lamberton and others about thinking of information as a form of capital that is central to the structure of all economic relations, rather than simply a factor in market exchange relations, has become more pressing as innovation has become more central to economic growth and corporate competitive strategy, as ICTs become more central to the economy as a whole, and as knowledge flows proliferate with the emergence of the Internet (Giddens 1998; Lamberton 1999; David & Foray 2002; Haltiwanger & Jarmin 2003; OECD 2003). Two research questions have been central to these discussions. The first concerns the nature of *digital goods* to the new economy. Quah (2003) defines digital goods as 'bitstrings, sequences of 0s and 1s, that have economic value', and identifies them as including 'ideas and knowledge, computer software, digital images, music, databases, video games, blueprints, recipes, DNA sequences [and] codified messages' (2003: 289, 293). Quah argues that digital goods possess five characteristics that challenge conventional understandings of the economics of goods and services. For Quah, they are:

1   non-rival: use by one agent does not degrade its usefulness to other agents
2   infinitely expansible: every user can make and distribute as many copies of the digital good as they choose
3   discrete: they show indivisibility, so that only the whole digital good contains all of its value (i.e. the whole of a film such as *Titanic* has value over and above that of its component parts)
4   a-spatial: they exist in cyberspace, and are both everywhere and nowhere on the digital network simultaneously

5   recombinant: they arise in part from drawing together existing
    elements in new forms that have features that were absent from the
    original, parent digital goods.

The second key set of issues surround the rise of endogenous growth
theory or *new growth economics*. Economists from Stanford University such as
Paul Romer (1994, 1995, 2007) and Paul David (1985, 1999) have argued that
technological change and economic growth need to be seen as intrinsically
connected, in contrast to the conventional approach that treats technology
as an 'exogenous variable' to growth models. Romer (2007) proposes that
'economic growth springs from better recipes, not just from more cooking',
or that it arises not from the discovery of new resources (labour, capital,
or physical resources), but rather from those occasions where 'people take
resources and rearrange them in ways that are more valuable'. Romer argued
that the central economic change of the last two decades has been the shift
from people being primarily involved in the production of physical objects to
the discovery and design of ideas and new ways of doing things, so that 'the
whole economy will start to look like Microsoft, with a very large fraction
of people engaged in discovery as opposed to production' (1995: 70). David
(1999) has argued that it may take up to a generation for the longer-term
economic impacts of new technologies to become apparent, not least because
the nature of what needs to be measured changes as the structure of economic
production and consumption changes, and growth is increasingly driven by
the 'hard-to-measure' sectors of services and information.

The Internet makes many of these issues more pressing, as it is the largest
repository of information gathered through a networked infrastructure in
human history. It is estimated that there were about 30 billion Web pages in
existence on over 108 million websites in February 2007 (Boutell.com 2007),
all of which may lay claim to providing at least some information that is of
interest to someone. All of this information is not, however, knowledge, so the
distinction between the two becomes vital. Brown and Duguid (2000) point
out that, at an epistemological level, knowledge is distinguished from information on the basis of the personal dimensions of ownership of knowledge,
the difficulties in disembedding knowledge from those who possess it, and
the need for knowledge transfer to involve a learning process. Arguing that
a knowledge economy is different not only from an industrial economy but
also from an information economy, they emphasise how 'the importance of
people as creators and carriers of knowledge is forcing organisations to realise
that knowledge lies less in its databases than in its people' (2000: 121). In this

sense, knowledge is embodied in persons and practices, whereas information is captured and stored in databases and is readily accessible and increasingly reproducible through the Internet. Howells argues that, in contrast to information, knowledge requires 'cognitive structures which can assimilate information and put it in a wider context, allowing actions to be undertaken from it' (Howells 2000: 53).

This embodiment of knowledge in people and practices as distinct from its capture and storage in databases becomes more significant when we consider the distinction between explicit and tacit knowledge. *Explicit knowledge* is knowledge that is codified (i.e. written or recorded in some form as data), that can be formally taught and learned, and readily transferred from one context to another. The Internet is a remarkably cost-effective means of codifying, reproducing, and distributing explicit knowledge worldwide. As the Internet makes explicit knowledge more readily available, however, it raises the significance of tacit knowledge. *Tacit knowledge* is knowledge derived from direct experience, and the processes through which it is required are often intuitive, habitual, and reflexive, best learned through practices of doing something and the trial-and-error processes associated with learning-by-doing. Both Leadbeater (2000) and Romer (2007) refer to the significance of cooking in this respect, as an activity that involves both the application of explicit knowledge, codified in the form of recipes, and forms of tacit knowledge, such as knowing when pasta is *al dente*, or the quantity of a dab of butter or a smidgen of salt. Leadbeater (2000: 28–30) sees celebrity chefs such as Jamie Oliver as paradigmatic *knowledge entrepreneurs* in this sense, because they trade in both formal knowledge, which is acquired by purchasing their recipe books, and tacit knowledge, acquired by watching them cook these recipes on TV. By contrast, the challenge for large organisations, in both the public and private sectors, is that their strength in the production, dissemination, and use of explicit knowledge, and the factors that work to their advantage with the handling of information—large-scale, ability to preserve information over time, and the capacity to distribute it across large distances (all of which are exponentially enhanced with the Internet)—are those factors that make the capture of tacit knowledge so difficult.

A final important distinction exists between incremental and radical knowledge creation. *Incremental knowledge creation* is knowledge that is embodied in organisations, into which those who enter the organisation are inducted, and gradually add to. Within a company such as Disney, whose theme parks are the largest single-site employers of labour in the USA, there is a strong emphasis on the induction of new staff, who are not only trained in skills required to do their jobs, but in understanding the 'Disney way', which the company believes to be service that exceeds consumer expectations. Workers therefore bring both explicit and tacit knowledge to the performance of their roles in Disney, but the knowledge comes in forms that have been 'pre-packaged' by the Disney Corporation for mass distribution. By contrast, *radical knowledge creation* is based on extensive experimentation and testing, and explicit recognition of the likelihood of ideas failing. Leadbeater argues that large companies will find it hard to dominate sectors such as computer software, communications, and biotechnology, because the speed with which new ideas are being generated exceeds the capacity of such large companies to adopt new processes and unlearn previous practices. The relationship between the four forms of knowledge is outlined in Table 10.2. What is apparent is that the latter category, radical knowledge creation based on tacit knowledge and unproven assumptions, is unlikely to thrive within large organisations, but is increasingly important to competitive strategy in the new economy, particularly in knowledge-intensive industries: 'Big companies in knowledge-intensive fields will resemble a mother ship with a flotilla of smaller companies around it. To be creative a big company needs to be linked into a knowledge-creating network outside it, which gives it access to the places where counter-intuitive, unconventional ideas are being created' (Leadbeater 2000: 105).

Table 10.2 Forms of knowledge and organisational strategy

	Formal knowledge	Tacit knowledge
Incremental knowledge creation	Organisational training	Induction into organisational culture
Radical knowledge creation	Promotion and distribution of 'best practice' knowledge	Informal knowledge networks

Innovation and the 'innovator's dilemma'

The significance of both tacit knowledge and radical knowledge creation is drawn into even sharper focus when we consider the changing nature of innovation, or the application of new knowledge to new products, processes, and services. Dodgson and colleagues (2002) have referred to a *fifth-generation innovation process*, linked to the rise of *disruptive technologies* that undercut established products, management practices, and industry players (Bower & Christensen 1999), and the greater role played by both global markets and end-users in the innovation process. In contrast to ideas-push or demand-pull models of innovation, or the recent focus on national innovation systems, fifth-generation innovation processes stress the links between suppliers and consumers, strategic integration through research and partnership networks, and technological integration through both the fusion of different technologies (e.g. the linking of electrical and mechanical technologies to develop the 'hybrid' car), and the development of new ICT-based 'toolkits' that promote global collaborative knowledge networks (Dodgson et al. 2002: 54–7).

Indicators of the increasing importance of innovation can be seen in shortened product development cycles, reduced product life cycles, a greater range of products to cater for discrete market segments, and the high 'market-to-book ratios' of many of the world's largest companies. Companies such as Microsoft and Nokia possess few physical assets relative to their market valuation as measured in their share capital, as compared to established manufacturers such as General Electric, General Motors, or Boeing, since much of their wealth creation arises from product innovation. But the challenge of innovation is not simply that it is both more complex and more vital to a firm or organisation's survival in increasingly competitive global markets. It also relates to what Clayton Christensen (2003) has famously referred to as the *innovator's dilemma*, or the traps that exist in following two long-established business orthodoxies: working to your established strengths, and listening to your customers.

The innovator's dilemma arises from the confluence of two factors that are common to products and services based on new technologies. The first, which is derived from Everett Rogers' (2003) model of the *diffusion of innovation*, as well as Donald Norman's (1998) work on technology users and their needs and expectations, leads to the model of the *technology S-curve* (Figure 10.4).

Figure 10.4 The technology S-curve

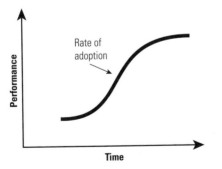

Source: Sood & Tellis 2005: 153

The technology S-curve takes the shape that it does for two reasons. First, from the point of view of technological innovators, early applications of the technology may possess significant 'bugs' or faults, or the relationship between the technology and its applications may remain unclear, but there is a threshold point where improvements are rapidly made to the technology as dominant standards emerge with the coalescence of product characteristics and consumer preferences, until the technology matures in a mass market stage as most users find its performance to be 'good enough' and the energies of researchers go to other, newer technologies. For example, the television would now be considered a mature technology, as most people now have one that is good enough for what they use it for, but developing mobile and wireless devices from which you can access television content is at an early development stage. The second factor in the technology S-curve relates to users, and the fivefold distinction noted in Chapter 3 between enthusiasts, early adopters, mainstream adopters, late adopters, and laggards, where, again, the bulk of the user population tend to sit in the middle rather than at either end of the spectrum, generating a bell-curve distribution.

The technology S-curve sits alongside the development of new technologies in terms of performance over time identified by Bower and Christensen (Figure 10.5).

Figure 10.5 Assessing disruptive technologies

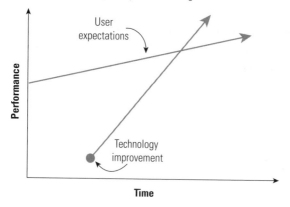

Source: Bower and Christensen 1999: 149

If we map these two diagrams onto one another, they demonstrate the innovator's dilemma, which is the risk on the one hand of providing a product or service that underperforms in terms of the expectations of early adopters in the early stage of the product life cycle, and on the other of providing a product or service that exceeds the needs of most users in the later stages of a product life cycle (Figure 10.6).

Figure 10.6 The innovator's dilemma

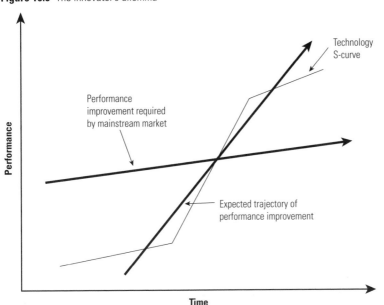

The reasons why this occurs in the first case is because new products often contain bugs or design flaws, to which early adopters are often particularly likely to draw attention. What is known as *first-mover advantage* can become *first-mover disadvantage*, or *second-mover advantage* as competitors who sub-sequently enter the market learn from the first mover's mistakes (Tellis & Golder 1996). Apple's attempts to capture the PDA market with the release of the Newton in 1993 suffered from such problems, and second mover products such as the Palm Pilot and Pocket PC took advantage of Apple's popularisation of the PDA concept, but with more stable products.

The second innovator's dilemma is a more complex one, and relates to the growing disjuncture over time between the trajectory of performance improvement for technologies, and the expectations of users over time as products and services become more mass-market commodities. It is quite clear, for example, that 95 per cent of the functionality of a software program such as Microsoft Excel is unlikely to be used by 95 per cent of its users, who are not specialists in statistics, finance, or such areas, and tend to use the program for a small number of basic tasks. Whether this matters depends in part on whether competitors identify an opportunity for a product or service that is less sophisticated but cheaper than the established market leaders, and can tap into unmet demand. The most famous instance of this is budget airlines such as Ryanair, Easyjet, and Virgin. They identified that while incumbent airlines such as QANTAS and British Airways were continually improving the quality of their in-flight service (better meals, more in-flight entertainment, complimentary drinks etc.), there was a very large class of potential airline users who had little interest in the quality of the in-flight experience, as long as they could get from one place to another more cheaply. As a result, they were able to create a new market segment of airline travellers who sought low-cost flights with lower expectations of the quality of the in-flight experience than the incumbents had assumed. The difficulty was that the incumbents had sought to improve what they were already good at, and to respond to the needs of their existing customer base, whereas the newer, disruptive innovators sought to fundamentally change the assumptions underpinning airline travel. Similar observations could be made in the personal computing industry by comparing Apple, which has continuously sought to innovate with the quality of its product, serving a sophisticated user community with high expectations of their personal computers, with a company such as Dell, which largely does not innovate with the quality of its computers, but rather has focused its innovation strategy on developing new, lower-cost distribution channels through the Internet that enabled it to deliver PCs cheaply and quickly.

CASE STUDIES: YOUTUBE AND JOOST

Over the course of the 2000s, far more people acquired access to high-speed broadband Internet connectivity. In many cases this was not connected to their home service subscription decisions, but rather to the availability of high-speed broadband access in workplaces, schools, universities, and other institutional sites. One consequence of access to high-speed broadband Internet is that access to audiovisual content becomes much more readily available, yet major film studios and television networks had been reluctant to put much of their content onto the Internet. The two main reasons for this were concerns about piracy and copyright infringement, and the potential for 'channel conflict' with their traditional distribution sites, such as cinemas, video and DVD outlets, and television channels, from which the bulk of their advertising revenue was derived. Yet it has been increasingly apparent that users are keen to access their media content through personal computers, particularly when they are able to rate, reuse, and distribute this content among their peers. Enter *YouTube* (www.youtube.com).

YouTube is a video-sharing site, where users can upload, share, rate, comment on, and distribute audiovisual material. Created in February 2005, it was ranked by *TIME* magazine as the 'Invention of the Year' for 2006, and was subsequently acquired by Google for US$1.65 billion. *YouTube* was a disruptive innovation in the sense discussed by Bower and Christensen (1999), because its developers identified that the Internet had made it far less costly to distribute audiovisual content, but this was not being exploited by established film and television industries because they had to recoup the high costs of production of their content through managed distribution via their existing channels. Drawing on the 'Pro-Am Revolution' identified by Leadbeater and Miller (2004), they also recognised that the production costs of making video had fallen, but that this was not recognised at the higher levels of the film and television industries, so *YouTube* encouraged the multitude of video producers to put their material up for distribution through the site.

It was estimated in 2007 that 100 million videos are downloaded through *YouTube* each day, and its audience was about 20 million people worldwide each month, with a strong skew towards younger people. *YouTube* also has an increasingly important function as a feedback loop into the mainstream media. In May 2007, the most viewed *YouTube* videos were Judson Laipply's 'Evolution of Dance' (over 48 million views), and the videos for My Chemical Romance's 'Famous Last Words' and Avril Lavigne's 'Girlfriend' (24–26 million viewings). My own experience of this feedback loop came during the English cricket team's tour of Australia in December 2006 to January 2007, where a blog site covering the tour revealed that Australian fast bowler (and sometime musician) Brett Lee had done a duet with the leading Indian singer Asha Bhosle on a 'Bollywood-themed' love duet ('Haan Main Tumhaara Hoon') that had screened on MTV India. Over the course of ten days, I was able to follow the passage of this video from a link on the UK *Guardian*'s website to the websites of Australian online news media, to becoming a lead story on television news, to being a feature of the websites in Australia devoted to the cricket tour itself.

CASE STUDIES (*cont.*)

Copyright infringement remains an ongoing issue for *YouTube*. In the case of some of the most popular material uploaded to the site, such as excerpts from television programs such as the *Jon Stewart Daily Show*, *The Simpsons*, and *South Park*, this is clearly more of an issue for the owners and distributors of the content, such as Viacom and News Corporation, than its own producers, who have long accepted that their material is accessed 'virally' through the Internet community. Nonetheless, the US media company Viacom initiated a $1 billion lawsuit against *YouTube* for breach of its copyright in February 2007, on the grounds that 160,000 video clips that were produced and initially distributed through Viacom have been collectively viewed more than a million times on *YouTube* without Viacom's permission (Kedrosky 2007).

It is in this context that the development of *Joost* (www.joost.com) can be understood. Established by Niklas Zennström and Janus Friis, the Netherlands-based founders of the Internet-based telephony service *Skype* (www.skype.com), their aim is to work with established media content providers, such as Warner Music, the television production company Endemol, and Viacom (which owns the Comedy Company and MTV networks), to distribute their licensed content over the Internet. *Joost* represents an archetypal case of second-mover strategy in this area, in that *YouTube* has created the demand for audiovisual content distributed through the Internet, but is vulnerable to the reaction of incumbent media providers who can use copyright and intellectual property laws to their own advantage. If US Supreme Court judgments are adverse to *YouTube*, as they were to *Napster* in the online distribution of music in 2000, then *Joost* has positioned itself to exploit second-mover advantage, as Apple was able to do with its *iTunes* music distribution network soon after the demise of *Napster*.

A creative economy?

It was noted in the previous chapter that the rise of the creative industries has drawn new attention to the relationship between creativity, innovation, and entrepreneurship in the new economy. While much policy attention in the 1990s was directed towards information policy, the need to develop skills and infrastructure for the ICT sector, and the promotion of electronic commerce, there is now a renewed focus on creativity and the unique skills and talents of individuals. Moreover, with the imperative to innovate becoming ever stronger, but with established models of research and development, based on incremental improvements, and direct response to existing customers proving vulnerable in the face of phenomena such as the innovator's dilemma, there is renewed interest in creativity and the creative process as a way of unlocking the potential for new knowledge to generate new and innovative products and services.

John Howkins, author of *The Creative Economy*, has captured this shift in thinking from an information society to a creative economy and society in a 2002 presentation to the London Development Agency:

> The information society that we've been speaking about and living in for 30–40 years, and which is symbolised by the boom in information technology, telecoms, media and financial services, is losing its grip on our imaginations and may, indeed, be coming to an end. I define an IS as a society characterised by people spending most of their time and making most of their money by handling information, usually by means of technology. *If I was a bit of data I would be proud of living in an information society. But as a thinking, emotional, creative being—on a good day, anyway—I want something better* … I am talking about a change of perspective, a shift of emphasis. Ideas and information are symbiotically intertwined. But when I say I have an idea I am expressing a more personal view, and making a different claim, from when I say I have some information … We need information. But we also need to be active, clever, and persistent in challenging this information. We need to be original, sceptical, argumentative, often bloody-minded and occasionally downright negative—in one word, creative. (Howkins 2005: 117–88; emphasis added)

The 'new economy' literature, from economics and other areas of the social sciences, sees the dynamics of the new economy as increasingly driven by creativity and culture. For 'new growth' economists, creativity and economic dynamism are best promoted by institutional and policy frameworks that promote a culture of innovation and entrepreneurship (PMSEIC 2005). Castells has proposed that the dynamics of the new economy are cultural as much as they are technological or economic, not only in the sense that economic growth is increasingly associated with the development and diffusion of new ideas, but also in the more anthropological sense that the dynamics of ICT development will be dependent on 'the culture of innovations, on the culture of risk, on the culture of expectations, and, ultimately, on the culture of hope in the future' (Castells 2001: 112). Mitchell and colleagues (2003) have argued that this requires a shift in the focus of policies to promote ICT development and measure its influence to move beyond productivity-based indicators, and to understand more fully the relationship between ICTs and new forms of creative practice. Venturelli has argued that culture and creativity are increasingly the 'gold' that nations possess in the global information economy:

> Culture can be seen as the key to success in the Information Economy, because for the very first time in the modern age, the ability to create new ideas and new forms of expression forms a valuable resource base of a society ... Cultural wealth can no longer be regarded in the legacy and industrial terms of our common understanding, as something fixed, inherited and mass-distributed, but as a measure of the vitality, knowledge, energy, and dynamism of the production of ideas that pervades a given community. (2005: 395–6)

Such arguments have been developed most strongly by Richard Florida, in *The Rise of the Creative Class* (2002). Florida proposes that, if the 19th and early 20th century was the heyday of industrial capitalism and the factory system, and the mid- to late 20th century was dominated by organisation and bureaucracy, the 21st century will mark the hegemony of the creative class, whose core values are a commitment to individuality, meritocracy, mobility, diversity, openness, and the self-formation of identities. The shift towards creativity becoming '*the* decisive source of competitive advantage' in the global economy has further implications since 'creativity has come to be the most highly prized commodity in our economy—and yet it is not a "commodity". Creativity comes from people. And while people can be hired and fired, their creative capacity cannot be bought and sold, or turned on and off at will' (2002: 5).

Tracking employment trends in the USA over the course of the 20th century, Florida argued that the *creative class* has grown from 10 per cent of the US workforce in 1900, to 21 per cent by 1970, and 30 per cent by 1999, thereby making it a larger group than the traditional working class (2002: 73, 330). Moreover, he identified that the creative sector accounts for 47 per cent of wealth generated in the US economy, so the creative class makes a disproportionately large contribution to contemporary economic growth (2007: 29). Defining creative work as that which 'produces new forms and designs that are readily transferable and widely useful' (2002: 7), he distinguished between a *super-creative core*—which consists of scientists and engineers, academics, writers, artists, entertainers, cultural figures, researchers, and 'thought leaders', who now make up about 12 per cent of the US workforce—and creative professionals who perform support work in knowledge-intensive or creative industries to facilitate and promote the creativity of others.

Despite criticisms of Florida's analysis and the policy implications derived from it (see e.g. Peck 2005; Kotkin 2006), one reason Florida's work has been so influential is that the notion of creative cities and regions links with arguments about the embodied nature of knowledge that is valuable in particular people and their skills and talents, and the embeddedness of particular forms of knowledge in certain geographical places. Theories of dynamic economic *clusters* aim to capture the correlation between agglomerations of related firms and industries and sectors and the economic success of particular cities and regions. Porter (1998) argued that successful geographical clusters generated sustained competitive advantage for the firms and institutions within them, by increasing productivity through access to specialist inputs, labour, knowledge, and technology, promoting innovation by making information about new opportunities more widely available, and promoting new business formation in related sectors through distinctive access to necessary labour, skills, knowledge, technology, and capital. Storper (1997) proposed that the interaction between new digital technologies, organisational changes such as networking, and competition among cities and regions to capture economic rents, means that sources of distinctiveness between cities and regions have become more, not less, relevant in the global economy. Scott (2004) has argued that the creative industries (or what he terms the cultural-products industries) demonstrate particularly strong tendencies towards location-based clustering due to:

1   the importance of specific forms of labour input, and the quality of such specialised labour and associated forms of tacit knowledge
2   the organisation of production in dense networks of SMEs that are strongly dependent on each other for the provision of specialised inputs and services
3   the employment relation in creative industries, which is frequently characterised by intermittent, project-based work, meaning that recurring job-search costs can be minimised through co-location in particular areas

4   the indirect, synergistic benefits that result from the interaction of individual creativity with collective learning, tacit knowledge, and historical memory, through the coexistence of people and enterprises engaged in interrelated activities

5   the development of associated services and institutional infrastructure, and the priority that the relevant industry sectors have in the thinking of local and regional governments.

The implication may well be, as Florida has argued, that the world is becoming *spiky*. What he means by this is that rather than globalisation and new media generating a levelling or equalising effect—the 'world is flat' argument proposed by Friedman (2005)—there is instead a clustering of innovation around a small but growing number of urban and regional centres. Because concentrations of creative, talented people become increasingly important to innovation, and because innovation is the principal driver of growth in a global knowledge economy, the phenomenon of clustering around innovation centres becomes ever more significant:

> Creative people cluster not simply because they like to be around one another or they prefer cosmopolitan centres with lots of amenities ... They and their companies also cluster because of the powerful productivity advantages, economies of scale, and knowledge spillovers such density brings ... Because globalisation has increased the returns to innovation, by allowing innovating products and services to quickly reach consumers worldwide, it has strengthened the lure that innovation centres hold for our planet's best and brightest, reinforcing the spikiness of wealth and economic production. (Florida 2007: xxii)

We are therefore presented with the *paradox of place* in relation to globalisation and new media. While new media in principle allow more and more activities to occur anywhere, the geographical dynamics of clustering and the changing nature and value of knowledge promote new forms of embeddedness of economic activity in a relatively small number of urban and regional centres. As a result, there is uneven development between cities, regions, and nations, and heightened inter-place competition.

USEFUL WEBSITES

E-marketer.com <www.emarketer.com>. Site that aggregates international trends in e-business and online marketing and online market trends, drawing from over 2800 worldwide sources.

Knowledge Assessment Methodology <web.worldbank.org/WBSITE/EXTERNAL/ WBI/WBIPROGRAMS/KFDLP>. A website developed by the World Bank as part of its 'Knowledge for Development' program that aims to benchmark countries in terms of their positioning in a knowledge economy. Interestingly, it found in 2006 that the five most advanced countries were Scandinavian (Denmark, Sweden, Finland, Iceland, Norway).

The Work Foundation—The Knowledge Economy <www.theworkfoundation.com/ futureofwork>. A major investigation into the nature of the global knowledge economy—with a particular focus on developments in Europe—that commenced in 2006.

11

internet law, policy, and governance

As a technology, the Internet has presented a boom for lawyers. The most cursory glance at the range of legal issues raised by the development of the Internet and networked ICTs indicates that they are enormous in their scope, domain of application, and implications for different individuals and groups within societies. Examples of some of the domains covered by 'cyberspace law' include:

- *cyberspace and business*: electronic commerce; online contract law; online financial law; online gambling; cyberfraud
- *cyberspace and medicine*: telemedicine; online prescribing; online pharmacies
- *cyberspace and equity*: broadband development and access; educational uses of the Internet; gender and race online; poverty and unequal access to the Internet (the 'digital divide')
- *cyberspace and education*: plagiarism; use of computers in schools; content filtering for minors
- *freedom of speech issues*: freedom of expression; obscenity, pornography and 'online indecency'; protection of children; cultural rights
- *intellectual property issues*: copyright law; patent law; trademark law; gifts and online exchange

- *privacy issues*: cryptography and privacy protection for online transactions; employment privacy; personal information privacy; data security
- *security issues*: cybercrime; 'spamming'; cyberstalking and online harassment; hacking; identity theft; the Internet and terrorism.

This is a lengthy list, and it could easily be added to. The legal implications of the Internet's rapid development are rendered even more complex by specific features of its relationship to existing laws, regulatory frameworks, and the ideas that underpin them. First, there are the unique characteristics of networked information, in that it is intangible, geographically distributed, recombinant, and continually changing in its form and character. This contrasts to the traditional bases of law where 'existing legislation depends upon clearly demonstrable, localisable and liable legal persons and ownership titles. Information and evidence have to be, or must be able to be, set down on a data carrier that has still to be comparable to printed paper' (van Dijk 1999: 116). This contrast between the fluidity of the online environment and the need for fixity and tangible links to legal subjects on which the legal system operates is compounded by the difficulties that arise in implementing laws, since activities in networks are frequently non-transparent, communication can be anonymous or very hard to trace back to an original source, and evidence can be destroyed, hidden, wiped, or altered by computer users and systems operators.

The second set of factors that greatly complicate Internet law arise from the global nature of the Internet and its network infrastructure, and the predominantly national basis of laws and legal systems. Froomkin (1997) observed that the transnational nature of the Internet as a communications medium promotes *regulatory arbitrage*, whereby people and corporations can, in certain circumstances, 'arrange their affairs so that they evade domestic regulations by structuring their communications or transactions to take advantage of foreign regulatory regimes' (1997: 129). The problem of Internet users and Internet service providers being able to evade national laws by accessing content or undertaking transactions through other territorial domains—or, as others would see it, the enhanced freedom of Internet users to evade domestic laws that they may deem inappropriate—is further promoted through the uncertainties surrounding legal and territorial jurisdiction in cyberspace. There have been many instances of jurisdictional conflict over content, ranging from attempts by the Chinese government to close down websites hosted in Taiwan and Hong Kong that promote the ideas of the Falun Gong movement (which is banned in China) (Kalathil & Boas 2003), attempts by the French government in 2000 to pressure the Yahoo! search engine into preventing French citizens from viewing Nazi memorabilia on its English-language auction sites (Stein & Sinha 2002), and the Australian government's attempts to prevent online casinos or websites with prohibited content from operating in Australia (Crawford 2003; Penfold 2003). A successful defamation case was pursued by Australian businessman Joseph Gutnick against the Dow Jones company; even though the material concerning Gutnick was written and published in the USA, Gutnick's legal team successfully argued that the material could be downloaded and read in Australia, and hence could be deemed to be defamatory under Australian law (Crawford 2003).[1]

The third issue is that Internet law, in a sense, does not exist. Just as the Internet marks out a convergent space between computing, telecommunications, and media, we also find that what we term 'Internet law' is marked by the application and extension of laws developed for other media and communications technologies, such as print, broadcasting, and telecommunications. It has also involved the extension, in a largely unplanned and incoherent manner, of areas of civil, criminal, and corporate law developed to address quite different issues from those presented by networked and convergent media. Similarly, what constitutes Internet policy in many countries is often an uncomfortable amalgam of policies developed for traditional media industries (most notably broadcasting), telecommunications policies, and policies to promote production in media content sectors, with defence and national security making an occasional appearance in the policy mix. The problem is not simply one of law and policy lagging behind technological developments, since this will to some extent inevitably be the case. Rather, as van Dijk (1999: 117) observed, legal and policy responses have largely been fragmentary and *ad hoc* adjustments that remain based on outdated assumptions: 'There is no internal readjustment. Instead, detailed alterations are made to existing legislation including technical definitions that will soon be outdated ... Fragmentary adjustments to legislation are not suitable for the regulation of large-scale networks and their far-reaching consequences to individuals and society at large.'

In the plethora of *national information policy* statements that emerged in the 1990s, there was also often a curious dualism. On the one hand, there was a confidence that the freely operating commercial market provided the best means of allocating resources and promoting technological development.

The Global Information Infrastructure proposed by the Clinton-Gore US administration in the 1990s gave primacy to the promotion of private investment, service development driven by free markets and competition, flexible regulatory systems, and the removal of barriers to foreign investment. In tandem with this, new international regulatory organisations such as the World Trade Organization (established in 1995) actively promoted the privatisation of public telecommunications monopolies and fostered the promotion of competition policy and free trade, with an underlying view that communications companies were market-based service providers with sharply delimited 'universal service' obligations (Winseck 2002b; Flew & McElhinney 2005). At the same time, through national information policies, many governments threw a lot of money at the ICT sectors in the hope of developing 'national champions' in global markets, and promoting a networked society and a Web-savvy population.[2] Melody (1996) observed at the time that, in many of these programs, there was a misplaced primacy given to development of information infrastructure as an end in itself, which was often accompanied by generous subsidies to multinational ICT corporations to produce locally, with insufficient attention being given to the relationship between content applications, user demand, and skills acquisition that would have provided a more sustainable, equitable, and democratic basis for Internet development policies (cf. Breen 2002).

Perspectives on Internet governance

It has been proposed that, rather than understanding regimes of Internet regulation in terms of law (which raises the question of the origins of current laws) or policy (which presumes a national territorial jurisdiction, as well as government stewardship of a global, predominantly commercial medium), it can be understood in terms of *governance*. The concept of governance does not draw a line between the public and private sectors, or between the market and the state: it recognises that markets themselves can constitute powerful governance structures, and that governments act as often to promote markets and private sector interests as they do to regulate and constrain them (Jessop 1998, 2000). Moreover, it enables a clearer understanding of the role played in Internet law and policy by non-government and non-corporate institutions and organisations of civil society and social movements, alongside the state/public and corporate interests, as well as the ways in which such processes increasingly cross territorial jurisdictions (Murphy 2002).

The concept of Internet governance is useful as a corrective to strong notions of *cyber-libertarianism*. Cyber-libertarianism has been a vision for an Internet commonly found among key user communities—particularly in the USA—that viewed the infrastructure as essentially being able to be managed by a self-governing community of users. It was a key tenet of Internet pioneers such as those associated with the Electronic Frontier Foundation (EFF), which saw in the Internet a 'platform which will allow every person to speak their mind and query the world to create their own point of view' (EFF n.d.). The non-hierarchical, decentralised, and networked nature of the Internet presented for groups such as the EFF the opportunity to develop self-governing online communities which, being finally free of state interference and censorship, could realise the freedom of speech principles embedded in the First Amendment of the US Constitution. John Perry Barlow (1996a) declared in his 'Declaration of the Independence of Cyberspace': 'We believe that from ethics, enlightened self-interest and the commonweal, our governance will emerge ... The only law that all of our constituent cultures would recognise is the Golden Rule'. Mike Godwin (1998: 23), counsel for the EFF in the famous case surrounding the US *Communications Decency Act* (1996), argued that:

> Give people a modem and a computer and access to the Net, and it's far more likely that they'll do good than otherwise. This is because freedom of speech is itself a good—the framers of the [US] Constitution were right to give it special protection, because societies in which people can speak freely are better off than societies in which they can't.

The cyber-libertarian perspective is no longer articulated as strongly as a model for Internet governance as it was in the mid-1990s. One reason has been that as the Internet has grown exponentially, and as the user base has become massively more diverse, the shared ethos that underpinned early forms of virtual communities is no longer as applicable or relevant (Davies 2003). More significantly, the cyber-libertarian perspective was also deeply ambivalent about its view of corporate power on the Internet. Authors and activists such as Lessig have noted the danger of the cyber-libertarian position and its neglect of questions of corporate power, observing that Internet activists operating from a cyber-libertarian position run the risk of 'winning the political struggle against state control so as to entrench control in the name of the market' (Lessig 2001: 267). Early critics of cyber-libertarianism such as Barbrook and Cameron (1995) noted how an anti-statist vision of

Internet self-governance (what they termed the 'Californian Ideology') was likely to experience deep ambivalence in determining its relationship to the rise of corporate power on the Internet and associated neo-liberal ideologies that critique state power in the name of the commercial global market (e.g. Dyson et al. 1994).

A very different perspective on Internet governance emerged from critical political economy. For Mosco (1997), McChesney (1999), and Schiller (2000), the early promise of the Internet as a democratic and decentralised alternative to commercial mass media was quickly swept aside as governments deregulated the communications system in the 1990s to give greater power to dominant commercial interests. These writers saw the emergent pattern of Internet governance as largely resembling that of the societies in which it operated, meaning that in corporate-dominated societies, it will be these powerful interests that will most effectively shape government policy to suit their interests. McChesney argued that 'if certain forces thoroughly dominate a society's political economy they will thoroughly dominate its communications system ... and so it is ... for the most part, with big business interests in the United States' (1999: 124–5). Schiller argued in *Digital Capitalism* (2000) that the development of the global Internet was best understood as being driven by the demands of transnational corporations and the US government for a globally integrated computing and communications network that could promote the expansion of operations and markets worldwide, minimising the capacity of national governments to regulate such activities in the public interest.

As the Internet has developed as a global, decentralised network it continues to challenge the two core tenets of nation-state sovereignty: sovereignty over territory, and sovereignty over citizens. Not only can cyberspace never be constituted as existing within national territory (unlike, say, air space), but the Internet itself not only enables, but actively promotes, communications activities and transactions that cross territorial boundaries (Kleinwächter 2002: 56–7). One attempt to develop a framework for global Internet governance has been the Internet Corporation for Assigned Names and Numbers. ICANN was established in 1998 to address a very new problem, which is how to govern the allocation of Internet domain names, or the addresses that people, organisations, and governments can adopt to direct people to their sites on the World Wide Web.

Before the mid-1990s, the allocation of Internet addresses had been a largely technical matter, undertaken by individuals or small groups with little discussion or controversy, and with little international consultation. As the Internet grew exponentially, this structure was increasingly inadequate. Commercial interests saw their domain name as increasingly a part of their branding and marketing strategies, and they sought to ensure that their 'brand', as embodied in their domain name, was protected in cyberspace. This was accentuated by the phenomenon of *cybersquatting*, where people would buy up potentially popular domain names, and perhaps use them for *culture-jamming* (Lasn 2000), or to direct unsuspecting users to pornography sites, or simply capture an asset that they could then profitably on-sell. Both the Brisbane City Council and the government of South Africa were surprised to find that the domain names *brisbane.com* and *southafrica.com* had already been bought by online speculators, who then sought to sell the domain name at an exorbitant price (Froomkin 2003; Rimmer 2003a). Clear limits have emerged to the idea of selling domain names to the highest bidder, and a range of powerful interests were seeking a more cohesive structure for domain name governance.

The ICANN is a private, non-profit agency which aims to represent both the global 'Internet community' and the global 'Internet business community', which includes both those involved in domain name registration and those seeking to register online domain names in order to pursue electronic commerce. While governments clearly have an interest in the outcomes of ICANN decision-making, it seeks to maintain an advisory, 'back seat' function for governments (Kleinwächter 2002: 66). It has aimed to develop an approach to dispute resolution that is non-legalistic, and based on a quick and low-cost resolution of disputes on the basis of whether a domain name registrant can be considered to have acted in 'bad faith'.

Paré (2003) and Froomkin (2003) have found that both the structure and conduct of ICANN have in practice been heavily influenced by the US government in representing business interests in trademark and intellectual property protection. They question the claim that ICANN has evolved a new form of decentralised global Internet governance that transcends national interests and appeals to the distinctive ethos of a global Internet community. Indeed, Paré argued that the consensus-oriented politics of ICANN have in fact generated a crisis of legitimacy for the organisation, because it is seen as 'a private organisation which is exerting global public authority over a key information and communication resource in a manner that appears to be inconsistent with both the way in which decisions have traditionally been made in the public domain and the traditional norms and values associated with internetworking' (Paré 2003: 169). This crisis of legitimacy of ICANN was identified at the World Summits on the Information Society (WSIS) in Geneva (2003) and Tunis (2005), where developing countries and civil society organisations in particular argued the need for an alternative framework for Internet governance over issues such as domain names, where the organisations of the United Nations would play a leading role (Froomkin 2003; Ó Siochrú et al. 2003; Ó Siochrú 2004).

Copyright and intellectual property law: An overview

Copyright and intellectual property law has become, in many respects, the crucible for many of the issues and challenges presented by the development of new media for law and policy. These legal and policy issues are being played out in a variety of national and international forums, and are at the core of how the global knowledge economy or creative economy will develop. Among the issues raised are:

1 the balance between public good and private benefit criteria for use of, and access to, information
2 the balance between individual rights of ownership and social use for common benefit
3 the nature of knowledge as both a commodity for commercial exploitation and as a public good for common use
4 the best ways in which to promote and equitably share the benefits of creativity in an age of digital networks for people, communities, nations, and global humanity.

Copyright law as we understand it today was first enacted in Britain in 1709 with the *Statutes of Anne*, which established a term of protection for the author of an original work of 14 years as an incentive to produce new works, and set a limit to the time in which control over the rights to previously published works was ceded from publishers to the 'public domain' of 21 years. The US Congress, in one of its first legislative acts after the Declaration of Independence, passed the *Copyright Act* of 1790, as an enactment of the principle established under Article 1, Section 8 of the Constitution to give Congress the power to 'promote the Progress of Science and useful Arts, by securing for limited Times to Authors and Inventors the exclusive Right to their respective Writings and Discoveries', both providing protection to the creators of original works ('Authors and Inventors'), and setting statutory limits to the time before such rights passed into the public domain. James Madison, one of the original drafters of the US Constitution, saw in this an outcome where 'the public good fully coincides … with the claims of individuals' (quoted in Vaidhyanathan 2001: 45).

Copyright law is derived from the principle that neither the creator of a new work nor the general public should be able to appropriate all of the benefits that flow from the creation of a new, original work of authorship. It presumes that original forms of creative expression can belong to individuals, who have both a moral right to ownership and a legitimate economic right to derive material benefit from the use of these ideas and works by others as an incentive to create further original works. It also presumes that the use of their original ideas and works should be subject to the laws of free and fair exchange, that there should be adequate compensation of use by others, and there should be safeguards against misuse. At the same time, it recognises that original ideas and works are drawn from an existing pool of knowledge and creativity, and that there is therefore a need to guarantee that such ideas and works exist in the public domain for fair use by others. Moreover, since such information is the lifeblood of democracy, commerce, and the development of future knowledge, broad access by the community to the widest possible pool of information, knowledge, and forms of creative expression is a valuable end in itself, as a condition for participation in public life and the development of new knowledge. In order to balance these competing claims on knowledge, copyright law divides up the possible rights in and uses of a work, giving control over some of these rights to the creators and distributors and control over others to the general public (Litman 2001: 16).

The neat distinctions that copyright law seeks to make between private ownership and public use have often been difficult to sustain in practice. Three areas of distinction have been particularly contentious. First, facts, ideas, and concepts are not themselves copyrightable—they cannot be owned by individuals. What copyright protects is original forms of creative expression of such facts, ideas, concepts, and so on, or the ways in which they are expressed, selected, and arranged by individuals through physical works such as books, publications, artistic works, etc. Second, what the author or creator has an exclusive right to is the creative expression contained in a work, but not the physical form in which that work is produced and distributed. In the case of a book, for example, the original author retains exclusive ownership of the forms of creative expression that constituted that book, but is assumed to have contractually assigned the rights of reproduction of that book to a publisher, and in turn derives subsequent benefit from that publisher's activities in distributing the book, in the form of royalties or other forms of financial remuneration. Finally, there has developed alongside copyright law a series of exceptions where it is deemed to be in the public interest to make material more widely available at no cost. These *fair use* or fair dealing provisions for private, non-commercial uses without authorisation, have been typically applied to the photocopying of works in public libraries, but are now extensively applied in the copying of software applications, and the placing of materials on the World Wide Web (e.g. sections from books and academic journals used for teaching purposes). Embedded within copyright more generally are two competing normative visions of intellectual property, as something that can be privately owned as property, and as something that is central to the principles of freedom of speech, equitable access to public information, and economic efficiency (Table 11.1).

Table 11.1 Two visions of intellectual property

	Information as public resource	Information as private property
Normative starting point	Free speech and free circulation of ideas and information in society	Individual property rights and rights of personal privacy
Vision of production of ideas	Draws primarily upon existing materials	Individual creativity and originality
Economic perspective	Information and efficiency	Innovation and incentives
Principal concern	Inequitable access to information in society	Denial of individual rights and creativity

Source: Adapted from Boyle 1997: 156

It is notable that the US *Copyright Act* of 1790 constructed issues relating to copyright upon what can be described as a horizontal axis of content creators, distributors, and users, where each was a broadly equal player in terms of power resources. Subsequently, in a process tracked by authors such as Bettig (1996), Vaidhyanathan (2001), and Perelman (2002), this horizontal axis has been overlaid by a vertical axis, whereby those who have established ownership of copyrighted works—who are, by the nature of contracts in the creative industries, typically the distributors of creative content rather than its originators—have constituted themselves as a powerful interest group whose interests sit over and above, and frequently in opposition to, the much larger, but far more dispersed, group of end-users of copyrighted or copyrightable material (Figure 11.1).

Figure 11.1 Relations within copyright and intellectual property regimes

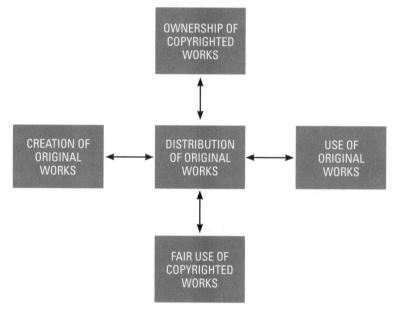

Copyright and new media

Of the many issues that render copyright law ever more complex and significant in an age of new media and the Internet, four stand out. First, the rapid development and mass dissemination of technologies that enable low-cost reproduction of data and information has dramatically changed the issues arising in copyright law. Whereas copyright law developed at a time when the reproduction of a work bore some costs (e.g. the costs of reprinting a book), the development of low-cost duplication technologies readily available at home, work, or school/university has meant that more and more people have the ability to copy materials at near-zero cost. With the development of the Internet, email, and file-sharing technologies, these copies can be distributed to any number of people across electronic networks.

Second, the rise of a knowledge-based or creative economy has seen intellectual property rights become a key source of new corporate wealth. The commercial creative industries are characterised by high costs of production of original material, a high failure rate for new commercial product, and near-zero costs of content reproduction (Caves 2000; Hesmondhalgh 2007). As a result, a very high premium is attached to successful creative product that is likely to accrue economic rents over time. The value of Mickey Mouse to the Disney Corporation, or the value of the Beatles' back catalogue of songs, remains high decades after the content was originally produced. Associated with the enhanced economic value of intellectual property rights has been the rise of the *copyright industries*, defined as those industries 'engaged primarily in the generation, production, and dissemination of new copyrighted material' (Siwek 2002: 9).

Third, copyrighted products are now a part of global popular culture to a historically unprecedented degree. Corporate trademarks are reproduced and often parodied, musical fragments are sampled, references to other pop-culture forms are frequently made in TV programs such as *The Simpsons* and *South Park*, films and TV programs increasingly feed off generic conventions established in other films and TV programs, and advertising undertakes a relentless 'bower-birding' of cultural referents derived from other media. Coombe (1998) observed that the growth and extension of legal protections to intellectual property has occurred at a time when 'the texts protected by intellectual property laws *signify*: they are cultural forms that assume local meaning in the life worlds of those who incorporate them into their daily lives' (1998: 7).

Finally, copyright and intellectual property law has been progressively globalised over time. The European states agreed on a common framework for copyright law through the Berne *Convention for the Protection of Literary and Artistic Works* (1886), although the USA was a conspicuous non-signatory to this convention (Drahos & Braithwaite 2002: 34–5). In more recent times, the USA has been a leader in promoting international intellectual property regimes, not least because its copyright industries are seen as most at risk from product piracy. The US-based Software Protection Agency estimated in 1994 that as much as 98 per cent of software used on computers in China was pirated, as was 95 per cent of computer software used in Russia and 92 per cent of that used in Thailand (Baase 1997: 174–5), and the International Intellectual Property Alliance estimated that the cost to the US economy of intellectual property piracy has been about $40 billion annually (Boyle 1997: 121). As the world's leading net exporter of intellectual property rights, the USA has been the principal driver of the Trade-Related Aspects of Intellectual Property Rights (TRIPS) Agreement, signed by more than one hundred nations in 1994 after agreement by the signatories to the General Agreement on Trade in Services (GATS). Entry of China into the World Trade Organization is perhaps particularly significant in this regard, as China has been seen, particularly by US interests, as the nation that is most frequently in breach of copyright and intellectual property law (Montgomery & Keane 2006; Zhang, Y 2006).

Cyber-libertarians such as John Perry Barlow predicted the collapse of copyright law under the weight of new media, arguing that 'Intellectual property law cannot be patched, retro-fitted or expanded to contain the gasses of digitised expression … We will need to develop an entirely new set of methods as befits this entirely new set of circumstances' (Barlow 1996b: 10). Copyright and intellectual property law have not only proved more resilient; they have in fact been strengthened since the rise of the Internet, raising the different question of how best to manage the balance of interests identified in Figure 11.1. above. Litman (2001) has observed that the problem with applying old rules to new media is that they are likely to inhibit the development of new technologies in the short term, and to fail completely in the medium term. At the same time, the call for a generalised copyright exemption for new media developments, which follows from the cyber-libertarian position, is unlikely to satisfy the creators of copyrightable content, who are concerned about who would pay for their work, and the ability to continue in creative or intellectual pursuits, if content was made more freely available to users. Litman instead proposed that there is a need for more direct dialogue between the creators and users of copyrightable content, or between creative people and the wider public, because their interests are less clearly opposed than is presented to be the case by content distributors. Initiatives such as the Creative Commons digital content licensing scheme have sought to address such concerns, in ways that are both legally robust and readily understood and applicable to producers of original content in the creative industries and related sectors.

Recent developments in international copyright and intellectual property law

The 1990s saw two very significant extensions of both the scope and domain of application of copyright law. In the USA, the *Digital Millennium Copyright Act* was passed by the US Congress in 1998, along with the *Sonny Bono Copyright Term Extension Act* 1998. The latter was presented to Congress by the late Sonny Bono, a Californian Congressman and former member of the pop group Sonny & Cher, which extended term of copyright protection for copyright works from the life of the author plus 50 years to the life of the author plus 70 years. Despite widespread criticism of these legislative initiatives as poor from both a legal and policy perspective (see e.g. Litman 2001; Vaidhyanathan 2001; Perelman 2002; Rimmer 2003b), their impact has been significant both within and outside the USA. Cases such as *Eldred v. Ashcroft* were unsuccessful in challenging the extension of copyright, despite 17 leading American economists, including five Nobel Laureates, contesting the claim that such copyright extension was not in the nation's economic interest (Moore 2005). Rimmer (2003b) termed the *Sonny Bono Copyright Extension Act* a 'Mickey Mouse Bill' because it arose at a time when Disney was facing the imminent expiry of copyrights on Mickey Mouse and its other famous cartoon characters, but the resultant legislative changes have guaranteed that Mickey Mouse will not pass into the public domain until 2023.

The second major development was the passing of the TRIPS Agreement in 1995, at the conclusion of the Uruguay Round of trade negotiations that led to the formation of the World Trade Organization. The TRIPS Agreement was signed by over a hundred countries in April 1994, and all members of the WTO are bound by the conditions of the TRIPS Agreement, including recent members such as China (Braithwaite & Drahos 2000: 57). Unlike previous multilateral conventions governing intellectual property, such as the Paris and Berne Conventions struck by the European powers in the late 19th century, TRIPS is not based on the setting of minimum standards and mutual adjustment of national laws over time. Rather, it establishes a global framework for the protection of intellectual property to which significant legal and economic sanctions can be applied to nations that fail to comply with its highly prescriptive standards to protect the rights of those holding patents, copyright, trademarks, and trade secrets. Sell described TRIPS as:

> A stunning triumph for commercial interests and industry lobbyists who had worked so tirelessly to achieve the global agreement. TRIPS institutionalized a conception of intellectual property based on protection and exclusion rather than competition and diffusion. By extending property rights and requiring high substantive levels of protection, TRIPS represented a significant victory for U.S. private sector activists from knowledge-based industries. (2002: 172)

One of the factors that links US legislation and developments through TRIPS and the World Intellectual Property Organization (WIPO) is the impact of bilateral free-trade agreements. TRIPS established an important beachhead for uniformity in international patent legislation through the Patent Cooperation Treaty, which enables developers of patentable products to file an international patent application through the WIPO; this has force in 136 member nations in 2007, who agree that, if the application is accepted, the patent is binding in all of those nations. Bilateral free-trade agreements between the USA and other nations have typically involved the extension of US-based forms of copyright protection to the signatory nations, which included Australia when it signed on to the US–Australia Free Trade Agreement in 2004 (Moore 2005).

Two critical questions arise from these measures to both extend copyright protection into the indefinite future, and to establish a legally binding global intellectual property regime. The first is whether it is beneficial to society as a whole. The economic argument for copyright protection has revolved around the rights of content creators to receive remuneration for the expression of their ideas and concepts in so far as they are of appeal in the commercial market, and the need for such returns in order to provide incentives for future development of new ideas. Critics have argued that while these are valid arguments in principle, the extension of copyright protection through recent legislation shifts the balance too far away from other users and heightens the possibility of inadvertent copyright infringement, and is also a hindrance to economic and social innovation. In relation to the former, the digital media environment is particularly significant, as it promotes collaboration, content sharing, content reuse and repurposing, and P2P filesharing. Since it has been argued that P2P is 'both the origin and the future of the Internet' (Haussmann 2002), the case can be made that the media and entertainment industries would be better served by fostering such networks, rather than seeking to restrict or criminalise such activities (Vaidhyanathan 2001, 2004; Perelman 2002; Lessig 2004; Benkler 2006). Moreover, the economic case for extending copyright protection is weak. The 17 leading American economists whose statement was lodged in *Eldred v. Ashcroft 2002* argued that the extension of copyright protection to 70 years under the *Sonny Bono Copyright Extension Act* would only provide an increase in compensation to creators of less than 1 per cent (cited in Moore 2005: 74). This needs to be balanced against the economic costs of extending copyright protection and extending the capacity to extract monopoly rents for existing copyright holders over time, in ways that would be likely to be detrimental to the creation of new works. In its criticism of these changes, the US Committee for Economic Development emphasised how copyright law can inhibit the capacity of 'follow-on' and 'second' innovators to build upon copyrighted innovations, thereby dampening the overall scope for innovation by artificially restricting the public domain (CED 2004). Perelman (2002: 178) has argued that information is not only a public good, and hence warranting government oversight of how it is produced and distributed, but is in fact a *metapublic good*, which generates positive benefits to a community when it is freely available in ways that cannot be calculated, since 'information is not scarce, except to the degree that society allows agents to create artificial scarcity through secrecy and property rights ... as the economy becomes increasingly dependent on information, the traditional system of property rights applied to information becomes a costly fetter on our development'.

When extended to the global realm, the issues that arise from the global application of US-derived copyright and intellectual property laws, as pursued through agreements such as TRIPS, are considerable (see e.g. Bannermann 2006; Shanker 2006). These tend to involve debates about the equity of such arrangements between economically developed and developing countries, for two reasons. First, the vast bulk of intellectual property rights are held in a small number of countries; in 2004, five patent offices (Japan, USA, South Korea, China, and Europe) accounted for 75 per cent of patent applications and 74 per cent of patents granted worldwide (WIPO 2006). Second, the near-zero costs of reproduction of digital goods enabled by new media technologies create strong incentives in lower-wage countries to copy such materials (DVDs, computer software programs, etc.) and resell them at substantially lower prices than those offered to consumers in higher-wage nations. Drahos and Braithwaite (2002: 188–9) have drawn attention to the paradox identified in this chapter, which is that 'strong' protection of intellectual property rights may lead to monopolies, while 'weak' protection may lead to 'free-riding' on the innovations of others, and underinvestment in innovation. Drahos and Braithwaite also identify a positive correlation between democratic societies and efficient intellectual property rights, but note that this is in turn dependent on (1) an inclusive policy culture, where all relevant interests participate in negotiation of the final outcomes; (2) full provision of information to all relevant parties; and (3) the absence of coercive power by one party over others. Significantly, they find all of these to be absent from international negotiations about the TRIPS Agreement, since developing countries were largely excluded from the forums in which TRIPS was debated, awareness of possible adverse consequences of TRIPS (e.g. on the availability of low-cost generic drugs to address the AIDS crisis in Africa) was low, and the USA in their view threatened trade sanctions and foreign aid withdrawals for nations that did not share its views on the merits of a uniform multilateral agreement on intellectual property rights (Drahos & Braithwaite 2002: 189–92). Using the public goods framework derived from economic theory, Drahos and Braithwaite conclude that current tendencies on copyright and intellectual property law have the potential to lead to *information feudalism* on a global scale. They characterise information feudalism as involving the use of intellectual property rights to inhibit competition (e.g. through the patenting of basic business processes); the withholding of valuable information about diseases and suitable treatments from poorer developing nations; and the locking up of basic research outcomes from institutions that have once treated knowledge as a pure public good for social use, such as universities.

CASE STUDY: CREATIVE COMMONS

Creative Commons (CC) is a worldwide project that aims to make copyright material more accessible, and its terms of access more negotiable in the digital environment (Creative Commons 2007a). In order to do this, Creative Commons asks content owners who wish to contribute to the commons to generically give permission in advance to certain types of reuse of their content, through the labelling of their content with a CC badge and an agreement in advance of individual use to the legal terms and conditions attached to this use through a legally binding CC licence. It aims to overcome three bottlenecks that current copyright and intellectual property laws present in the digital environment: the difficulties faced by reusers of already existing content in locating and negotiating with the initial content creators; the question of rights and conditions attached to reuse of existing digital content in other domains, for commercial or non-commercial purposes; and the extent to which existing copyright and intellectual property laws circumvent direct negotiation between content creators and prospective users of copyrighted material through the assignation of rights to content distributors, who then manage all legal aspects of content reuse and repurposing rather than the direct producers of the original content.

Creative Commons was founded in 2001 by a series of high-profile intellectual property experts and creative practitioners including Lawrence

Lessig, James Boyle, Hal Abelson, Eric Saltzman, Joi Ito, and Eric Aldred, with financial support from the Centre for the Public Domain and other organisations. It is currently supported in the USA by the Berkman Center for Internet and Society at Harvard Law School and Stanford Law School Center for Internet and Society, and Creative Commons licences had been developed in May 2007 in 35 countries outside the USA, including Argentina, Australia, Austria, Slovenia, South Africa, South Korea, Spain, Sweden, and Switzerland, with a further 14 countries being in discussion (Creative Commons 2007c). Central to this international expansion of Creative Commons has been initiatives to ensure that CC licences achieve legally effective harmonisation of the Creative Commons licence to the specific national legislation that governs copyright and intellectual property law within different countries.

A key aim of Creative Commons has been to simplify the range of choices available to creative people across the artistic, educational, scientific, and digital production domains about how they can designate in advance, and independently of those who distribute their content as commercial product, rights to reuse and repurposing. There are four categories of Creative Commons licence that are available to those who choose to place their content under a CC licence:

1 *Attribution*: Content developers allow others to copy, distribute, display, and perform your copyrighted work—and derivative works based upon it—but only if they give credit to your original work in the way that you requested.

2 *Non-commercial*: Others are permitted to copy, distribute, display, and perform your work—and derivative works based upon it—but only if it is for non-commercial purposes. If there is an intention to use the work for commercial purposes, then there needs to be a different legal basis for discussion. An example of this would be Alberto Korda's famous photograph of Che Guevara in 1960, which has been made freely available to radical organisations and groups that broadly share Che's ideals. Korda successfully defended the right for this image not to be used by the Smirnoff company to promote its vodka product in 2000, as he argued that this was clearly at odds with Che's own socialist ideals and Korda's moral rights as the photographer.

CASE STUDY (*cont.*)

3 *No Derivative Works*: Others are permitted to copy, distribute, display, and perform only verbatim copies of your work, but not derivative works based upon it. In this way, the integrity of the original work can be preserved, as well as the moral rights of the original creator.

4 *Share Alike*: Original content creators allow others to distribute derivative works only under a licence identical to the licence that governs their own work. It should be noted that a licence cannot feature both the Share Alike and No Derivative Works options, since the Share Alike requirement applies only to derivative works.

Creative Commons describes its purpose as being to provide 'free tools that let authors, scientists, artists, and educators easily mark their creative work with the freedoms they want it to carry', so that creative producers can 'use CC to change your copyright terms from "All Rights Reserved" to "Some Rights Reserved"' (Creative Commons 2007b). In doing so, the aim has also been to dramatically simplify the plethora of legal questions that face providers of original creative content about how to deal with others who draw upon their creative work in ways that avoid complex and costly legal disputes. As Fitzgerald puts it: 'Models such as Creative Commons rely on the power of copyright ownership and law to structure access downstream. In this sense CC is not anti-copyright. Rather, it uses copyright as the basis for structuring open access. However, CC is designed to provide an alternative for managing copyright in digital content' (2006: 222).

Further reading
Lessig 2004; Orlowski 2005; Flew 2005b; Fitzgerald 2006

Digital gatekeepers and the open source movement

While the challenges of copyright in a digital age have generated different responses both within and across the creative industries, responses in the media and entertainment sectors have often been reactive and defensive. They have frequently involved legal action against those perceived to be transgressors of their copyrighted material, as seen in the successful legal action against the music file-sharing service *KaZaA* pursued through the Federal Court of Australia (*Universal Music Australia Pty Ltd v. Sharman Licence Holdings Ltd* [2005]), and the recent $US1 billion lawsuit lodged by Viacom against *YouTube* (*Viacom v. YouTube* [2007]) (cf. Butt & Bruns 2005; O'Brien 2007), as well as the heavy lobbying of legislators to receive favourable legal and policy environments noted above.

At the technological level, there has also been a focus on the development of Technological Protection Measures (TPMs) generally, and Digital Rights Management (DRM) in particular (Flew 2005b; Flew et al. 2006). DRM can be defined as the set of technical and legal mechanisms applied to help control access to, and distribution of, copyrighted and other protected material in the digital environment. Development of DRM systems are technically complex, requiring client rendering devices with trusted processing, input, and output paths, as well as modifications to current personal computing architecture. A key question arising from DRM strategies as a means to regulate access to digital content is whether or not the costs of DRM, and the more general strategy of *defence-in-depth* of the current copyright regime, justifies its status as the primary solution to the current dilemma. The DRM-driven approach is not a viable solution, as it has at least three adverse consequences:

· diminished consumer privacy, as DRMs generate significantly increased functional capability to monitor online user behaviour
· reduced innovation potential, as the development of new methods to attack peer-to-peer file-sharing networks and applications can inhibit the capacity for 'follow-on' or 'second' innovators to build on copyrighted innovations, as noted above
· greater imbalances in the relationship between copyright holders and users of copyrighted materials; it is impossible to program 'fair use' exceptions into DRM systems, since 'fair use' is a complex legal mechanism, with outcomes dependent on individual aspects of each case.

An important alternative paradigm, and one that is very much grounded in the collaborative, DIY ethos that has underpinned the Internet from its inception (Castells 2001; Flichy 2007), is that arising from the open source movement. The 'open software' and 'free software' movements[3] have pioneered decentralised, networked, and collaborative initiatives to develop new forms of software, licensed through non-proprietorial General Purpose

Licences (GPLs). This means not only that users can acquire the software without cost, but also acquire access to the source code, which they can in turn apply, modify, or reconfigure. The influence of open source thinking can be seen throughout the Web 2.0 environment, with the idea that 'back-end' systems should be relatively open and flexible.

Underpinning the emergence of this large community of software developers, from which software such as the Linux operating system has emerged as a major alternative to proprietorial systems such as those developed by Microsoft, are a series of broad principles whose domain of application moves well beyond the realm of software. The first is a general belief in freely available content. This is not, as Lessig has pointed out in *Free Culture*, free as in 'free beer', or no one having to pay for anything, but in the sense that creativity and innovation are best served by information and culture that is as widely available as possible, 'to guarantee that follow-on creators and innovators remain *as free as possible* from the control of the past' (Lessig 2004: xiv). In this respect, belief in the intrinsic value of an 'information commons' or a 'creative commons' is threatened by recent initiatives to strengthen the intellectual property rights regime, which is seen as presenting the danger of creating 'a "permission culture"—a culture in which creators get to create only with the permission of the powerful, or of the creators of the past' (2004: xiv). Second, there is a belief that collaborative, non-proprietorial initiatives ultimately generate better product, and that open source has a compelling commercial as well as a moral logic. Eric Raymond has contrasted the 'cathedral' model of corporate- or government-controlled initiatives to that of the 'bazaar', or initiatives generated by cooperating autonomous communities such as software developers. Raymond (1998) argues that 'perhaps in the end the open source culture will triumph not because cooperation is morally right or software "hoarding" is morally wrong … but simply because the commercial world cannot win an evolutionary arms race with open source communities that can put orders of magnitude more skilled time into a problem'. Finally, there is an implicit belief in the value of a *gift economy*, whereby people will freely choose to participate in a collaborative initiative on the basis that sharing and collaboration are good things to do, and that the benefits they derive from such participation can be principally non-material in form (Best 2003).

The rise of the open source movement has focused attention on different possible Internet futures, and the varying layers of control over digital communications networks—control over physical infrastructure and code, as well as over content. It sharpened the distinction between a policy moment that could reproduce the *ancien régime* of broadcast media, with its high barriers to entry for new competitors and its sharp demarcation between content producers and consumers, and an uncertain but potentially more open and democratic future based around the collective empowerment of users of digital media backed by an open and robust public information domain. Yochai Benkler (2001: 90) identified the *new public interest* in policies to develop open source and an information commons in these terms:

> We are in the midst of a pitched battle over the spoils of the transformation to a digitally networked environment and the information economy. Stake-holders from the older economy are using legislation, judicial opinions and international treaties to retain the old structure ... As economic policy, letting yesterday's winners dictate the terms of tomorrow's economic competition is disastrous. As social policy, missing an opportunity to enrich our freedom and enhance our justice while maintaining or even enhancing our productivity is unforgivable.

Rennie (2003: 56) has also termed this a 'new public interest' model that 'involves embracing a range of possible publics that may conflict with or contradict each other. There is no claim to what the "good" is, only a striving for it: more players and more ideas means a greater chance that some kind of progress will emerge, either in the form of economic advancement or the advancement of democracy'.

More generally, the open source movement is characterised by its bias towards the new and towards innovation. As Lawrence Lessig put it, 'We as a society should favour the disrupters. They will produce movement toward a more efficient, prosperous economy' (2001: 92). What this produces is not Left/Right politics as it has been traditionally defined—the state versus the market, the public sphere versus commercialisation, capitalism versus socialism—but rather a shifting field of more contingent alliances, which recognises the capacity of incumbent interests, both public or private, to effectively block innovation in order to protect existing monopoly privileges, and the difficulties in forming constituencies for change where the outcomes are uncertain. It is argued that creativity and innovation are best served by information and culture that is as widely available as possible, 'to guarantee that follow-on creators and innovators remain *as free as possible* from the control of the past' (Lessig 2004: xiv).

INTERVIEW: PROFESSOR BRIAN FITZGERALD,
SCHOOL OF LAW, QUEENSLAND UNIVERSITY
OF TECHNOLOGY[4]

Brian Fitzgerald is Professor of Law at Queensland University of Technology, and the author of leading texts and journal articles on Internet law, intellectual property law, and e-commerce and the law. He has been an author or co-author of *Cyberlaw: Cases and Materials on the Internet, Digital Intellectual Property and E-Commerce* (2002); *Jurisdiction and the Internet* (2004); *Intellectual Property in Principle* (2004); and *Internet and E-Commerce Law* (2007). He is also a Chief Investigator in the Australian Research Council Centre of Excellence for Creative Industries and Innovation, leading projects on 'Creative Commons and Open Content Licensing (OCL) Models' and 'Digital Liberty: Reconciling Rights of Creators, Owners, Citizens and Consumers'.

Can you tell us something about how you came to be involved in the area of internet law?

[BF:] I first came across Internet or cyber law back in the mid-1990s, when I was doing a Masters degree at Harvard University Law School and I took a course on Internet Law and Society ... At Harvard they just rolled in all of these names that are now luminaries in the Internet sphere, John Perry Barlow and people like that, and I thought it was great. I came back to Australia in 1996 and started teaching cyberlaw and I've been researching and teaching in relation to the Internet, especially intellectual property issues for over ten years now.

Your current research is around the concept of open content licensing. Would you like to say what open content licensing is?

[BF:] The basic rule is that to reproduce or communicate someone's copyright material you need to have their permission (in legal terms we might call this a 'licence') unless there is some exception to this rule under the law. The digital environment exacerbates this process because in the digital environment of the Internet 'use' automates reproduction or communication and thereby everything we do needs permission. The idea behind Creative Commons (CC) is to provide a permission in advance. This is done by stamping material (that people who own it are willing to share) with a CC badge—openly licence it—so others know what they can do with it without having to ring up the copyright owner—say in the US—and ask permission to be able to reuse it. Over 150 million links back to CC licences worldwide show it has been very effective. At least 30 million of those are on *Flickr*, the online photo repository. If I search the Internet for a photo of Byron Bay licensed under a CC licence and I find one that says it is licensed under a CC BY-NC-SA licence—I know I can reproduce and communicate (reuse) it on the condition that I must acknowledge the creator, use it only in a non-commercial manner and share improvements back to the world.

The photo is said to be openly licensed (to the whole world)—in that it can be accessed and reproduced without the need for any further permission. Open licensing allows for you to share your copyright material with the world on certain conditions without having to give it away. It differs from the traditional All Rights Reserved model in that you allow Internet users the right to do some things with the material but maybe not everything. As openly licensed content is more easily accessed and reused there is real potential for new business models to harness the benefits of this greater usability and profile. In fact some websites like *Revver.com* are building business models around openly licensed material.

Open content then is not only good for users, but it also has downstream economic and other benefits?

[BF:] It could be good for creators, it could be good for users, it could be good for the population generally. One of the things that governments have to consider at the moment is that they hold enormous amounts of data and copyright material. If they charge a cent for access to every piece they own, then there will be innovation but it will be limited to those that can afford to pay the entrance fee. If this data is allowed to flow out of government in an open manner, and people are allowed to use it in new and innovative ways, government might actually sponsor much more innovation. Therefore the idea of allowing everyone to access publicly funded copyright material through the Internet in an open access model is a very important ingredient of the innovation system.

Hal Varian and Carl Shapiro in their seminal work *Information Rules* (Shapiro & Varian 1999) sum this up in the slogan 'maximise value, not protection'. That is if you seek rent/money at the gate you may cut off some of the ideas but if you allow everyone through the gate you may multiply downstream quantifiers—sometimes you can get untold innovation that you may not otherwise have got.

When you look at the initial copyright balance, the aim was to get a balance between the rights to the original producer or generator of the idea, and the users of that idea. We often hear from creative people, artists, writers, etc., that we need copyright law, for how else would we make a living out of what we do?

[BF:] Everyone wants to be able to seek a livelihood. As a creator, the most important thing that I want to do is to have other people listen or see or share in the value of that creativity. Now that's the primary thing; but as a self-interested wealth maximiser, I'm also going to say that I'd also like to make some money out of that. Hence there are competing interests but ultimately I think with creators, it's always about the creativity—that is to reach the broadest possible connection with an audience, and with the hyper-distribution that the Internet allows we can now let many more people share in our creativity. It's building the business back-end to that which is the real challenge. But the bottom line is that the Internet allows all level of creators the ability to reach the whole wide world as an audience cheaply and quickly and what we really need to do is work on the business models that support that 'long tail'.

The problem with copyright law has been, at least in the 20th century, that it really has been used as a rent-seeking model for large corporations, which means that the people who really make money out of copyright are not necessarily the creators, but the companies who actually take on the role of marketing and commercialising creativity. While that seems reasonable to a point, the creators, unless they are at the very top of the tree, often do not see great reward. That is why people are talking in quite an enthusiastic way about the new possibilities the Internet might offer creators. Does the new user generated Web 2.0 model actually allow creators broader scope to participate in a revenue stream? And what role for copyright law?

To be their own distributors?

[BF:] Yes. It may or may not be successful. You are still going to need some traditional marketing activities, for a while, at least. But I think there is a lot of scope there for new opportunities because, call it 'long tail theory' [Anderson 2006] or whatever you want, we know there are lots of people out there who are creative and would like to receive some revenue who do not receive it. Because a lot of the revenue is generated by a very small handful of people who are marketed very well. Increasingly the Internet is challenging us to think about how we can do a better deal for everybody.

I don't know if we are really going to see a creative 'utopia' in the new environment, but some people certainly hold out strong hope that the copyright law may actually, in the future, bring better revenue to the creators. To do that, I think you've got to fundamentally change the way we are doing the business.

You've had an association with establishing Creative Commons in Australia. Do you want to say more about how Creative Commons aims to work with some of those balances?

[BF:] Creative Commons is an international open licensing project. The figurehead is Lawrence Lessig at Stanford University, and a number of people, prominent people, throughout the world have endorsed and have participated in the project.

Creative Commons licences provide a facility for copyright owners in all sectors to exercise their fundamental and democratic freedom to share their copyright for ideological, cultural, economic, and/or social reasons.

An interesting example in Australia is the Picture Australia project run by the National Library of Australia where they ask people to contribute photos to chronicle Australian life and they do that by encouraging people to upload those photos to the Internet photo repository *Flickr* where they have a Picture Australia user group in which they encourage people to use a Creative Commons licence. What does that do? It gives people the ability to reuse, reutilise and/or repurpose some of that material.

Wikipedia is another classic example. It uses the GNU Free Documentation Licence (GFDL) to negotiate copyright issues with a minimum of fuss. People are contributing copyright material, remixing it and editing it, and the GFDL allows the usability and flexibility of the material by providing the permission in advance to use the copyright material.

How do you perceive the growing use of Creative Commons licensed material in commercial media?

[BF:] The commercial media are now using Creative Commons licensed material—especially photos—on a regular basis. As the copyright owner you have the choice. Release your material under an attribution only licence which allows others to use it commercially with no obligation to pay you anything. This may satisfy your wish to be famous and may even provide commercial reward indirectly. However, if you want to control commercial exploitation you would need to release under a non-commercial licence. In this case anybody wanting to reuse your material commercially must come back and strike a special commercial licensing deal with you. In essence you reserve the commercial rights while releasing to the Internet world on a non-commercial basis.

Can you elaborate on that in light of the Viacom case against YouTube?

[BF:] *YouTube* is a phenomenal success, a leading example of the power of social networking, and a tremendous innovation that could not previously have been imagined. It happened by serendipity but also through a lot of money put into the infrastructure and marketing of it. But what's also happened is a lot of copyright material has been put up on *YouTube* without permission, and even though *YouTube* now has a 10-minute limit for videos, there's nothing to stop someone putting up a 25-minute episode of *The Simpsons* by putting it up in three different segments. If you go to *YouTube* you'll see a lot of what is unauthorised copyright material—it's copyright material that no-one's given the permission to put up there.

Viacom has come along to *YouTube* and said you don't really have the right to put that material up there, it's ours, you haven't got our permission, and there's no fair use involved. *YouTube* has tried to cut deals with most of the big content providers, either video or music players, producers, and recording companies, but Viacom has held out and I suppose the strategy with Viacom is that it seems *YouTube* hasn't offered them enough of the advertising revenue that *YouTube* is making.

To this end we are really witnessing a ground-breaking piece of litigation. On the one hand we have a really big traditional distributor (Viacom) saying we are the dominant player here. On the other side we have got the new access corporation (*YouTube*) that has a whole business model which is based around building access to content. This is a clash of ideology—one is control, one is open access—and we are going to see the law as the battleground for this. How it will play out in fine detail is that in 1998 with the DMCA (*Digital Millennium Copyright Act*), the US introduced what they called safe harbours, which basically says that the intermediary can have a level of safety or immunity from liability if it goes through a certain number of activities and one of those is not knowing that the content was infringing and another registering [for notice and takedown notices], and really what the Viacom and *YouTube* case is going to come down to is whether those safe harbours are broad enough to protect *YouTube*.

Two things are apparent in this field. One is that the user community gravitates to open-source models, and moves in swarms to open-source models, but also that traditional media, entertainment, and copyright industries, have great

*influence over the legislature. It seems that that influence and legislature
trumps the other providers in the legal framework, whether it be* **Napster,
KaZaA,** *and so on. How significant do you think the forces are for change in the
copyright balance?*

[BF:] What we've seen up until now are companies that are smaller, that have
sometimes been branded as illegitimate, that are easily knocked over. They are
the 'other', if you like, in the whole discourse. But with Google and Yahoo! and
companies like that, we've now got large mainstream, Western, US-based corporations that can stand and fight, if they want to, against similar large corporations
that are promoting the traditional idea of copyright management.

Out of the Viacom and *YouTube* case, we will probably see a fundamental
shift, where the big traditional players engaging in a process of litigation that they
can probably never really completely win. Although they may win at a legal level,
some might say it's a hollow victory in the sense that the world around them
keeps changing, and they may have to come back and reassess, and say 'Well we
won this one, but we really haven't won back the revenue stream'.

I think to have such legitimate and wealthy corporations like Google involved in
this mix, we do really have two different, if I can use crude terms, groups of rent-
seekers. We've got the traditional copyright owning group, and now we've got the
group that wants to drive access. Does that mean the user wins? Does that mean
the creator wins? They are questions that I think still need to be answered.

In relation to Google's project around digitising libraries in the US, the Google
Print Project, ultimately I think it would make a lot of content more accessible to
us so there I think the users would be a winner. Would complete open access
to everything necessarily be the best way to manage copyright? Still a difficult
question to call, but we know that in certain areas, it is probably the better
approach.

*In the 20th century, it seems much of what happened internationally in terms
of copyright was influenced by what happened in the USA with the TRIPS
Agreement probably being the ultimate symbol of that. From your work in other
countries, are you seeing different notions of the copyright balance emerging,
are developing countries essentially adopting the Western models?*

[BF:] Some have called the period from 1980–2005 the Age of America in terms
of IP law and policy but there has recently been a weakening of that position.
Whether it's because the US has had to invest their funds into fighting terrorism or
that they've had their eyes on other things, there's no doubt that the development

agenda joined with the access agenda has really opened up a whole new domain of discussion. The development agenda from countries like Brazil, Chile, and to some extent India and China, has really started to rattle the cage. They want more balance and equity in the IP system. Along with that you've got major corporations like Google promoting an open access agenda for clear and in many instances persuasive commercial reasons.

The developing countries have directed their claims at the WIPO (World Intellectual Property Organization), and it was interesting that in February 2007, WIPO came back and said that it would actually invest a significant amount of time looking at the development agenda in much more detail. Now that might be just lip-service or it might be a fundamental change—to say that there's going to be some loosening of the boundaries. As these emergent countries become increasingly important players in the global digital economy, such trends are likely to continue.

 ## USEFUL WEBSITES

Berkman Centre for Internet Law and Society <cyber.law.harvard.edu/home>. Resource site developed at Harvard Law School that is a leader in addressing intellectual property issues, as well as a range of areas of Internet law and policy. It is the host site for a series of major international research initiatives, including the Centre for Citizen Media, FreeCulture, and the OpenNet Initiative.

Oxford Internet Institute <www.oii.ox.ac.uk>. Major site for international and inter-disciplinary Internet research, based within the University of Oxford. Key research strands include Internet governance and democracy, the Internet and everyday life, and the wider implications of the open source software movement.

World Intellectual Property Organization <www.wipo.int/portal/index.html.en>. A specialist agency of the United Nations responsible for information gathering and promotion of shared international intellectual property standards. The major source of information on what copyright, patents, and trademarks are, how they are distributed worldwide, and how policy and regulation is developing on an international scale.

12

conclusion

New Media: An Introduction has highlighted the extent to which, in the two decades in which the Internet and digital media technologies have established themselves as dominant media and communication forms, there have been major transitions with those technologies and how they are used. In particular, the rise of social media and Web 2.0 technologies has accelerated trends towards the users of digital media also being its primary content producers. While the 1990s saw concepts such as convergence, interactivity, and the virtual dominating both popular and academic discourse, in the 2000s we are increasingly focused on participation, collaboration, collective intelligence, and user-led innovation.

At the heart of this lies the Internet as a dense, ubiquitous, and global socio-technical network. While early Internet studies posed the question of the relationship of this technology to the culture that surrounds it, it is now clearly embedded in global media culture to the extent that, as Manuel Castells observed, we now live in a network society. This has a range of economic, cultural, political, legal, and other implications. In the economic sphere, it is linked to the shift towards a global knowledge economy, or an economy increasingly driven by knowledge-based and creative industries, and by user-led innovation, rather than industrial production, science-based research and development, and mass consumption. Culturally, it has allowed participatory culture to flourish through blogs, social media sites, and DIY media production and distribution outlets such as *YouTube*. Politically, it presents a challenge to established sites of institutional authority, be they governments, political parties, and indeed the traditional news media, as looser, more fluid collaborative networks constitute increasingly dynamic sites of innovation and the generation of new ideas, information, and forms of power, resistance, and activism. In the legal domain, remix culture and the almost limitless scope for repurposing and remediation of digital content come up against traditional copyright and intellectual property laws. Indeed, in terms of our very identities, these are increasingly located within global networks of information and communication, whether through our own online affiliations, or from the information that is stored about us on various databases as a result of our electronic transactions.

The rise of social media, blogs, and social software is connected to what Benkler (2006) terms the rise of types of *social production* that are collaborative in form, strongly motivated by non-market behavioural factors, and difficult to directly claim ownership of or control over. Benkler argues that social production models find their most favourable ecologies in industries that are connected to information, communication, communications, culture, and creativity, meaning that they are having their most significant impact in knowledge-based, media, and creative industries, but that the ruptures they promote in these industries resonate throughout the economic system. This is particularly the case as forms such as information and attributes such as creativity have become, as authors such as Howkins (2001) and Florida (2002, 2007) have argued, the core productive forces of the 21st-century global economy. Benkler observes that the more important non-contractual factors such as gift relations, reciprocity, and trust are to an economic relationship, the more social production will flourish, and the more of a challenge these new models will present to incumbent producers: the rise and rise of *Wikipedia* and *YouTube* are perhaps the most graphic examples of this. The core contradiction is, not surprisingly, around the status and application of copyright and intellectual property laws in this environment, and it is notable that both the laws themselves have been strengthened over the last decade, and the propensity among incumbent media and information companies to seek their enforcement has increased, even as alternative socio-legal models such as Creative Commons have been evolving.

The copyright wars, or the tensions that exist between information and creative content as both public resources and private property, are salutary reminders that we need to avoid being overly drawn into new media hype, and that empirically grounded analysis of trends in new media is required.

This becomes particularly apparent if we consider two boom areas in the new media environment, multiplayer online games and new forms of news production such as citizen journalism. In the case of online games, the dynamism of the sector and the pleasurable experiences of gaming need to be considered alongside issues such as exploitative working conditions in the industry leading to high staff turnover and burn-out, as well as the ongoing debates about ownership of user-generated content in the online games themselves. The online environment has also spawned new forms of journalism and news production, with the shifts in production infrastructures associated with Web 2.0, as well as new patterns of distribution and use, leading to the rise of what has been termed citizen journalism. While citizen journalism emerges in a context where there are growing questions of journalism as a professional ideology and tendencies to 'capture' by powerful sources, there is also the concern that eroding traditional revenue bases for news organisations may see an undermining of news values in the online space, as lower-cost alternatives such as celebrity blogging are more tightly aligned to demographic profiling driven by the marketing divisions of news organisations. Both instances remind us that an understanding of the political economy of new media remains vitally important, even as new opportunities for participatory media culture and the expression of what Leadbeater (2007) terms mass creativity are emerging and multiplying.

To conclude *New Media*, I wish to touch upon five emergent phenomena whose significance and implications warrant further consideration as new media technologies morph and evolve.

Mobility

After some false starts, it is clear that one of the accelerating trends in new media is for data and digital content to be accessed from handheld mobile devices. While the rise in mobile phone ownership and use has been one of the great phenomena of the period since the early 1990s, phones have for the most part functioned as devices for voice communication and simple text messaging (and increasingly photography and video), while more complex data, such as Web content, continued to be largely accessed from personal computers. The fuller development of 3G (3rd generation) wireless networking and the wiring up of spaces (particularly cities) has been accompanied by the development of devices which fully integrate phone, computing, and PDA functions, such as RIM's Blackberry, the Samsung Blackjack, and the Apple iPhone.

The implications of mobile computing becoming a user expectation are only now being considered. One implication may be that wireless networking access will inform locational decisions made by people and organisations, as part of the global competition for talent that Florida (2007) refers to. Another may be further 'nomadism' in terms of when and where people undertake work-related activities. It will also impact on how people consume leisure and entertainment products, with access to major sporting events already proving to be a major driver of demand for wireless handheld devices. We also need to consider how relentless access to networked information impacts on its users; some have already dubbed the Blackberry the 'Crackberry' because it generates addiction to email and other forms of text messaging.

Always on

The rise of mobile computing intersects with another major trend in new media, which is that growing access to high-speed broadband services, the costs of Internet access associated with usage time, network infrastructure constraints, download times, and storage device capacity are all rapidly diminishing. As a result, it is becoming the norm for more and more people to simply leave their computers on at all times, and to download an ever increasing amount of material—and increasingly audio and video material—onto their computers. The broader socio-cultural implications of ever increasing speed and volume of communications or what can be termed 'always on' culture, both for users and for the wider communications ecology, is thus becoming an increasingly significant research question.

One implication is that it promotes the 'long tail' phenomenon identified by Anderson (2006) where businesses can increasingly profit from low-volume sales to niche consumers based on a wider inventory of 'virtual' product (as seen with Amazon and eBay). Another implication has been in the area of news production, where a 24/7 news cycle is now the norm, rather than the traditional news cycles of print or broadcast news production. There are also questions about the quality of communication: if people are receiving 100+ emails a day, and there is an expectation from senders that these will be read and responded to quickly, will the quality of responses deteriorate as people lack the time away from work that was traditionally the basis of leisure and well-being? Will it see more people choose to 'downsize', accepting a lower income as a necessary condition for an enhanced quality of life?

Meeting people is easy

If it is estimated that there are about 100 million bloggers worldwide, and social media sites such as *MySpace* are claiming to have over 100 million accounts, then the critical mass of people involved in online activities that involve routine interaction with others has reached a substantial level. Yet we know little beyond the consistency of such trends with meta-theories such as those of the network society, participatory culture, or social production about what the implications are of such a critical mass of online networkers using social media.

I would suggest that social researchers should consider how one establishes empirical measures for identifying the significance of these trends. We know, for instance, that open source software development is effective because it can produce a powerful operating system such as Linux. What are our equivalents for social media? Do bands and musicians that have *MySpace* sites achieve more sales and downloads for their music than those who don't? Does a *MySpace* or *Facebook* page matter in terms of electoral politics? Do people with a personal social networking site do better in the employment market? What are the reasons that people have for going into these online spaces, and how do they know if they have made an impact? There is some evidence of bloggers making a difference to political agendas and news agendas, but more systematic and sustained research on these questions would greatly advance our conceptual understanding of these notable new media phenomena.

Critical information studies

Vaidhyanathan (2006) has proposed that the complex set of legal, social, political, economic, and cultural issues arising from new media should be approached from a multidisciplinary perspective that he has termed critical information studies (CIS). He proposes that CIS would consider 'the ways in which culture and information are regulated, and thus the relationships among regulation and commerce, creativity, science, technology, politics, and other human affairs' (2006: 293). Identifying how this would translate more specifically into research agendas, Vaidhyanathan proposes the following:

- the abilities and liberties to use, revise, criticise, and manipulate cultural texts, images, ideas, and information

- the rights and abilities of users (or consumers or citizens) to alter the means and techniques through which cultural texts and information are rendered, displayed, and distributed
- the relationship between information control, property rights, technologies, and social norms
- the cultural, political, social, and economic ramifications of global flows of culture and information (2006: 293).

He observes that an interdisciplinary framework such as CIS not only makes it more exciting to research a field such as digital copyright law, as it enmeshes researchers in debates across cultural studies and political economy as well as law and information studies. It also presents the possibility that such scholarly research will engage quite directly with issues that are in the public domain:

As the sets of cultural producers and consumers intersect, the marginal price of distribution of information and cultural products drops to zero, and global communication networks link disparate bodies of work and people who engage with that work. More people take an interest in the policies that govern how information and information technology get distributed and used (Vaidhyanathan 2006: 303).

In addition, such questions link up this research with the activities of various public interest organisations, legal groups and policy-makers, as well as providing academic researchers with direct questions about how they wish their own work to circulate in the public domain (e.g. should it have a Creative Commons licence? Should it be published in 'Open Content' journals?).

The possibilities of CIS as an emergent field of critical and inter-disciplinary socio-legal research are considerable, and it both draws from and contributes to a rich range of knowledges from across a variety of other academic disciplines. At the same time, Vaidhyanathan identifies three key challenges for those working within this emergent field. The first is that it is dominated by research from the English-speaking world, and most particularly the USA. As the Internet has increasingly become a genuinely global domain, he notes that some of the underlying assumptions may 'ring flat in parts of the world where liberalism is not taken for granted', pointing to a need for 'CIS [to] get beyond its American roots and consider how every change in the information ecosystem is global' (2006: 306). A second challenge relates to the institutional location of many researchers within universities that increasingly see themselves, not simply as the users and providers of information that is in the public domain, but as significant holders of copyright materials in their own right, from which they extract revenues and develop research commercialisation strategies. Finally, there is the question of whether scholars committed to a CIS agenda would practise what they preach by only dealing with publishers and journals that enable more open access to scholarly materials through legal mechanisms such as Creative Commons licences.

Dewesternising Internet studies

Following Curran and Park's (2000) proposal that there is a need to dewesternise media studies, the data provided in Chapter 1 of this book on trends in global Internet use point to a similar need in relation to understanding new media and the Internet. The fastest growth in global Internet use is happening in Asia, Africa, Latin America, the Caribbean, and the Middle East, and North America, Europe, and Australia/New Zealand are moving from a position of dominance in the 1990s to one where these parts of the world are becoming, or may indeed have become, a minority of the global Internet community. The majority of the world's Internet users do not communicate primarily through the English language, yet we understand little about how this is changing the nature of the global new media ecology.

Just as Curran and Park noted that early paradigms in global media and communications tended to understand much of the world's media as an underdeveloped or state-controlled other to a Western (typically American) norm, Internet studies is still strongly influenced by its emergence in the USA in the free-wheeling decade that was the 1990s. One example of this is the degree of focus on Internet censorship in a number of countries, with China being the largest and perhaps most significant. It is certainly the case that there are varying degrees of censorship, state control, and surveillance of online communication in many parts of the world, and that this may well run at odds with the democratising potential of new media. Yet this is not the whole picture, and it only addresses some aspects of new media use in some parts of the world. Establishing the significance of state control over the Internet in China, for instance, tells us little about how the Internet is developing as a new media form in countries such as India, Korea, Brazil, and Russia, to take some examples. It also acts as a filter to more grounded case studies of comparative new media use in different socio-cultural and political-economic environments.

The problems here are, I believe, twofold. The first arises from the strong historical association of the Internet with libertarian discourses (Flichy 2007). As the Internet was first popularised in the USA, and the first major political campaigns around the new media tended to focus on questions of free speech, there has been a tendency in Internet studies to focus on the more heroic, political, or resistant aspects of use of the medium, as opposed to more mundane, everyday, convivial, or conversational uses (Burgess 2006). This is not to say that we should not draw attention to Internet censorship in different parts of the world, or that we should not be supporting those who seek to use the new media to achieve a legitimate right to free expression of opinion and ideas. It is to say, however, that to focus only on this may lead to some significant omissions in our understanding of new media use in cross-cultural perspectives. The enthusiasm of Chinese Internet users to vote in televised talent programs, to take one example, may tell us something interesting about how a popular demand for the right to vote may be expressing itself in that country, if we choose to give it significance as an aspect of new media use.

The second gap is clearly that of language, interspersed with isolation between different research communities, and an associated reluctance on the part of Western new media researchers to learn from developments in other parts of the world. South Korea provides a fascinating case study of how digital media content may evolve where there is near-universal access to high-speed broadband networks, yet published research in English-language new media journals on developments in Korea is patchy and sporadic. To make these points is not to devalue what is most valuable in the Western intellectual and political traditions, such as the right to free speech and free expression of ideas and opinions. It is to say that more should be done to foster international and intercultural research and collaboration in the new media field, so that patterns of mutual learning and dialogue can emerge that are more reflective of the dynamics of global new media production, distribution, and use. My hope is that this book has made a modest contribution to that spirit of collaboration and dialogue.

endnotes

Chapter 1

1. The term 'information' is being defined broadly as all forms of message and symbol that are communicated to others, which include those forms that can be considered original knowledge, but also a vast range of other forms that are communicated. One of the difficulties in use of the term in relation to new media, such as theories of the 'information society', is that it implies a second, narrower definition, where information is associated with forms of knowledge that advance the understanding of the receiver of their social and physical environment. Any cursory glance at the World Wide Web, or any other digital media platform, will find an abundance of content that would constitute information in the former sense, but not in the latter. The common tendency to conflate access to more information with greater personal and social knowledge has been widely critiqued (e.g. Castells 1999; Graham 1999).

2. The best histories of the Internet have been written by those directly involved in its development, such as Leiner et al. (2003), Berners-Lee (2000), and Gillies and Cailliau (2000), who provide important insiders' accounts of the development of the World Wide Web. A useful chronology of the development of computers that is very much informed by the development of the Internet can be found in Hirst and Harrison (2006: 207–12).

3. This question is discussed in Rheingold (1994), Hafner and Lyon (1996), Castells (1996a: 41–6; 2001: 39–46), Leiner et al. (2003), and Hassan (2004). Castells (2001) argues that it is more useful to see the culture of early Internet developers as being a techno-meritocratic one, strongly grounded in academic protocols of shared pursuit of science, peer review, and sharing research findings, rather than

a culture grounded in military service. The research centres of universities such as MIT, Harvard, and Stanford were central points for its development.

4. The number of Internet hosts is inevitably less than the number of Internet users, since multiple users will access the Internet from a single host. At the same time, users will access the Internet from more than one host, as seen in the worldwide proliferation of Internet cafés for travellers. The number of Internet hosts, or sites from which connection to a server is made, is easier to measure than the number of people who access the Internet.

5. Douglas Engelbart was a computer scientist whose work on the interaction between computers and human intelligence, and his applications of such work in the early development of human–computer interfaces, was central to the development of Graphical User Interfaces, at a time when computers were not envisaged as a personal or mass media device. One of Engelbart's major research papers, 'Augmenting Human Intellect: A Conceptual Framework', written in 1962, can be found at <www.bootstrap.org/augdocs/friedwald030402/augmentinghumanintellect/ahi62index.htm>.

6. The InterPlanetary Internet Project is a Special Interest Group of the Internet Society whose aim is to define the architecture and protocols necessary to permit interoperation of the Internet resident on Earth with other remotely located internets resident on other planets or spacecraft in transit. For more information, see <www.ipnsig.org/home.htm>.

Chapter 2

1. The full name of this legislation is the *Uniting and Strengthening America by Providing Appropriate Tools Required to Intercept and Obstruct Terrorism Act of 2001* (Public Law 107-56), also known as *USA PATRIOT Act* or simply the *Patriot Act*, which was passed into US law by President George W. Bush on 26 October 2001, after being passed by overwhelming majority vote in the US House of Representatives and Senate.

Chapter 5

1. Sociologists such as Granovetter (1985) and Podolny and Page (1998) have argued that economists such as Williamson have consistently underestimated the significance of relations of trust, reciprocity, and co-operation to how market economies actually work.

2. In their *Global Analysis of World Cities* (GAWC) project, Taylor and colleagues (2002) distinguished between alpha world cities, that displayed all world-city characteristics; beta world cities, that displayed about two-thirds of the characteristics of a world city; and gamma world cities or cities with some evidence of world city formation. The characteristics sought were leadership in the global service industry sectors of accountancy, advertising, banking and finance,

and law. According to this criterion, the *alpha world cities* were London, Paris, New York, Tokyo, Chicago, Frankfurt, Hong Kong, Los Angeles, Milan, and Singapore, and the *beta world cities* were San Francisco, Sydney, Toronto, Zurich, Brussels, Madrid, Mexico City, São Paulo, Moscow, and Seoul. Another 102 cities according to this study have some claims to world city status (Taylor et al. 2002: 99–101).

Chapter 7

1. Hollywood and the games world have of course had more successful subsequent liaisons, most notably with the *Lara Croft* films, starring Angelina Jolie as the versatile action heroine.
2. It is estimated, for instance, that Microsoft lost $1.5 billion in the first 18 months of the launch of its Xbox, but saw this as a necessary condition for its being able to capture market share from more established players like Sony and Nintendo, as well as establishing its credibility in the games development community as an industry player in for the long haul, and hence with developing content for its Xbox games console.
3. For a fascinating account of the difficulties in presenting academic research on games to politicians and in the media that does not draw on the 'moral panic', cause-and-effect model, see Henry Jenkins' (2006c) description of his appearance before the US Congress shortly after the Littleton shootings.
4. The pink software movement was a focus of this particular debate. In the 1990s a number of companies were formed to make 'pink' software—games that were designed to appeal to girls. The most notable of these was *Purple Moon*. However, there was much disagreement about whether creating 'special' games for girls had the effect of marginalising them, and a better tactic would rather integrate different styles into more mainstream games. It was also disputed that current games were not appealing to girls (de Castell & Bryson 1998) and that the nature of play was in fact gendered at all.

Chapter 8

1. The Iraq war has been something of a high point for blogging, with the widespread demand for alternative information sources generated from commentators in Iraq whose reports were not filtered through media organisations, such as the pseudonymous blogger Salam Pax (Redden 2003).
2. In Australia, the value of federal government advertising went from $5–10 million in the first half of the 1990s to $20–100 million in the late 1990s and 2000s under the Howard government. $100 million was spent on advertising in June 2000 when the new Goods and Services Tax was introduced, and advertisements to publicise new government policies involved $60 million of expenditure at the time of the 2001 and 2004 federal elections (Ward 2003; Young 2006).

Chapter 9

1.   The 'arts multiplier' refers to those studies that seek to demonstrate that investment of public funds in arts activities generates economic and non-economic benefits greater than the cost of the original investment (e.g. tourism benefits from hosting a major festival). Seaman (2000) has argued that such studies are plagued by the problem of double-counting, and the tendency to ignore what economists term *opportunity cost*, or the question of whether the same investment of funds on another activity may have generated greater benefits. The fact that such studies are usually linked to advocacy on the part of a particular arts organisation or arts funding agency has not helped to diminish their reputation among economists for being a form of industry special pleading that lacks methodological rigour (cf. Madden 2001).

Chapter 11

1.   It is worth noting that Gutnick's defamation case against Dow Jones would probably not have succeeded if pursued in the US courts. Australia has unusually restrictive defamation laws, which require that the defendant prove that a statement is true, rather than the plaintiff having the burden of proof of establishing that the statements were false.

2.   Among the key national information policy statements of the 1990s were the US government's *National Information Infrastructure Task Force* (1993); the European Union's *Europe and the Information Superhighway* (Bangemann Report) (1994); Singapore's *IT200—A Vision of an Intelligent Island* (1992); the Canadian government's *The Canadian Information Highway: Building Canada's Information and Communications Infrastructure* (1994); Japan's *Program for Advanced Information Infrastructure* (1994); the Australian government's *Creative Nation* (1994) and *Networking Australia's Future* (1995) reports; the Malaysian government's *Multimedia Super Corridor* strategy (1995); Korea's *Infomatization Strategies for Promoting National Competitiveness* (1996); and the OECD's *Global Information Infrastructure—Global Information Society* report (1997). See Northfield 1999 for an extended commentary on these; cf. Barr 2000: 169–74.

3.   The underlying principle of open software is not simply that it is freely available, but that the source code is made available to all users, who can modify it accordingly. The concept of 'free software' has been associated with Richard Stallman, who founded the Free Software Foundation and developed the GNU General Purpose Licence in 1983. Stallman and his followers have largely pursued a moral case that free access to software and source code is a basic right of a free society. While most open source software initiatives are consistent with the principles of free software, open source advocates tend to stress the technical superiority of the software developed by such means rather than the moral right to free software, and argue more of an economic case for adopting open source models. In practice, both groups can be seen to be pursuing broadly similar objectives.

4. Legal cases cited in this interview include: *A&M Records, Inc. v. Napster, Inc.* [2001] (U.S. Ninth Circuit Court required closedown of *Napster* online music distribution site); *Universal Music Australia Pty Ltd v Sharman License Holdings Ltd* [2005] (Federal Court of Australia required closedown of *KaZaA* online music distribution site); *Viacom International Inc, Comedy Partners, Country Music Television Inc, Paramount Pictures Corporation and Black Entertainment Television LLC v YouTube Inc, YouTube LLC and Google Inc.* ($US1 billion litigation case launched by Viacom and its subsidiaries against *YouTube* and its owner, Google, in March 2007).

bibliography

Aarseth, Espen 2001, 'Computer Game Studies: Year One', *Game Studies: The International Journal of Computer Game Research* 1(1) <www.gamestudies.org/0101/>, accessed 25 April 2007.

Abramovitz, Moses, and David, Paul 2001, *Two Centuries of American Macroeconomic Growth: From Exploitation of Resource Abundance to Knowledge-Driven Development*, SIEPR Discussion Paper No. 01–05, Stanford Institute for Economic Policy Research, Stanford University, Stanford CA.

Akerlof, George 1970, '"The Market for "Lemons": Quality Uncertainty and the Market Mechanism', *Quarterly Journal of Economics* 84(3): 488–500.

Aksoy, Asu, and Robins, Kevin 1992, 'Hollywood for the 21st Century: Global Competition for Critical Mass in Image Markets', *Cambridge Journal of Economics* 16(1): 1–22.

Aldridge, Stephen, Halpern, David, and Fitzpatrick, Sarah 2002, *Social Capital: A Discussion Paper*, Performance and Innovation Unit, London, April.

Amabile, Teresa 1996, *Creativity in Context*, Westview Press, Boulder CO.

——2004, 'The Six Myths of Creativity', *Fast Company* 89, December <www.fastcompany.com/magazine/89/creativity.html>, accessed 22 April 2007.

Americans for the Arts 2007, 'Research Services: Creative Industries', <www.artsusa.org/information_resources/research_information/services/creative_industries/default.asp>, updated 12 March, accessed 3 May 2007.

Amin, Ash, and Thrift, Nigel (eds) 2004, *The Cultural Economy Reader*, Blackwell, Oxford.

Anderson, Chris 2006, *The Long Tail: Why the Future of Business is Selling Less of More*, Random House, New York.

Arnison, Matthew 2003, 'Open Publishing is the same as Free Software', <www.purplebark.net/maffew/cat/openpub.html>, first published March 2001, accessed 28 April 2007.

Arthur, W. Brian 1999, 'Competing Technologies and Economic Prediction', in D. MacKenzie and J. Wacjman (eds), *The Social Shaping of Technology*, 2nd edn, Open University Press, Buckingham.

Atton, Chris 2001, 'Approaching Alternative Media: Theory and Methodology'. Paper presented to *Our Media, Not Theirs*, International Communications Association pre-conference, Washington DC, 24 May <www.ourmedianet.org/papers/om2001/Atton.om2001.pdf>, accessed 1 May 2007.

——2002, *Alternative Media*, Sage, London.

——2004, *An Alternative Internet*, Edinburgh University Press, Edinburgh.

Australian, The 2007 'Ghosts of Blogging Haunt Net Celebrity', <www.theaustralian. news.com.au/story/0,20867,21445581-2703,00.html>, posted 26 March 2007, accessed 26 March 2007.

Australian Broadcasting Corporation 2001, 'This Time It's Different', broadcast on *Four Corners*, 30 April, <www.abc.net.au/4corners/dotcom/>.

Australian Research Council Centre of Excellence for Creative Industries and Innovation 2005, *CCI National Mapping Project: Conceptual Background* <https://wiki.cci.edu.au/display/NMP/Conceptual+Background>, created 11 November, accessed 12 December 2006.

Baase, Sara 1997, *A Gift of Fire: Social, Legal, and Ethical Issues in Computing*, Prentice-Hall, Upper Saddle River NJ.

Bannermann, Sara 2006, 'Copyright and the Common Good: An Examination of "the Public Interest" in International Copyright Regimes', in P.N. Thomas and J. Servaes (eds), *Intellectual Property Rights and Communications in Asia: Conflicting Traditions*, Sage, New Delhi, pp. 58–78.

Barber, Benjamin 2000, 'Jihad versus McWorld', in F. Lechner and J. Boli (eds), *The Globalization Reader*, Blackwell, Oxford, pp. 21–6.

Barbrook, Richard, and Cameron, Andy 1995, 'The Californian Ideology', *Muse* 3: 3–17.

Barlow, John Perry 1995, 'Is There a There in Cyberspace?', *UTNE Reader*, March-April, pp. 31–6.

——1996a, 'A Declaration of the Independence of Cyberspace', <www.eff.org/pub/Publications/John_Perry_Barlow>, accessed 22 January 2001.

——1996b, 'Selling Wine Without Bottles: The Economy of Mind on the Global Net', in P. Ludlow (ed.), *High Noon on the Electronic Frontier*, MIT Press, Cambridge MA, pp. 9–34.

Barney, Darin 2004, *The Network Society*, Polity Press, Cambridge.

Barr, Trevor 2000, *newmedia.com.au*, Allen & Unwin, Sydney.

Bassett, Caroline 2007, 'Cultural Studies and New Media', in G. Hall and C. Burchall (eds), *New Cultural Studies: Adventures in Theory*, Edinburgh University Pres, Edinburgh, pp. 220–37.

Batterham, Robin 2000, *The Chance to Change: Discussion Paper by the Chief Scientist*, August, <www.isr.gov.au/science/review/ChanceToChange_17aug.pdf.>, accessed 1 June 2002.

Baudrillard, Jean 1988a, 'For a Critique of the Political Economy of the Sign', in M. Poster (ed.), *Jean Baudrillard: Selected Writings*, Polity Press, Cambridge, pp. 57–97.

——1988b, 'Simulacra and Simulations', in M. Poster (ed.), *Jean Baudrillard: Selected Writings*, Polity Press, Cambridge, pp. 166–84.

Baym, Nancy 2005, 'Interpersonal Life Online', in L. Lievrouw and S. Livingstone (eds), *The Handbook of New Media: Social Shaping and Consequences of ICTs*, 2nd edn, Sage, London, pp. 35–54.

BBC (British Broadcasting Corporation) 2005, 'Building Public Value: Review of the BBC's Royal Charter', May <www.bbc.co.uk/info/policies/bpv.shtml>, accessed 22 April 2007.

——2006, 'Blogosphere Sees Healthy Growth', <http://news.bbc.co.uk/2/hi/technology/6129496.stm>, accessed 17 March 2007.

——2007, 'What is Digital Storytelling?', <www.bbc.co.uk/wales/digitalstorytelling/about.shtml>, accessed 22 April 2007.

Bell, Daniel 1974, *The Coming of Post-Industrial Society*, Penguin, Harmondsworth.

Bell, Steven, and Kellner, Douglas 1991, *Postmodern Theory: Critical Interrogations*, Macmillan, London.

Beniger, James 1986, *The Control Revolution: Technological and Economic Origins of the Information Society*, Harvard University Press, Cambridge MA.

Benkler, Yochai 2001, 'The Battle for the Institutional Ecosystem in the Digital Environment', *Communications of the ACM* 44(2): 84–90.

——2006, *The Wealth of Networks: How Social Production Transforms Markets and Freedom*, Yale University Press, New Haven CN.

Bennett, Tony 1994, 'Research and Cultural Development', in M. Breen (ed.), *Enhancing Cultural Value: Narrowcasting, Community Media and Cultural Development*, Centre for International Research on Communications and Information Technologies, Melbourne, pp. 17–23.

——1998, *Culture: A Reformer's Science*, Allen & Unwin, Sydney.

Berland, Jody 1992, 'Angels Dancing: Cultural Technologies and the Production of Space', in L. Grossberg, C. Nelson, and P. Treichler (eds), *Cultural Studies*, Routledge, New York, pp. 38–55.

Berners-Lee, Tim 2000, *Weaving the Web: The Past, Present and Future of the World Wide Web by its Inventor*, Texere, London.

Best, Kirsty 2003, 'Beating Them at Their Own Game: The Cultural Politics of the Open Source Movement and the Gift Economy', *International Journal of Cultural Studies* 6(4): 449–70.

Bettig, Ronald 1996, *Copyrighting Culture: The Political Economy of Intellectual Property*, Westview Press, Boulder CO.

Bilton, Chris 2007, *Management and Creativity: From Creative Industries to Creative Management*, Blackwell, Oxford.

——, and Leary, Ruth 2002, 'What Managers can do for Creativity: Brokering Creativity in the Creative Industries', *International Journal of Cultural Policy* 8(2): 49–64.

Blumler, Jay, and Coleman, Stephen 2001, *Realising Democracy Online: A Civic Commons in Cyberspace*, Institute for Public Policy Research, London.

Bocock, Robert 1992, 'Consumption and Lifestyles', in R. Bocock and K. Thompson (eds), *Social and Cultural Forms of Modernity*, Open University Press, Cambridge, pp. 119–67.

Boden, Margaret 1990, *The Creative Mind: Myths and Mechanisms*, Cardinal, London.
——1995, 'Creativity and Unpredictability', *Stanford Humanities Review* 4(2), <www.stanford.edu/group/SHR/4-2/text/boden.html>, accessed 22 April 2007.
Bolter, Jay David, and Grusin, Richard 2000, *Remediation: Understanding New Media*, MIT Press, Cambridge MA.
Boutell.com 2004, 'WWW FAQs: How many Web sites are there?', <www.boutell.com/newfaq/misc/sizeofweb.html>, accessed 19 December 2006.
Boutell.com 2007, 'WWW FAQs: How many Web sites are there?', <www.boutell.com/newfaq/misc/sizeofweb.html>, accessed 19 May 2007.
Bower, Joseph, and Christensen, Clayton 1999, 'Disruptive Technologies: Catching the Wave', in *Harvard Business Review on Managing Uncertainty*, Harvard Business School Press, Cambridge MA, pp. 147–73.
Bowman, Shayne and Willis, Chris 2003, *WeMedia: How Audiences are Shaping the Future of News and Information*, The Media Centre, American Press Institute, July.
Boyle, James 1997, *Shamans, Software, and Spleens: Law and the Construction of the Information Society*, Harvard University Press, Cambridge MA.
Braithwaite, John, and Drahos, Peter 2000, *Global Business Regulation*, Cambridge University Press, Melbourne.
Brand, Jeffrey 2007, *Interactive Australia 2007. Facts About the Australian Computer and Video Game Industry*, Interactive Entertainment Association of Australia, Sydney.
Breen, Marcus 2002, 'Convergence Policy: It's Not What You Dance, It's the Way You Dance It', in G. Elmer (ed.), *Critical Perspectives on the Internet*, Rowman & Littlefield, Lanham MD, pp. 165–82.
Brockman, John 1996, *Digerati: Encounters with the Cyber Elite*, Orion Business Books, London.
Brook, James and Boal, Iian (eds) 1995, *Resisting the Virtual Life: The Culture and Politics of Information*, City Lights, San Francisco.
Brown, John Sealy, and Duguid, Paul 2000, *The Social Life of Information*, Harvard Business School Press, Boston MA.
Bruns, Axel 2005, *Gatewatching: Collaborative Online News Production*, Peter Lang, New York.
——2006, 'Wikinews: The Next Generation of Alternative Online News?', *SCAN: Journal of Media Arts Culture* 3(1) <scan.net.au/scan/journal/display.php?journal_id=69>, accessed 28 April 2007.
——, and Jacobs, Joanne 2006, 'Introduction', in A. Bruns and J. Jacobs (eds), *Uses of Blogs*, Peter Lang, New York, pp. 1–7.
Bryce, Jo, and Rutter, Jason 2002, 'Killing Like a Girl: Gendered Gaming and Girl Gamers' Visibility', in F. Mayra (ed.), *Computer Games and Digital Cultures Conference Proceedings*, Tampere University Press, Tampere, Finland.
Buckingham, David 2000, *After the Death of Childhood: Growing Up in the Age of Electronic Media*, Polity Press, Cambridge.
——2005, 'Children and New Media', in L. Lievrouw and S. Livingstone (eds), *Handbook of New Media*, 2nd edn, Sage, London, pp. 75–91.
Burgess, Jean 2006, 'Hearing Ordinary Voices: Cultural Studies, Vernacular Creativity and Digital Storytelling', *Continuum: Journal of Media and Cultural Studies* 20(2): 201–14.

——, Foth, Marcus, and Klaebe, Helen 2006, 'Everyday Creativity as Civic Engagement: A Cultural Citizenship View of New Media'. Paper presented to *Communications Policy and Research Forum 2006*, Sydney, Australia, 25–26 September, <eprints.qut.edu.au/archive/00005056/>, accessed 22 April 2007.

Burnett, Ron, and Marshall, P. David 2003, *Web Theory: An Introduction*, Routledge, London.

Bush, Vannevar 1996, 'Excerpt from "As we may think"', in M. Stefik (ed.), *Internet Dreams: Archetypes, Myths, and Metaphors*, MIT Press, Cambridge MA, pp. 15–22.

Butt, Danny and Bruns, Axel 2005, 'Digital Rights Management and Music in Australia', *Media and Arts Law Review* 10(4): 265–78.

Cahoone, Lawrence 2003, *From Modernism to Postmodernism: An Anthology*, Blackwell, Malden MA.

Cairncross, Frances 1998, *The Death of Distance: How the Communications Revolution will Change our Lives*, Orion Business Books, London.

Calabrese, Andrew 1999, 'The Information Age According to Manuel Castells', *Journal of Communication* 49(3): 172–86.

Callinicos, Alex 2001, *Against the Third Way: An Anti-capitalist Critique*, Polity Press, Cambridge.

Campbell, Cole 2000, 'Citizens Matter; And this is why Public Journalism Matters', *Journalism Studies* 1(4): 689–94.

Carey, James 1992, *Communication as Culture*, Routledge, New York.

——1995, 'The Press, Public Opinion, and Public Discourse', in T.L. Glasser and C.T. Salmon (eds), *Public Opinion and the Communication of Consent*, Guilford Press, New York.

——, and Quirk, John J. 1992, 'The History of the Future', in J. Carey, *Communication as Culture*, Routledge, New York, pp. 173–200.

Carr, Diane, Burn, Andrew, Buckingham, David, Schott, Gareth, and Thompson, John (eds) 2006, *Computer Games: Text, Narrative, and Play*, Polity Press, Cambridge.

Carr, Nicholas 2005, 'The Amorlaity of Web 2.0', <http://roughtype.com/archives/2005/10/the_amorality_o.php>, accessed 17 March 2007.

Cassell, Justine, and Jenkins, Henry 1998, *From Barbie to Mortal Kombat. Gender and Computer Games*, MIT Press, Cambridge MA.

Castells, Manuel 1977, *The Urban Question: A Marxist Approach*, trans. A. Sheridan, Edward Arnold, London.

——1978, *City, Class, and Power*, Macmillan, London.

——1983, *The City and the Grassroots: A Cross-Cultural Theory of Urban Social Movements*, Edward Arnold, London.

——1989, *The Informational City: Information Technology, Economic Restructuring, and the Urban-Regional Process*, Blackwell, Oxford.

——1996, *The Rise of the Network Society*, vol. 1 of *The Information Age: Economy, Society and Culture*, Blackwell, Malden MA.

——1998, *The Power of Identity*, vol. 2 of *The Information Age: Economy, Society and Culture*, Blackwell, Malden MA.

——1999, 'Flows, Networks, and Identities: A Critical Theory of the Informational Society', in M. Castells, R. Flecha, P. Freire, H.A. Giroux, D. Macedo, and

P. Willis, *Critical Education in the New Information Age*, Rowman & Littlefield, Lanham MD.

——2000a, *End of Millennium*, vol. 3 of *The Information Age: Economy, Society and Culture*, Blackwell, Malden MA.

——2000b, 'Materials for an Exploratory Theory of the Network Society', *British Journal of Sociology* 51(1): 5–24.

——2001, *The Internet Galaxy: Reflections on Economy, Society and Culture*, Oxford University Press, Oxford.

——2004, 'Afterword: Why Networks Matter', in H. McCarthy, P. Miller, and P. Skidmore (eds), *Network Logic: Who Governs in an Interconnected World?*, DEMOS, London, pp. 221–4.

——, and Aoyama, Yuku 1994, 'Paths Towards the Informational Society: Employment Structure in G-7 Countries, 1920–90', *International Labour Review* 133(1): 5–33.

Castronova, Edward 2005, *Synthetic Worlds: The Business and Culture of Online Games*, University of Chicago Press, Chicago.

Caves, Richard 2000, *Creative Industries: Contracts Between Art and Commerce*, Harvard University Press, Cambridge MA.

CCPR (Centre for Cultural Policy Research) 2003, Baseline Study of Hong Kong's Creative Industries, University of Hong Kong, September.

CDS (Centre for Digital Storytelling) 2007, 'What is Digital Storytelling?', <www.storycenter.org/whatis.html>, accessed 22 April 2007.

CED (Committee for Economic Development) 2004, *Promoting Innovation and Economic Growth: The Special Problem of Digital Intellectual Property*, Report by the Digital Connections Council for the Committee for Economic Development, CED, Washington DC.

Centre for Citizen Media 2007, 'About the Centre', <www.citmedia.org/about>, accessed 28 April 2007.

Chakravartty, Paula, and Sarikakis, Katharine 2006, *Media Policy and Globalization*, Edinburgh University Press, Edinburgh.

Chandler, Alfred 1977 *The Visible Hand: The Managerial Revolution in American Business*, Harvard University Press, Cambridge MA.

Cho, Kevin 2006, 'Samsung, SK Telecom, Shinhan Sponsor South Korean Alien Killers', *Bloomberg News* <www.bloomberg.com/apps/news?pid=email_us&refer=asia&sid=a2JvzciDnpB4>, posted 15 January, accessed 15 July, 2007.

Christensen, Clayton 2003, *The Innovator's Dilemma*, HarperCollins, New York.

Christopherson, Susan, and Storper, Michael 1986, 'The City as Studio, the World as Back Lot: The Impact of Vertical Disintegration on the Location of the Motion Picture Industry', *Environment and Planning D: Society and Space* 4: 305–20.

Clift, Stephen 2000, 'The E-Democracy E-Book: Democracy is Online 2.0', <www.publicus.net/ebook/edemebook.html>, accessed 7 April 2002.

Coleman, Stephen 2006, 'New Mediation and Direct Representation: Reconceptualising Representation in the Digital Age', *New Media and Society* 7(2): 177–98.

——, and Gøtze, John 2001, *Bowling Together: Online Public Engagement in Policy Deliberation*, Hansard Society, London.

Collins, Jim 1992, 'Postmodernism and Television', in R.C. Allen (ed.), *Channels of Discourse, Reassembled*, Routledge, London, pp. 327–53.

Community Broadcasting Foundation 2007, 'What is Community Broadcasting?', <www.cbf.com.au/Content/templates/sector.asp?articleid=30&zoneid=13>, accessed 1 May 2007.

Coombe, Rosemary 1998, *The Cultural Life of Intellectual Properties: Authorship, Appropriation, and the Law*, Duke University Press, Durham NC.

Cortada, James 2006, *How Computers Changed the Work of American Financial, Telecommunications, Media, and Entertainment Industries*, vol. 2 of *The Digital Hand*, Oxford University Press, Oxford.

Couldry, Nick 2002, 'The Digital Divide', in D. Gauntlett and R. Horsley (eds), *Web Studies*, Arnold, London, pp. 185–94.

—— 2003, 'Beyond the Hall of Mirrors? Some Theoretical Reflections on the Global Contestation of Media Power', in N. Couldry and J. Curran (eds), *Contesting Media Power: Alternative Media in a Networked World*, Rowman & Littlefield, Lanham MD, pp. 39–54.

Cowan, Ruth Schwartz 1997, *A Social History of American Technology*, Oxford University Press, New York.

Cox, Melissa 2000, 'The Development of Computer-Assisted Reporting'. Paper presented to the Association for Education in Journalism and Mass Communication, University of North Carolina, Chapel Hill NJ.

Crandall, Robert, and Sidak, J. Gregory 2006, 'Video Games: Serious Business for the U.S. Economy', *Entertainment Software Alliance*, <www.theesa.com/archives/files/2006%20WHITE%20PAPER%20FINAL.pdf>, accessed 30 April 2007.

Cranny-Francis, Anne 2005, *Multimedia: Texts and Contexts*, Sage, London.

Crawford, Kate 2003, 'Control-SHIFT: Censorship and the Internet', in C. Lumby and E. Probyn (eds), *Remote Control: New Media, New Ethics*, Cambridge University Press, pp. 173–88.

Creative Commons 2007, 'Creative Commons', *Creative Commons*, <creativecommons.org>, accessed 24 April 2007.

Creeber, Glen, and Hills, Ben 2007, 'Editorial—TV III', *New Review of Film and Television Studies* 5(1): 1–4.

Critcher, Chas (ed.) 2006, *Critical Readings: Moral Panics and the Media*, Open University Press, Maidenhead.

Cross, Robert 2004, *The Hidden Power of Social Networks: Understanding How Work Really Gets Done in Organizations*, Harvard Business School Press, Boston.

Csikszentmihalyi, Mihaly 1996, *Creativity: Flow and the Psychology of Discovery and Invention*, Harper Collins, New York.

Cubitt, Sean 2006, 'Tactical Media', in K. Sarikakis and D. Thussu (eds), *Ideologies of the Internet*, Hampton Press, Cresskil NJ, pp. 35–46.

Cunningham, Stuart 2002, 'From Cultural to Creative Industries: Theory, Industry and Policy Implications', *Media International Australia* 102, February: 54–65.

——2005, 'Creative Enterprises', in J. Hartley (ed.), *Creative Industries*, Blackwell, Oxford, pp. 282–98.

——2006, *What Price a Creative Economy?*, Sydney, Currency Press, Platform Paper No. 9.

——2007 (forthcoming), 'Creative Industries Policy Discourse outside of the United Kingdom', *Global Media and Communication* 3(3).

——, and Potts, Jason 2007, Four Models of the Creative Industries. Unpublished paper.

——, Cutler, Terry, Hearn, Greg, Ryan, Mark, and Keane, Michael 2004, 'An Innovation Agenda for the Creative Industries: Where is the R&D?', *Media International Australia* 112: 174–85.

Curran, James, and Park, Myung-Jin (eds) 2000, *Dewesternizing Media Studies*, Routledge, London.

Curtin, Michael 2007, *Media Capitals: The Cultural Geography of Globalization*, Blackwell, Oxford.

Cutler & Company 2002, *Producing Digital Content: A Report for the Department of Communications, Information Technology, and the Arts*, Melbourne, August.

David, Paul 1985, 'Clio and the Economics of QWERTY', *American Economic Review* 75(2): 332–7.

——1999, 'Digital Technology and the Productivity Paradox: After Ten Years, What has been Learned?' Paper prepared for *Understanding the Digital Economy: Data, Tools and Research*, held at US Department of Commerce, Washington DC, 25–26 May.

David, Paul, and Foray, Dominique 2002, 'An Introduction to the Economy of the Knowledge Society', *International Social Science Journal* 171: 9–23.

Davies, William 2003, *You Don't Know Me But ... Social Capital and Social Software*, iSociety, London.

DCMS (Department of Culture, Media, and Sport) 1998, *Mapping the Creative Industries*, <www.culture.gov.uk/creative/creative_industries.html>, accessed 5 May 2001.

de Bono, Edward 1995, *Serious Creativity*, Harper Collins, London.

de Castell, Suzanne, and Bryson, Mary 1998, 'Retooling Play: Dystopia, Dysphoria, and Difference', in J. Cassell and H. Jenkins (eds), *From Barbie to Mortal Kombat: Gender and Computer Games*, MIT Press, Cambridge MA, pp. 232–61.

de Certeau, Michel 1984, *The Practice of Everyday Life*, University of California Press, Berkeley.

de Kerckhove, Derrick 1998, *Connected Intelligence: The Arrival of the Web Society*, Kogan Page, London.

Department of Communications and the Arts 1994, *Creative Nation: Commonwealth Cultural Policy*, AGPS, Canberra.

Deuze, Mark 2003, 'The Web and its Journalisms: Considering the Consequences of Different Types of News Media Online', *New Media and Society* 5(2): 203–30.

——2005, 'What is Journalism? Professional Identity and Ideology of Journalists Reconsidered', *Journalism* 6(4): 442–64.

——2006, 'Participation, Remediation, Bricolage: Considering Principal Components of a Digital Culture', *The Information Society* 22: 63–75.

DiMaggio, Paul, Hargittai, Eszter, Neuman, W. Russell, and Robinson, John P. 2001, 'Social Implications of the Internet', *Annual Review of Sociology* 27: 307–36.

Disappearing Computer 2004, 'The Disappearing Computer Initiative', <www.disappearing-computer.net/artefacts.html>, accessed 20 December 2006.

Dobb, Maurice 1973, *Theories of Value and Distribution since Adam Smith: Ideology and Economic Theory*, Cambridge University Press.

Doctorow, Cory 2006, 'Technorati State of the Blogosphere, Q3 2006', posting to *BoingBoing: A Directory of Wonderful Things* <www.boingboing.net/2006/11/07/technorati_state_of_.html>, accessed 26 March 2007.

Dodgson, Mark, Gann, David, and Salter, Ammon 2002, 'The Intensification of Innovation', *International Journal of Innovation Management* 6(1): 53–83.

Donald, James 2004, 'What's New: A Letter to Terry Flew', *Continuum: Journal of Media and Cultural Studies* 18(2): 235–46.

Doremus, Paul, Keller, William, Pauly, Lewis, and Reich, Simon 1998, *The Myth of the Global Corporation*, Princeton University Press, Princeton NJ.

Dovey, Jon, and Kennedy, Helen 2006, *Game Cultures: Computer Games as New Media*, Open University Press, Maidenhead.

Drahos, Peter, and Braithwaite, John 2002, *Information Feudalism: Who Owns the Knowledge Economy?*, Earthscan, London.

Du Gay, Paul, and Pryke, Michael 2002, 'Cultural Economy: An Introduction', in P. du Gay and M. Pryke (eds), *Cultural Economy: Cultural Analysis and Commercial Life*, Sage, London, pp. 1–19.

Dyer-Witheford, Nick 2002, 'E-Capital and the Many-Headed Hydra', in G. Elmer (ed.), *Critical Perspectives on the Internet*, Rowman & Littlefield, Lanham MD, pp. 129–63.

Dyson, Esther 1999, *Release 2.0: A Design for Living in the Digital Age*, Broadway Books, New York.

——, Gilder, George, Keyworth, George, and Toffler, Alvin 1994, 'Cyberspace and the American Dream: A Magna Carta for the Knowledge Age', <www.pff.org/issues-pubs/futureinsights/fi1.2magnacarta.html>, accessed 3 February 2000.

Eco, Umberto 1976, *A Theory of Semiotics*, Indiana University Press, Bloomington IN.

Economist, The 1999, 'The Net Imperative', *Economist Survey: Business and the Internet*, 26 June, pp. 3–5.

Electronic Frontier Foundation (no date), 'Preserving Free Expression: Our Fundamental Rights of Freedom of Speech and Press', <www.eff.org/freespeech.html>, accessed 20 July 2001.

Elmer, Greg (ed.) 2002, *Critical Perspectives on the Internet*, Rowman & Littlefield, Lanham MD.

El-Nawawy, Mohammed, and Iskandar, Adel 2002, *Al Jazeera: How the Free Arab News Network Scooped the World and Changed the Middle East*, Westview Press, Cambridge MA.

El Oifi, Mohammed 2005, 'Influence without Power: Al Jazeera and the Arab Public Sphere', in M. Zayani (ed.), *The Al Jazeera Phenomenon: Critical Perspectives on New Arab Media*, Pluto Press, London, pp. 66–79.

Engelbart, Douglas 1962, 'Augmenting Human Intellect: A Conceptual Framework', October <www.bootstrap.org/augdocs/friedewald030402/augmentinghumanintellect/ahi62index.html>, posted September 1997, accessed 23 April 2007.

Ernst, Dieter, and Kim, Lin Su 2002, 'Global Production Networks, Knowledge Diffusion, and Local Capacity Formation', *Research Policy* 31: 1417–29.

ESA (Entertainment Software Alliance) 2006, 'Essential Facts about the Computer and Video Games Industry', <www.theesa.com/archives/files/Essential% 20Facts%202006.pdf>, accessed 6 April 2007.

Farmer, James 2006, 'Citizen Journalism Sucks', *The Age*, <blogs.theage.com.au/ media/archives/2006/10/citizen_journal.html>, posted 5 October, accessed 27 April 2007.

Feenberg, Andrew 2003, 'Democratic Rationalization: Technology, Power, and Freedom', in R.C. Scharff and V. Dusek (eds), *Philosophy of Technology: The Technological Condition*, Blackwell, Malden MA, pp. 652–65.

Feldman, Curt, and Thorsen, Tor 2004, 'Employees readying Class-action Lawsuit against EA', *Gamespot*, 11 November, <au.gamespot.com/news/2004/11/11/ news_6112998.html>, accessed 7 April 2007.

Fiske, John 1987, *Television Culture*, Routledge, London.

——1992, 'The Cultural Economy of Fandom', in L.A. Lewis (ed.), *The Adoring Audience: Fan Culture and Popular Media*, Routledge, London, pp. 30–54.

Fitzgerald, Brian 2006, 'Creative Commons: Accessing, Negotiating and Remixing Online Content', in P. Thomas and J. Servaes (eds), *Intellectual Property Rights and Communications in Asia*, Sage, New Delhi, pp. 219–25.

Flew, Terry 2001, 'The "New Empirics" in Internet Studies and Comparative Internet Policy', in H. Brown, G. Lovink, H. Merrick, N. Rossiter, D. Teh, and M. Willson (eds), *Fibreculture Reader: Politics of a Digital Present*, Fibreculture Publications, Melbourne, pp. 105–13.

——2002, *New Media: An Introduction*, 1st edn, Oxford University Press, Melbourne.

——2004a, 'Creativity, the "New Humanism" and Cultural Studies', *Continuum: Journal of Media and Cultural Studies* 18(2): 161–78.

——2004b, 'Creativity, Cultural Studies and Services Industries', *Communication and Critical/Cultural Studies* 1(2): 176–93.

——2005a, *New Media: An Introduction*, 2nd edn, Oxford University Press, Melbourne.

——2005b, 'Creative Commons and the Creative Industries', *Media and Arts Law Review* 10(4): 257–64.

——2005c, 'Creative Economy', in J. Hartley (ed.), *The Creative Industries Reader*, Blackwell, London, pp. 344–60.

——2007, *Understanding Global Media*, Palgrave Macmillan, Basingstoke.

——, and McElhinney, Stephen 2005, 'Globalisation and the Structure of New Media Industries', in L.A. Lievrouw and S.M. Livingstone (eds), *The Handbook of New Media: Social Shaping and Consequences of ICTs*, 2nd edn, Sage, London, pp. 287–96.

——, and Sternberg, Jason 1999, 'Media Wars: Media Studies and Journalism Education', *Media International Australia* 90, February: 9–14.

——, Hearn, Greg, and Leisten, Susanna 2006, 'Alternative Intellectual Property Regimes in the Global Creative Economy', in P.N. Thomas and J. Servaes (eds), *Intellectual Property Rights and Communications in Asia: Conflicting Traditions*, Sage, New Delhi, pp. 226–40.

——, Sternberg, Jason, and Adams, Debra 2007, 'Revisiting the "Media Wars" Debate', *Australian Journal of Communication* 33(1) (forthcoming).

Flichy, Patrice 2005a, 'New Media History', in L.A. Lievrouw and S.M. Livingstone (eds), *The Handbook of New Media: Social Shaping and Consequences of ICTs*, 2nd edn, Sage, London, pp. 185–204.

——2005b, 'Internet: The Social Construction of a "Network Ideology"', in O. Couthard, R. Hanley, and R. Zimmerman (eds), *Sustaining Urban Networks: The Social Diffusion of Large Technical Systems*, Routledge, London, pp. 103–16.

——2007, *The Internet Imaginaire*, MIT Press, Cambridge MA.

Florida, Richard 2002, *The Rise of the Creative Class, and How it's Transforming Work, Leisure, Community and Everyday Life*, Basic Books, New York.

——2007, *The Flight of the Creative Class: The New Global Competition for Talent*, HarperCollins, New York.

Friedman, Thomas 2005, *The World is Flat: A Brief History of the 21st Century*, Farrar, Straus & Giroux, New York.

Friel, Brian 2002, 'Hierarchies and Networks', *Openflows*, <www.openflows.org/article.pl?sid=02/08/02/2118227&mode=nocomment&tid=12>, posted 2 August 2002, accessed 21 January 2007.

Froomkin, Michael 1997, 'The Internet as a Source of Regulatory Arbitrage', in B. Kahin and C. Neeson (eds), *Borders in Cyberspace*, MIT Press, Cambridge MA, pp. 129–64.

——2003, 'International and National Regulation of the Internet', <http://law.tm/docs/International-regulation.pdf>, published 8 December, accessed 21 May 2007.

Frow, John 1994, *When was Postmodernism?*, Local Consumption Publications, Sydney.

——1995, *Cultural Studies and Cultural Value*, Clarendon Press, Oxford.

Galperin, Hernan 2004, *New Television, Old Politics: The Transition to Digital TV in the United States and Britain*, Cambridge University Press.

Gandy, Oscar 2002, 'The Real Digital Divide: Citizens versus Consumers', in L. Lievrouw and S. Livingstone (eds), *Handbook of New Media*, Sage, London, pp. 448–60.

García, Beatriz 2004, 'Urban Regeneration, Arts Programming and Major Events: Glasgow, 1990, Sydney, 2000, Barcelona, 2004', *International Journal of Cultural Policy* 10(1): 103–18.

Garnham, Nicholas 1987, 'Concepts of Culture: Public Policy and the Cultural Industries', *Cultural Studies* 1(1): 23–37.

——2004, 'Information Society Theory as Ideology', in F. Webster (ed.), *The Information Society Reader*, Routledge, London, pp. 166–83.

——2005, 'From Cultural to Creative Industries: An Analysis of the Implications of the "Creative Industries" Approach to Arts and Media Policy Making in the United Kingdom', *International Journal of Cultural Policy* 11(1): 15–29.

Gary, Loren 1999, 'Beyond the Chicken Cheer: How to Improve Your Creativity', *Harvard Management Update*, July.

Gates, Bill 1999, *Business @ the Speed of Thought: Succeeding in the Digital Economy*, Penguin, London.

Gauntlett, David 2000, *Web.Studies: Rewiring Media Studies for the Digital Age*, Arnold, London.

——2004, 'Web Studies: What's new', in D. Gauntlett and R. Horsley (ed.), *Web Studies*, 2nd edn, Arnold, London, pp. 2–18.

——, and Horsley, Ross (eds) 2002, *Web Studies*, 2nd edn, Arnold, London,

GBN (Global Business Network) 2002, *Social Software and the Next Big Phase of the Internet*, interview of Clay Shirky by Peter Leyden, <www.gbn.com/>, December 2002, accessed 8 November 2005.

George, Cherian 2006, *Contentious Journalism and the Internet: Towards Democratic Discourse in Malaysia and Singapore*, Singapore University Press.

Giarini, Orio 2002, 'The Globalisation of Services in Economic Theory and Economic Practice: Some Conceptual Issues', in J.R. Cuadrado-Roura, L. Rubalcaba-Bermejo, and J.R. Bryson (eds), *Trading Services in the Global Economy*, Edward Elgar, Cheltenham, pp. 58–77.

Gibson, William 1984, *Neuromancer*, Gollancz, London.

Giddens, Anthony 1998, *The Third Way*, Polity Press, Cambridge.

Gilder, George 1994, *Life After Television*, W.W. Norton & Co., New York.

Gill, Rosalind 2002, 'Cool, Creative and Egalitarian? Exploring Gender in Project-Based New Media Work in Europe', *Information, Communication, and Society* 5(1): 70–89.

——2006, *Technobohemians or the New Cybertariat? New Media Work in Amsterdam a Decade after the Web*. Report prepared for the Institute of Network Cultures, Amsterdam.

Gillies, James, and Cailliau, Robert 2000, *How the Web was Born: The Story of the World Wide Web*, Oxford University Press, Oxford.

Gillmor, Dan 2006, *We the Media: Grassroots Journalism by the People, for the People*, O'Reilly, Sebastopol CA.

Glasser, Theodore 2000, 'The Politics of Public Journalism', *Journalism Studies* 1(4): 683–96.

Gitelman, Lisa, and Pingree, Geoffrey 2003, *New Media 1740–1915*, MIT Press, Cambridge MA.

Gleick, James 2000, *Faster: The Acceleration of Just About Everything*, Vintage, New York.

Godwin, Mike 1998, *Cyber Rights: Defending Free Speech in the Digital Age*, Times Books, New York.

Golding, Peter, and Murdock, Graham 2000, 'Culture, Communications, and Political Economy', in J. Curran and M. Gurevitch (eds), *Mass Media and Society*, 3rd edn, Arnold, London, pp. 60–83.

Gore, Al 1994, 'Remarks Prepared for Delivery by Vice-President Al Gore to the International Telecommunications Union', 21 March, <www.goelzer.net/telecom/al-gore.html>, accessed 26 December 2006.

Graham, Gordon 1999, *The Internet: A Philosophical Inquiry*, Routledge, London.

Graham, Philip 2000, 'Hypercapitalism: A Political Economy of Informational Idealism', *New Media and Society* 2(2): 131–56.

——2006, *Hypercapitalism: Language, New Media, and Social Perceptions of Value*, Peter Lang, New York.

Gramsci, Antonio 1971, *Selections from the Prison Notebooks of Antonio Gramsci*, in Q. Hoare and G. Nowell-Smith (eds), International Publishers, New York.

Granovetter, Mark 1985, 'Economic Action and Social Structure', *American Journal of Sociology* 91: 481–510.

Gray, Carole 2006, 'A Different Way of Knowing: Inquiry Through the Creative Arts', Proceedings of 1st International Symposium of Visual Studies, Production as Research, Centro de las Artes, Monterrey, April, <publicoutputs.rgu.ac.uk/CREDO/open/additionalpublication.php?id=3661>, accessed 22 April 2007.

Green, Lelia 2002, *Technoculture*, Allen & Unwin, Sydney.

Grossman, Lev 2006, 'Time's Person of the Year: You', *TIME* <www.time.com/time/magazine/article/0,9171,1569514,00.html>, published 13 December, accessed 17 March 2007.

Habermas, Jürgen 1995, 'Institutions of the Public Sphere', in O. Boyd-Barrett and C. Newbold (eds), *Approaches to Media: A Reader*, Hodder, London, pp. 235–44.

Hafner, Katie, and Lyon, Matthew 1996, *When Wizards Stay Up Late: The Origins of the Internet*, Simon & Schuster, New York.

Hague, Barry, and Loader, Brian (eds) 1999, *Digital Democracy: Discourse and Decision Making in the Information Age*, Routledge, London.

Hague, Barry, and Loader, Brian 1999. 'Digital democracy: An introduction', in B.N. Hague and B.D. Loader (eds), *Digital Democracy: Discourse and Decision Making in the Information Age*, Routledge, London, pp. 3–22.

Hall, Peter 2000, 'Creative Cities and Economic Development', *Urban Studies* 37(4): 639–49.

Hall, Stuart 1982, 'The Rediscovery of "Ideology": Return of the Repressed in Media Studies', in M. Gurevitch, T. Bennett, J. Curran, and J. Woollacott (eds), *Culture, Society and the Media*, Methuen, London, pp. 56–90.

——1986, 'Cultural Studies: Two paradigms', in R. Collins, J. Curran, N. Garnham, P. Scannell, P. Schlesinger, and C. Sparks (eds), *Media, Culture and Society: A Critical Reader*, Sage, London, pp. 33–48.

Hallin, Daniel 1994, *We Keep America on Top of the World: Television Journalism and the Public Sphere*, Routledge, London.

Haltiwanger, John, and Jarmin, Ron 2003, 'A Statistical Portrait of the New Economy', in D.C. Jones (ed.), *New Economy Handbook*, Elsevier, Amsterdam, pp. 3–24.

Hardt, Michael, and Negri, Antonio 2000, *Empire*, Harvard University Press, Cambridge MA.

——2005, *Multitude*, Penguin, London.

Hargreaves, Ian 1999, 'The Ethical Boundaries of Reporting', in M. Ungersma (ed.), *Reporters and the Reported*, Centre for Journalism Studies, Cardiff, pp. 1–15.

Hartley, John 1999a, *Uses of Television*, Routledge, London.

——1999b, 'The Frequency of Public Writing: Time, Tomb and Tome as Technologies of the Public', presented to MIT Media-in-Transition Conference, 8 October, <http://web.mit.edu/comm-forum/papers/hartley.html>, accessed 17 August 2001.

——2003, *A Short History of Cultural Studies*, Sage, London.

——2005, 'Creative Industries', in J. Hartley (ed.), *Creative Industries*, Blackwell, Oxford, pp. 1–39.

——2008, 'Journalism as a Human Right: The Cultural Approach to Journalism', in M. Löffelholz and D. Weaver (eds), *Global Journalism Research*, Blackwell, Oxford, pp. 39–51.

——, and Keane, Michael 2006, 'Creative Industries and Innovation in China', *International Journal of Cultural Studies* 9(3): 259–62.

Harvey, David 1990, *The Condition of Postmodernity*, Blackwell, Oxford.

Haseman, Brad 2006, 'A Manifesto for Performative Research', *Media International Australia* 118, February: 98–106.

Hassan, Robert 2004, *Media, Politics and the Network Society*, Open University Press, Maidenhead.

Haussmann, Frank 2002, 'Protecting Intellectual Property in the Digital Age', in A. Thierer and C.W. Crews (eds), *Copy Fights: The Future of Intellectual Property in the Information Age*, Cato Institute, Washington DC, pp. 205–20.

Hawn, Carleen 2004, 'If He's So Smart … Steve Jobs, Apple, and the Limits of Innovation', *Fast Company*, 78, January, <www.fastcompany.com/magazine/78/jobs.html>, accessed 22 April 2007.

Healy, Kieran 2002, 'What's New for Culture in the New Economy?', *Journal of Arts Management, Law, and Society* 32(2): 86–103.

Hearn, Greg, Ninan, Abraham, Rogers, Ian, Cunningham, Stuart, and Luckman, Susan 2004, 'From the Margins to the Mainstream: Creating Value in Queensland's Music Industry', *Media International Australia* 112: 101–14.

Heilbroner, Robert 2003 [1967], 'Do Machines Make History?', in R.C. Scharff and V. Dusek (eds), *Philosophy of Technology: The Technological Condition*, Blackwell, Malden MA, pp. 398–404.

Held, David, and McGrew, Anthony (eds) 2002, *Governing Globalization: Power, Authority and Global Governance*, Polity Press, Cambridge.

——(eds) 2003, *The Global Transformations Reader: An Introduction to the Globalization Debate*, Polity Press, Cambridge.

——, McGrew, Anthony, Goldblatt, David, and Perraton, Jonathon 1999, *Global Transformations: Politics, Economics, and Culture*, Polity Press, Cambridge.

Hermes, Joke 2005, *Re-Reading Popular Culture*, Blackwell, Oxford.

Herring, Susan 2004, 'Slouching Towards the Ordinary: Current Trends in Computer-Mediated Communication', *New Media and Society* 6(1): 26–36.

Herz, J.C. 2002, 'The Bandwidth Capital of the World', *WIRED*, no. 10.08, August, <www.wired.com/wired/archive/10.08/korea.html>, accessed 30 April 2007.

——2005, 'Harnessing the Hive', in J. Hartley (ed.), *Creative Industries*, Blackwell, Oxford, pp. 327–41.

Hesmondhalgh, David 2007, *The Cultural Industries*, 2nd edn, Sage, London.

——, and Pratt, Andy 2005, 'Cultural Industries and Cultural Policy', *International Journal of Cultural Policy* 11(1): 1–13.

Hill, David, and Sen, Krishna 2005, *The Internet in Indonesia's New Democracy*, Routledge, London.

Hirst, Martin, and Harrison, John 2006, *Communication and New Media: From Broadcast to Narrowcast*, Oxford University Press, Melbourne.

Hirst, Paul, and Thompson, Grahame 1996, *Globalization in Question*, Polity Press, Cambridge.

Hodgson, Geoffrey 2000, 'Socio-Economic Consequences of the Advance of Complexity and Knowledge', in *Organisation for Economic Co-operation and Development, The Creative Society of the 21st Century*, OECD, Paris, pp. 89–112.

Hofstede, Geert 1980, *Culture's Consequences: International Differences in Work-Related Values*, Sage, London.

Horst, Heather, and Miller, Daniel 2006, *The Cell Phone: An Anthropology of Communication*, Berg, Oxford.

Howells, Jeremy 2000, 'Knowledge, Innovation, and Location', in J.R. Bryson, P. Daniels, N. Hentry, and J. Pollard (eds), *Knowledge, Space, Economy*, Routledge, London, pp. 50–62.

Howkins, John 2001, *The Creative Economy: How People Make Money From Ideas*, Allen Lane, London.

——2005, 'The Mayor's Commission on the Creative Industries', in J. Hartley (ed.), *Creative Industries*, Blackwell, Oxford, pp. 117–23.

Hudson, Heather 2002, 'Universal Access to the New Information Infrastructure', in L. Lievrouw and S. Livingstone (eds), *Handbook of New Media*, Sage, London, pp. 369–83.

Human Rights Watch 2006, 'How Censorship Works in China: A Brief Overview', <www.hrw.org/reports/2006/china0806/3.htm>, August, accessed 5 May 2007.

Humphreys, Sal 2004, 'Productive Players: Online Computer Games' Challenge to Conventional Media Forms', *Communication and Critical/Cultural Studies* 2(1): 37–51.

IGDA (International Game Developers Association) 2004, *Quality of Life in the Game Industry: Challenges and Best Practices*, <www.igda.org/qol/whitepaper.php>, accessed 26 April 2007.

Innis, Harold 1951, *The Bias of Communication*, University of Toronto Press, Toronto.

Internet Software Consortium (ISC) 2006, *Internet Domain Name Survey* <www.isc.org/index.pl?/ops/ds>, accessed 3 December 2006.

Internet World Stats 2006, *Internet Usage Statistics—The Big Picture, World Internet Users and Population Stats* <www.internetworldstats.com/stats.htm>, accessed 3 December 2006.

Intven, Hank (ed.) 2000, *Telecommunications Regulation Handbook*, prepared for World Bank, Washington DC.

ITU (International Telecommunications Union) 2004, 'The Evolution to 3G Mobile-Status Report', <www.itu.int/itunews/issue/2003/06/thirdgeneration.html>, accessed 9 April 2004.

Jacobs, Jane 1994 [1961], *The Death and Life of American Cities*, Penguin, Harmondsworth.

Jameson, Fredric 1992, *Postmodernism, or, the Cultural Logic of Late Capitalism*, Verso, London.

Jenkins, Henry 1992, *Textual Poachers: Television Fans and Participatory Culture*, Routledge, New York.

——2006a, *Convergence Culture: When Old and New Media Collide*, New York University Press.

——2006b, *Fans, Bloggers and Gamers: Exploring Participatory Culture*, New York University Press.

Jessop, Bob 1998, 'The Rise of Governance and the Risks of Failure: The Case of Economic Development', *International Social Science Journal* 50(1): 29–45.

——2000, 'The State and the Contradictions of the Knowledge-Driven Economy', in J.R. Bryson, P.W. Daniels, N. Henry, and J. Pollard (eds), *Knowledge, Space, Economy*, Routledge, London, pp. 63–78.

Johnson, Steven 2005, *Everything Bad is Good for You: How Today's Popular Culture is Actually Making Us Smarter*, Riverhead Books, New York.

Jones, Steven G. (ed.) 2003, *Encyclopedia of New Media*, Sage, Thousand Oaks CA.

Juul, Jesper 2003, 'The Game, the Player, the World: Looking for a Heart of Gameness', in M. Copier and J. Raessens (eds), *Level Up: Digital Games Research Conference Proceedings*, University of Utrecht, pp. 30–47.

Kahn, Robert, and Cerf, Vinton 1996, 'Excerpt from The Digital Library Project vol. 1: The World of Knowbots', in M. Stefik (ed.), *Internet Dreams: Archetypes, Myths, and Metaphors*, MIT Press, Cambridge MA.

Kalathil, Shanthi, and Boas, Taylor 2003, *Open Networks, Closed Regimes: The Impact of the Internet on Authoritarian Rule*, Carnegie Endowment for International Peace, Washington DC.

Keane, Michael 2004, 'Brave New World: China's Creative Vision', *International Journal of Cultural Policy* 10(3): 265–79.

——2007, *Created in China: The New Great Leap Forward*, RoutledgeCurzon, London.

Kedrosky, Paul 2007, 'Viacom v. YouTube: The Real Issue is a Consumer Rebellion, Not Intellectual Property', *OpinionJournal*, <www.opinionjournal.com/editorial/feature.html?id=110009788>, published 15 February, accessed 20 May.

Keen, Andrew 2007, *The Cult of the Amateur: How Today's Internet is Killing Our Culture*, Doubleday, New York.

Kelly, Kevin 1997, 'New Rules for the New Economy', *WIRED*, no. 5.09, September, <www.wired.com/wired/archive/5.09/newrules.html>, accessed 9 January 2001.

Kenney, Keith, Gorelik, Alexander, and Mwangi, Sam 2000, 'Interactive Features of Online Newspapers', *First Monday* 5(1), <http://firstmonday.org/issues/issue5_1/kenney/index.html>, accessed 27 December 2006.

Kerr, Aphra 2006, *The Business and Culture of Digital Games: Gamework/Gameplay*, Sage, London.

Kingston, Margo 2003, 'Diary of a Webdiarist: Ethics Goes Online', in C. Lumby and E. Probyn (eds), *Remote Control: New Media, New Ethics*, Cambridge University Press, pp. 159–72.

Kitchin, Rob 1998, *Cyberspace: The World in the Wires*, John Wiley & Sons, Chichester.

Klein, Naomi 2000, *No Logo*, Flamingo, London.

Kleinwächter, Wolfgang 2002, 'Trilateralism, Co-regulation and Governance in the Global Information Society', in M. Raboy (ed.), *Global Media Policy in the New Millennium*, University of Luton Press, pp. 55–76.

Kline, Stephen, Dyer-Witheford, Nick, and de Peuter, Greg 2003, *Digital Play: The Interaction of Technology, Culture and Marketing*, McGill-Queen's University Press, Montreal and Kingston.

Knights, David, Noble, Faith, Vurdubakis, Theo, and Willmott, Hugh 2002, 'Allegories of Creative Destruction: Technology and Organisation in Narratives of the e-Economy', in S. Woolgar (ed.), *Virtual Society? Technology, Cyberbole, Reality*, Oxford University Press, Oxford, pp. 99–114.

Kong, Lily, Gibson, Chris, Khoo, Louisa-May, and Semple, Anna-Marie 2006, 'Knowledges of the Creative Economy: Towards a Relational Geography of Diffusion and Adaptation in Asia', *Asia Pacific Viewpoints* 47(2): 173–94.

Kotkin, Joel 2006, *The City: A Global History*, New York, Modern Library, New York.

Kress, Gunther 1997, 'Visual and Verbal Modes of Representation in Electronically Mediated Communication: The Potentials of New Forms of Text', in I. Snyder (ed.), *From Page to Screen: Taking Literacy into the Electronic Era*, Allen & Unwin, Sydney, pp. 53–79.

Kumar, Krishan 1995, *From Post-Industrial to Post-Modern Society: New Theories of the Contemporary World*, Blackwell, Oxford.

——2005, *From Post-Industrial to Post-Modern Society: New Theories of the Contemporary World*, 2nd edn, Blackwell, Oxford.

Kuo, David 2001, *Dot.Bomb: My Days and Nights as an Internet Goliath*, Brown & Co., New York.

Lambert, Joe 2002, *Digital Storytelling: Capturing Lives, Creating Community*, Digital Diner Press, Berkeley CA.

Lamberton, Don 1971, 'Introduction', in D. Lamberton (ed.), *Economics of Information and Knowledge*, Penguin, London, pp. 5–17.

——1999, 'Information: Pieces, Batches, or Flows?', in S.C. Dow and P.E. Earl (eds), *Economic Organization and Economic Knowledge: Essays in Honour of Brian J. Loasby*, vol. 1, Edward Elgar, Cheltenham, pp. 209–24.

Landry, Charles 2000, *The Creative City*, Earthscan, London.

——2005, 'London as a Creative City', in J. Hartley (ed.), *Creative Industries*, Blackwell, Oxford, pp. 233–43.

Lash, Scott 1994, *Economies of Signs and Space*, Sage, London.

——2002, *Critique of Information*, Sage, London.

——, and Urry, John 1989, *The End of Organised Capitalism*, Polity Press, Cambridge.

Lasn, Kalle 2000, *Culture Jam*, Quill, New York.

Lapsley, Robert, and Westlake, Michael 2006, *Film Theory: An Introduction*, 2nd edn, Manchester University Press.

Lavery, David (ed.) 2002, *This Thing of Ours: Investigating the Sopranos*, Columbia University Press, New York.

Leadbeater, Charles 2000, *Living on Thin Air: The New Economy*, Penguin, London.

——2007, *We-Think: The Power of Mass Creativity*, <www.wethinkthebook.net/home.aspx>, accessed 18 April 2007.

——, and Miller, Paul 2004, *The Pro-Am Revolution: How Enthusiasts are Changing our Economy and Society*, DEMOS, London.

Lee, Terence 2006, 'Going Online: Journalism and Civil Society in Singapore', in A. Romano and M. Bromley (eds), *Journalism and Democracy in Asia*, Routledge, London, pp. 15–27.

Leo, Patrice, and Lee, Terence 2004, 'The "New" Singapore: Mediating Culture and Creativity', *Continuum: Journal of Media and Cultural Studies* 18(2): 205–18.

Legrain, Philippe 2002, *Open World: The Truth About Globalisation*, Abacus, London.

Leiner, Barry, Cerf, Vinton, Clark, David, Kahn, Robert, Kleinrock, Leonard, Lynch, Daniel, Postel, Jon, Roberts, Larry, and Wolff, Stephen 2003, 'A Brief History of the Internet', <www.isoc.org/internet/history/brief.shtml>, Version 3.32, last revised 10 October 2003, accessed 3 December 2006.

Lenhart, Amanda, and Fox, Susannah 2006, *Bloggers: A Portrait of the Internet's New Story Tellers*, Pew Internet and American Life Project, Washington DC, <www.pewinternet.org/PPF/r/186/report_display.asp>, published 19 July, accessed 25 March 2007.

Lessig, Lawrence 2000, *Code and other Laws of Cyberspace*, Basic Books, New York.

——2001, *The Future of Ideas: The Fate of the Commons in a Connected World*, Vintage Books, New York.

——2004, *Free Culture: How Big Media Uses Technology and the Law to Lock Down Culture and Control Creativity*, Penguin, New York.

Levinson, Paul 1997, *The Soft Edge: A Natural History and Future of the Information Revolution*, Routledge, New York.

Lévy, Pierre 1997, *Collective Intelligence: Mankind's Emerging World in Cyberspace*, Plenum Trade, New York.

——1998, *Becoming Virtual: Reality in the Digital Age*, Plenum Trade, New York.

Lewis, Justin 1990, *Art, Culture and Enterprise: The Politics of Art and the Cultural Industries*, Routledge, London.

Lewis, Michael 2001, *The Future Just Happened*, Coronet Books, London.

Liestøl, Eve 2003, 'Computer Games and the Ludic Structure of Interpretation', in G. Liestøl, A. Morrison, and T. Rasmussen (eds), *Digital Media Revisited*, MIT Press, Cambridge MA, pp. 327–57.

Lievrouw, Leah, and Livingstone, Sonia 2005, 'Introduction to the Updated Student Edition', in L. Lievrouw and S. Livingstone (eds), *The Handbook of New Media: Social Shaping and Consequences of ICTs*, 2nd edn, Sage, London, pp. 1–14.

Lister, Martin, Dovey, Jon, Giddings, Seth, Grant, Iain, and Kelly, Kieran 2003, *New Media: A Critical Introduction*, Routledge, London.

Litman, Jessica 2001, *Digital Copyright*, Prometheus Books, Amherst NY.

Livingstone, Sonia 1998, *Making Sense of Television*, 2nd edn, Routledge, London.

——1999, 'New Media, New Audiences', *New Media and Society* 1(1): 59–68.

——2002, *Young People and New Media*, Sage, London.

——2005, 'Critical Debates in Internet Studies: Reflections on an Emergent Field', in J. Curran and M. Gurevitch (eds), *Mass Media and Society*, 4th edn, Hodder Arnold, London, pp. 9–28.

Lockard, Joseph 1997, 'Progressive Politics, Electronic Individualism and the Myth of Virtual Community', in D. Porter (ed.), *Internet Culture*, Routledge, New York, pp. 219–32.

Lovink, Geert 2002, *Dark Fiber: Tracking Critical Internet Culture*, MIT Press, Cambridge MA.

Lovelock, Peter, and Ure, John 2002, 'The New Economy: Internet, Telecommunications and Electronic Commerce?', in L. Lievrouw and S. Livingstone (eds), *Handbook of New Media*, Sage, London, pp. 350–68.

Lyon, David 1988, *The Information Society: Issues and Illusions*, Polity Press, Cambridge.

——2002, *Surveillance Society: Monitoring Everyday Life*, Open University Press, Buckingham.

MacKenzie, Donald, and Wacjman, Judy 1999, 'Introductory Essay: The Social Shaping of Technology', in D. MacKenzie and J. Wacjman (eds), *The Social Shaping of Technology*, 2nd edn, Open University Press, Milton Keynes, pp. 3–27.

Madden, Christopher 2001, 'Using "Economic" Impact Studies in Arts and Cultural Advocacy: A Cautionary Note', *Media International Australia* 98, February: 161–78.

Malaysiakini 2007, 'About Malaysiakini.com', <www.malaysiakini.com/pages/general/>, accessed 27 April 2007.

Malmstein, Ernst 2001, *Boo Hoo: A Dotcom Story from Concept to Catastrophe*, Random House, New York.

Mander, Jerry, and Goldsmith, Edward 1996, *The Case Against the Global Economy: And for a Turn Toward the Local*, Sierra Club Books, San Francisco.

Marshall, David (ed.) 2006, *The Celebrity Culture Reader*, London, Routledge.

Marvin, Carolyn 1988, *When Old Technologies Were New: Thinking about Electric Communication in the 19th Century*, Oxford University Press, New York.

Mattelart, Armand 2003, *The Information Society: An Introduction*, trans. S.G. Taponier and J.A. Cohen, Sage, London.

Mayfield, Antony 2007, 'What is Social Media?', *Spannerworks e-Books*, <www.spannerworks.com/ebooks>, accessed 28 April 2007.

Mayfield, Ross 2006, 'Power Law of Participation', *Ross Mayfield's Weblog: Markets, Technology and Musings*, <http://ross.typepad.com/blog/2006/04/power_law_of_pa.html>, published 27 April, accessed 27 December 2006.

McChesney, Robert W. 1999, *Rich Media, Poor Democracy: Communication Politics in Dubious Times*, New Press, New York.

——2000, 'So Much for the Magic of Technology and the Free Market: The World Wide Web and the Corproate Media System', in A. Herman and T. Swiss (eds), *The World Wide Web and Contemporary Cultural Theory*, Routledge, New York, pp. 5–35.

——2003, 'Corporate Media, Global Capitalism', in S. Cottle (ed.), *Media Organization and Production*, Sage, London, pp. 27–40.

——, and Schiller, Dan 2003, *The Political Economy of International Communciation: Foundations for the Emerging Global Debate about Media Ownership and Regulation*, United Nations Research Institute for Social Development, Technology, Business and Society Programme Paper No. 11, October.

McKay, George 1998, 'DIY Culture: Notes Towards an Intro', in G. McKay (ed.), *DIY Culture: Party and Protest in Nineties Britain*, Verso, London.

McLuhan, Eric, and Zingrone, Frank (eds) 1997, *Essential McLuhan*, Routledge, London.

McLuhan, Marshall 1964, *Understanding Media: The Extensions of Man*, Mentor Books, New York.

——, and Fiore, Quentin 1967, *The Medium is the Message*, Bantam, New York.

McMillan, Sally 2005, 'Exploring Models of Interactivity from Multiple Research Traditions; Users, Documents and Systems', in L. Lievrouw and S. Livingstone (eds), *Handbook of New Media*, 2nd edn, Sage, London, pp. 205–29.

McNair, Brian 2003, 'From Control to Chaos: Toward a New Sociology of Journalism', *Media, Culture and Society* 25(6): 547–55.

——2006, *Cultural Chaos: Journalism, News and Power in a Globalised World*, Routledge, New York.

McNamara, Andrew 2002, 'How "Creative Industries" Evokes the Legacy of Modernist Visual Art', *Media International Australia* 102, February: 66–76.

McPhail, Thomas, and McPhail, Brenda 1990, *Communication: The Canadian Experience*, Coop Clark Pitman, Toronto.

McQuail, Dennis 2002, *Mass Communication Theory*, 3rd edn, Routledge, London.

——2005, *McQuail's Mass Communication Theory*, 5th edn, Sage, London.

McQuire, Scott 2001, 'When is Art IT?', in H. Brown, G. Lovink, H. Merrick, N. Rossiter, D. Teh, and M. Willson (eds), *Fibreculture Reader: Politics of a Digital Present*, Fibreculture Publications, Melbourne, pp. 205–13.

McRobbie, Angela 2005, 'Clubs to Companies', in J. Hartley (ed.), *Creative Industries*, Blackwell, Oxford, pp. 375–93.

Meadows, Daniel 2003, 'Digital Storytelling: Research-based Practice in New Media', *Visual Communication* 2(2): 189–93.

Melody, William 1996, 'Towards a Framework for Designing Information Society Policies', *Telecommunciations Policy* 20(4): 243–59.

Menser, Michael, and Aronowitz, Stanley 1996, 'On Cultural Studies, Science, and Technology', in S. Aronowitz, B. Martinsons, and M. Menser (eds), *Technoscience and Cyberculture*, Routledge, New York, pp. 7–36.

Mercer, Colin 1994, 'Cultural Policy: Research and the Governmental Imperative', *Media Information Australia* 73, August, pp. 16–22.

Merrin, Chris 2005, *Baudrillard and the Media: A Critical Introduction*, Polity, Cambridge.

Miège, Bernard 2004, 'Capitalism and Communication: A New Era of Society or the Accentuation of Long-Term Tendencies?', in A. Calabrese and C. Sparks (eds), *Toward a Political Economy of Culture: Capitalism and Communication in the Twenty-First Century*, Rowman & Littlefield, Lanham MD, pp. 83–94.

Miles, Ian 1997, 'Cyberspace as Product Space: Interactive Learning about Interactive Media', *Futures* 29(9): 769–89.

Miller, Daniel 1998, 'Conclusion: A Theory of Virtualism', in J. Carrier and D. Miller (eds), *Virtualism: A New Political Economy*, Oxford, Berg, pp. 187–216.

——, and Slater, Don 2000, *The Internet: An Ethnographic Approach*, Routledge, London.

Miller, Paul 2004, 'The Rise of Network Campaigning', in H. McCarthy, P. Miller, and P. Skidmore (eds), *Network Logic: Who Governs in an Interconnected World?*, DEMOS, London, pp. 207–17.

Miller, Toby 2007, *Cultural Citizenship: Cosmopolitanism, Consumerism and Television in a Neoliberal Age*, Temple University Press, Philadelphia.

——, Govil, Nitin, McMurria, John, and Maxwell, Richard 2001, *Global Hollywood*, London, British Film Institute.

——, Govil, Nitin, McMurria, John, and Maxwell, Richard 2005, *Global Hollywood 2*, BFI Publishing, London.

Mills, C. Wright 1956, *The Power Elite*, Oxford University Press, New York.

Milner, Andrew 2006, 'Theorize This! Cultural Studies versus Utilitarianism', *Continuum: Journal of Media and Cultural Studies* 20(1): 111–25.

Mitchell, William, Inouye, Alan, and Blumenthal, Marjory 2003, *Beyond Productivity: Information Technology, Innovation, and Creativity*, National Research Council of the National Academies, National Academies Press, Washington DC.

MKW Wirtschaftsforschung GmbH 2001, *Exploitation and Development of the Job Potential in the Cultural Sector in the Age of Digitization: Final Report*. Commissioned by European Commission DG Employment and Social Affairs, MKWCmbH, Berlin, June.

MobileTracker 2005, 'Mobile Phone Users to hit 2 Billion this Year', 18 January <www.mobiletracker.net/archives/2005/01/18/2-billion-mobile-phones>, accessed 10 December 2006.

Mommaas, Hans 2004, 'Creative Clusters and the Post-Industrial City: Towards the Remapping of Urban Cultural Policy', *Urban Studies* 41(3): 507–32.

Montgomery, Lucy, and Keane, Michael 2006, 'Learning to Love the Market: Copyright, Culture and China', in P. Thomas and J. Servaes (eds), *Intellectual Property Rights and Communications in Asia*, Sage, New Delhi, pp. 130–48.

Moore, Christopher 2005, 'Creative Choices: Changes to Australian Copyright Law and the Future of the Public Domain', *Media International Australia* 114, February: 71–82.

Mosco, Vincent 1996, *The Political Economy of Communication*, Sage, Thousand Oaks CA.

——1997, 'Citizenship and the Technopoles', *Javnost (The Public)* 4(4): 35–46.

——2000, 'Webs of Myth and Power; Connectivity and the New Computer Technopoles', in A. Herman and T. Swiss (eds), *The World Wide Web and Contemporary Cultural Theory*, Routledge, New York, pp. 37–60.

——2004, *The Digital Sublime: Myth, Power and Cyberspace*, MIT Press, Cambridge MA.

MTI (Ministry of Trade and Industry) 2003, *Economic Contributions of Singapore's Creative Industries, Government of Singapore*, Economic Survey of Singapore First Quarter.

Murdock, Graham, and Golding, Peter 2004, 'Dismantling the Digital Divide: Rethinking the Dynamics of Participation and Excluson', in A. Calabrese and C. Sparks (eds), *Towards a Political Economy of Culture: Capitalism and Communication in the Twenty-first Century*, Rowman & Littlefield, Lanham MD, pp. 244–260.

Murphy, Brian Martin 2002, 'A Critical History of the Internet', in G. Elmer (ed.), *Critical Perspectives on the Internet*, Rowman & Littlefield, Lanham MD, pp. 27–45.

Murray, Janet H. 1997, *Hamlet on the Holodeck: The Future of Narrative in Cyberspace*, MIT Press, Cambridge MA.

Musser, John, and O'Reilly, Tim 2007, *Web 2.0: Principles and Practices*, O'Reilly Radar, San Francisco.

Nakamura, Lisa 2000, '"Where Do You Want to Go to Today?" Cybernetic Tourism, the Internet, and Transnationality', in B. Kolko, L. Nakamura, and G.B. Rodman (eds), *Race in Cyberspace*, Routledge, New York, pp. 15–26.

Negroponte, Nicholas 1995, *Being Digital*, Hodder & Stoughton, Sydney.

Negus, Keith, and Pickering, Michael 2004, *Creativity, Communication, and Cultural Value*, Sage, London.

Newson, Emily 2006, 'Celebrity Mags Embrace the Internet', *Cardiff University Online Journalism*, <journalism.cf.ac.uk/2007/online/index.php?id=parse-195-0-0-251&article=551&author=Emily+Newson>, posted 15 December, accessed 6 May 2007.

Newman, James 2002, 'The Myth of the Ergodic Videogame', *Games Studies* 2(1): 1–8.

Nie, Norman, and Erbring, Lutz 2000, *Internet and Society: A Preliminary Report*, Stanford Institute for the Quantitative Study of Society, Stanford CA.

Nielsen, Jakob 2000, *Designing Web Usability*, New Riders, Indianapolis IN.

Nielsén, Tobias 2004, *Understanding the Experience Economy: A Swedish Perspective on Creativity*, QNB Analys & Kommunikation AB, Stockholm.

Nip, Joyce 2006, 'Changing Connections: The News Media, the Government and the People in China's SARS Epidemic', in A. Romano and M. Bromley (eds), *Journalism and Democracy in Asia*, Routledge, London, pp. 28–40.

Noam, Eli 1991, *Television in Europe*, Oxford University Press, New York.

Nora, Simon, and Minc, Alain 1981, *The Computerisation of Society*, MIT Press, Cambridge MA.

Norman, Donald 1998, *The Invisible Computer*, MIT Press, Cambridge MA.

Norris, Pippa 2001, *Digital Divide: Civic Engagement, Information Poverty, and the Internet Worldwide*, Cambridge University Press.

Northfield, Dianne 1999, *The Information Policy Maze: Global Challenges—National Responses*, Centre for International Research into Communications and Information Technologies, Melbourne.

Nussbaum, Bruce 2005, 'Get Creative! How to Build Innovative Companies', *Business Week*, 1 August, <www.businessweek.com/magazine/content/05_31/b3945401.htm#>, accessed 29 December 2005.

Oakley, Kate 2004, 'Not So Cool Britannia: The Role of the Creative Industries in Economic Development', *International Journal of Cultural Studies* 7(1): 67–77.

O'Brien, Damien 2007, 'Viacom v. YouTube and Google: Copyright Challenges for User Generated Intermediaries'. Paper presented to ECUPL-QUT Legal and Policy Framework for the Digital Content Industry Conference, Shanghai, 28–29 May.

O'Connor, Justin 1999, 'Popular Culture, Reflexivity and Urban Change', in J. Verwijnen and P. Lehtovuori (eds), *Creative Cities*, University of Art and Design Publishing Unit, Helsinki.

——, and Gu, Xin 2006, 'A New Modernity? The Arrival of "Creative Industries" in China', *International Journal of Cultural Studies* 9(3): 271–83.

OECD (Organisation for Economic Co-operation and Development) 1996, *The Knowledge-Based Economy*, OECD, Paris.

——1999, *The Economic and Social Impacts of Electronic Commerce: Preliminary Findings and Research Agenda*, OECD, Paris.

——2003, *The e-Government Imperative*, OECD, Paris.

O'Neil, Mathieu 2006, 'Rebels for the System? Virus Writers, General Intellect, Cyberpunk and Criminal Capitalism', *Continuum: Journal of Media and Cultural Studies* 20(2): 225–41.

O'Regan, Tom 2002, 'Too Much Culture, Too Little Culture: Trends and Issues for Cultural Policy-Making', *Media International Australia* 102, February: 9–24.

O'Reilly, Tim 2005, 'What is Web 2.0: Design Patterns and Business Models for the Next Generation of Software', <www.oreillynet.com/pub/a/oreilly/tim/news/2005/09/30/what-is-web-20.html>, published 30 September, accessed 17 March 2007.

——2006, 'Web 2.0 Compact Definition: Trying Again', *O'Reilly Radar*, <http://radar.oreilly.com/archives/2006/12/web_20_compact.html>, posted 12 October, accessed 17 March 2007.

Orlowski, Andrew 2005, 'On Creativity, Computers, and Copyright', *The Register*, <www.theregister.co.uk/2005/07/21/creativity/>, published 21 July, accessed 22 May 2007.

Ó Siochrú, Seán, 2004, 'Civil Society Participation in the WSIS Process: Promises and Reality', *Continuum: Journal of Media and Cultural Studies* 18(3): 330–44.

——, and Girard, Bruce, with Mahan, Amy 2003, *Global Media Governance: A Beginner's Guide*, Rowman & Littlefield, Lanham MD.

Osborne, Thomas 2003, 'Against "Creativity": A Philistine Rant', *Economy and Society* 32(4): 507–25.

Outing, Steve 2005, 'The 11 Layers of Citizen Journalism', <www.poynter.org/content/content_print.asp?id=83126&custom=>, posted 11 June, accessed 28 April 2007.

Papacharissi, Zizi 2002, 'The Virtual Sphere: The Internet as a Public Sphere', *New Media and Society* 4(1): 9–27.

Paré, Daniel 2003, *Internet Governance in Transition: Who is the Master of this Domain?*, Rowman & Littlefield, Lanham MD.

Park, Myung-Jin, Kim, Chang-Mai, and Sohn, Byung-Woo 2000, 'Modernization, Globalization and the Powerful State: The Korean Media', in J. Curran and M.-J. Park (eds), *Dewesternizing Media Studies*, Routledge, London, pp. 111–23.

Peck, Jamie 2005, 'Struggling with the Creative Class', *International Journal of Urban and Regional Research* 29(4): 740–70.

Penfold, Carolyn 2003, 'Global Technology meets Local Environment: State Attempts to Control Internet Content', in K.C. Ho, R. Kluver, and K.C.C. Yang (eds), *Asia.com: Asian Encounters the Internet*, RoutledgeCurzon, London, pp. 83–96.

Penley, Constance, and Ross, Andrew 1991, *Technoculture*, University of Minnesota Press, Minneapolis MN.

Perelman, Michael 2002, *Steal This Idea: Intellectual Property Rights and the Corporate Confiscation of Creativity*, Palgrave, New York.

PMSEIC (Prime Minister's Science, Engineering, and Innovation Council) 2005, *The Role of Creativity in the Innovation Economy*, Imagine Australia, published 2 December.

Podolny, Joel, and Page, Karen 1998, 'Network Forms of Organization', *Annual Review of Sociology* 24: 57–76.

Pool, Ithiel de Sola 1983, *Technologies of Freedom*, Belknap Press, Cambridge MA.

Porter, Michael 1998, 'Clusters and the New Economics of Competition', *Harvard Business Review* 76(6): 77–91.

Poster, Mark 1990, *The Mode of Information: Poststructuralism and Social Context*, Polity Press, Cambridge.

——1995, *The Second Media Age*, Polity Press, Cambridge.

——2001, *What's the Matter with the Internet?*, University of Minnesota Press, Minneapolis MN.

——2005, 'Culture and New Media', in L. Lievrouw and S. Livingstone (eds), *Handbook of New Media*, 2nd edn, Sage, London, pp. 134–40.

——2006, *Information Please: Culture and Politics in the Age of Digital Machines*, Duke University Press, Durham NC.

Postman, Neil 1993, *Technopoly: The Surrender of Culture to Technology*, Vintage, New York.

Potts, Jason 2003, 'The *Prometheus* School of Information Economics', *Prometheus* 21(4): 477–86.

Pratt, Andy 1998, 'A "Third Way" for the Creative Industries?', *International Journal of Communications Law and Policy* 4(1), <www.digital-law.net/IJCLP/1_1998/ijclp_webdoc_4_1_1998.html>, accessed 29 May 2007.

Prensky, Marc 2001, 'Digital Natives, Digital Immigrants', <www.marcprensky.com/writing/Prensky%20-%20Digital%20Natives,%20Digital%20Immigrants%20-%20Part1.pdf>, accessed 2 December 2006.

Putnam, Robert 1995, 'Tuning In, Tuning Out: The Strange Disappearance of Social Capital in America', *Political Science and Politics* 28(4): 664–88.

——2000, *Bowling Alone: The Collapse and Revival of American Community*, Simon & Schuster, New York.

Quah, Danny 2003, 'Digital Goods and the New Economy', in D.C. Jones (ed.), *New Economy Handbook*, Elsevier, Amsterdam, pp. 289–321.

Rainie, Lee, and Bell, Peter 2004, 'The Numbers That Count', *New Media and Society* 6(1): 44–54.

Ramsay, Randolph 2007, 'GDC '07: Chris Taylor says "No more overtime"', *Gamespot AU*, 8 March, <au.gamespot.com/news/6167123.html?msg_sort=1>, accessed 7 April 2007.

Raymond, Eric 1998, 'The Cathedral and the Bazaar', *First Monday* 3(3), <www.firstmonday.dk/issues/issue3_3/raymond/>, accessed 28 December 2003.

Redden, Guy 2003, 'Read the Whole Thing: Journalism, Weblogs and the Re-Mediation of the War in Iraq', *Media International Australia*, 109: 153–65.

Redhead, Steve 2004, *Paul Virilio: Theorist for an Accelerated Culture*, Edinburgh University Press.

Reeves, Byron, and Nass, Clifford 2002, *The Media Equation: How People Treat Computers, Televisions, and New Media Like Real People and Places*, Cambridge University Press.

Rennie, Elinor 2003, '"Trespassers are Welcome": Access and Community Television Policy', *Javnost (The Public)* 10(1): 49–62.

——2006, *Community Media: A Global Introduction*, Rowman & Littlefield, Lanham MD.

Rheingold, Howard 1994, *The Virtual Community: Finding Connection in a Computerized World*, Secker & Warburg, London.

Rice, Ronald 1999, 'Artifacts and Paradoxes in New Media', *New Media and Society* 1(1): 24–32.

——2002, 'Primary Issues in Internet Use: Access, Civic and Community Involvement, and Social Interaction and Expression', in L. Lievrouw and S. Livingstone (eds), *Handbook of New Media*, Sage, London, pp. 105–29.

——, and Haythornthwaite, Carolyn 2005, 'Perspectives on Internet Use: Access, Involvement and Interaction', in L. Lievrouw and S. Livingstone (eds), *Handbook of New Media*, Sage, London, 2nd edn, pp. 92–113.

Ricks, Christopher 1968, 'McLuhanism', in R. Rosenthal (ed.), *McLuhan: Pro & Con*, Penguin, Baltimore MD.

Rifkin, Jeremy 2000, *The Age of Access: How the Shift from Ownership to Access is Transforming Modern Life*, Penguin, London.

Rimmer, Matthew 2003a, 'Virtual Countries: Internet Domain Names and Geographical Terms', *Media International Australia* 106, February: 124–36.

——2003b, 'The Dead Poets Society; The Copyright Term and the Public Domain', *First Monday*, <www.firstmonday.org/issues/issue8_6/rimmer/index.html>, 8(6), accessed 25 August 2003.

Robins, Kevin, and Webster, Frank 1999, *Times of the Technoculture: From the Information Society to the Virtual Life*, Routledge, London.

Robinson, Evan 2005, 'Why Crunch Mode Doesn't Work: 6 Lessons', *International Game Developers Association—Articles*, <www.igda.org/articles/erobinson_crunch. php>, accessed 7 April 2007.

Robinson, Ken 2001, *Out of Our Minds: Learning to be Creative*, Capstone, Oxford.

Rogers, Everett 2003, *Diffusion of Innovations*, 5th edn, Free Press, New York.

Rogers, Mark, Epstein, Michael, and Reeves, Jimmie 2002, 'The Sopranos as HBO Band Equity: The Art of Commerce in the Age of Digital Reproduction', in D. Lavery (ed.), *This Thing of Ours: Investigating the Sopranos*, Columbia University Press, New York, pp. 42–57.

Romano, Angela 2003, *Politics and the Press in Indonesia: Understanding an Evolving Political Culture*, RoutledgeCurzon, London.

Romer, Paul 1994, 'The Origins of Endogenous Growth', *Journal of Economic Perspectives* 8(1): 3–22.

——1995, 'Interview with Peter Robinson', *Forbes* 155(12): 66–70.

——2007 'Economic Growth', in D. Henderson (ed.), *The Concise Encyclopedia of Economics*, <www.econlib.org/library/enc/EconomicGrowth.html>, accessed 14 February 2007.

Rosen, Jay 2000, 'Questions and Answers about Public Journalism', *Journalism Studies* 1(4): 679–83.

——2007, 'PressThink: Ghost of Democracy in the Media Machine', <journalism. nyu.edu/pubzone/weblogs/pressthink/>, accessed 28 April 2007.

Rossignol, Jim 2006, 'Sex, Fame and PC Baangs: How the Orient plays host to PC gaming's strangest culture', *PC Gamer UK*, <http://rossignol.cream.org/?p=284>, posted 4 January, accessed 15 July 2007.

Rossiter, Ned 2006, *Organised Networks: Media Theory, Creative Labour, New Institutions*, NAi Publishers, Institute of Network Cultures, Amsterdam.

Rushkoff, Douglas 1996, *Playing the Future: How Kids' Culture Can Teach Us to Thrive in an Age of Chaos*, HarperCollins, New York.

Rutter, Jason, and Bryce, Jo (eds) 2006, *Understanding Digital Games*, Sage, Thousand Oaks CA.

Sale, Kirkpatrick 1995, *Rebels Against the Future: The Luddites and the War on the Industrial Revolution—Lessons for the Computer Age*, Addison-Wesley, Reading MA.

Sassen, Saskia 1991, *The Global City: New York, London, Tokyo*, Princeton University Press.

——1999, 'The State and the New Geography of Power', in A. Calabrese and J.-C. Burgelman (eds), *Communication, Citizenship, and Social Policy: Rethinking the Limits of the Welfare State*, Rowman & Littlefield, Lanham MD, pp. 17–31.

——2001, *The Global City: New York, London, Tokyo*, Princeton University Press.

Sawyer, Ben 2002, 'The Next Ages of Games Development', *The Adrenalin Vault, Developer's Corner*, <www.avault.com/developer/>, posted 30 September, accessed 28 October 2002.

Schaffer, Jan 2007, *Citizen Media: Fad or the Future of News? The Rise and Prospects of Hyper-Local Journalism*, <www.kcnn.org/research/citizen_media_report/>, accessed 6 May 2007.

Schiller, Dan 2000, *Digital Capitalism: Networking the Global Market System*, MIT Press, Cambridge MA.

——2006, 'Digital Capitalism: A Status Report on the Corporate Commonwealth of Information', in A.N. Valdivia (ed.), *A Companion to Media Studies*, Blackwell, Malden MA., pp. 137–56.

Schiller, Herbert 1995, 'The Global Information Highway: Project for an Ungovernable World', in J. Brook and I.A. Boal (eds), *Resisting the Virtual Life: The Culture and Politics of Information*, City Lights, San Francisco, pp. 17–33.

Schuler, Douglas 1996, *New Community Networks: Wired for Change*, Addison-Wesley, Reading MA.

Sclove, Richard 1995, *Technology and Democracy*, Guilford Press, New York.

Scott, Allen 2004, 'Cultural-Products Industries and Urban Economic Development: Prospects for Growth and Market Contestation in Global Context', *Urban Affairs Review* 39(4): 461–90.

Scott, Ben 2005, 'A Contemporary History of Digital Journalism', *Television and New Media* 6(1): 89–126.

Scott, John 1986, *Capitalist Property and Financial Power: A Comparative Study of Britain, the United States, and Japan*, Harvester Wheatsheaf Press, Brighton.

——1991, *Social Network Analysis: A Handbook*, Sage, London.

Seaman, Bruce 2000, 'Arts Impact Studies: A Fashionable Excess', in G. Bradford, M. Gary, and G. Wallach (eds), *The Politics of Culture: Policy Perspectives for Individuals, Institutions and Communities*, New Press, New York, pp. 266–85.

Sell, Susan 2002, 'Intellectual Property Rights', in D. Held and A. McGrew (eds), *Governing Globalization: Power, Authority, and Global Governance*, Polity Press, Cambridge, pp. 171–88.

Seltzer, K., and Bentley, T. 2000, *The Creative Age: Knowledge and Skills for the New Economy*, DEMOS, London.

Shanker, Daya 2006, 'Copyright, Competition Policy and Prevention of Monopolistic Abuses in the TRIPS Agreement', in P.N. Thomas and J. Servaes (eds), *Intellectual Property Rights and Communications in Asia: Conflicting Traditions*, Sage, New Delhi, pp. 79–102.

Shapiro, Carl, and Varian, Hal 1999, *Information Rules: A Strategic Guide to the Network Economy*, Harvard Business School Press, Boston MA.

Shaw, Russell 2005, 'Web 2.0? It Doesn't Exist', <http://blogs.zdnet.com/ip-telephony/?p=805>, posted 17 December, accessed 17 March 2007.

Shenton, Karla, and McNeeley, Todd 1997, *The Virtual Communities Companion*, Coriolis Group Books, Albany NY.

Shirky, Clay 2003, 'Social Software and the Politics of Groups', <http://shirky.com/writings/group_politics.html>, posted 9 March 2003, accessed 8 November 2005.

Sholle, David 2002, 'Disorganizing the "New Technology"', in G. Elmer (ed.), *Critical Perspectives on the Internet*, Rowman & Littlefield, Lanham MD, pp. 3–26.

Silver, David 2000, 'Looking Backwards, Looking Forward: Cyberculture Studies 1990–2000', in D. Gauntlett (ed.), *Web.studies: Rewiring Media Studies for the Digital Age*, Arnold, London, pp. 19–30.

Siwek, Stephen 2002, *Copyright Industries in the U.S. Economy: The 2002 Report*, International Intellectual Property Alliance, Washington DC.

——2004, *Copyright Industries in the U.S. Economy*, prepared for the International Intellectual Property Alliance, Washington DC.

Slater, Don 2002, 'Social Relationships and Identity Online and Offline', in L. Lievrouw and S. Livingstone (eds), *The Handbook of New Media*, Sage, London, pp. 533–46.

Smith, Anthony 1991, 'Towards a Global Culture?', in M. Featherstone (ed.), *Global Culture, Nationalism, Globalization and Modernity*, Sage, London, pp. 171–92.

Sood, Ashish, and Tellis, Gerard 2005, 'Technological Evolution and Radical Innovation', *Journal of Marketing* 69, July: 152–65.

Stadler, Felix 2006, *Manuel Castells and the Theory of the Network Society*, Polity Press, Cambridge.

Stein, Joel 2007, 'Have Something to Say? I Don't Care', *LATimes.com*, <www.latimes.com/news/printedition/opinion/la-oe-stein2jan02,1,918996.column?track=rss&ctrack=1&cset=true>, published 2 January, accessed 28 April 2007.

Stein, Laura, and Sinha, Nikhil 2002, 'New Media and Communication Policy: The Role of the State in the Twenty-First Century', in L. Lievrouw and S. Livingstone (eds), *Handbook of New Media*, Sage, London, pp. 410–31.

Sternberg, Robert (ed.) 1999, *Handbook of Creativity*, Cambridge University Press.

Stevenson, Deborah 2004, '"Civic Gold Rush": Cultural Planning and the Third Way', *International Journal of Cultural Policy* 10(1): 119–31.

Stevenson, Nick 1995, *Understanding Media Culture: Social Theory and Mass Communication*, Sage, London.

Stokman, Franz, Ziegler, Rolf, and Scott, John 1985, *Networks of Corporate Power: A Comparative Analysis of Ten Countries*, Polity Press, Cambridge.

Stoll, Clifford 1995, *Silicon Snake Oil: Second Thoughts on the Information Highway*, Macmillan, London.

Storper, Michael 1997, *The Regional World*, Guilford, New York.

Streeter, Thomas 1987, 'The Cable Fable Revisited: Discourse, Policy, and the Making of Cable Television', *Critical Studies in Mass Communication* 4: 71–97.

——2004, 'Romanticism in Business Culture: The Internet, the 1990s, and the Origins of Irrational Exuberance', in A. Calabrese and C. Sparks (eds), *Towards a Political Economy of Culture: Capitalism and Communication in the Twenty-First Century*, Rowman & Littlefield, Lanham MD, pp. 286–306.

Streitz, Norbert, and Nixon, Paddy 2005, 'The Disappearing Computer', *Communications of the ACM* 48(3): 33–5.

Sunstein, Cass 2002, 'The Law of Group Polarization', *Journal of Political Philosophy* 10(2): 175–95.

Tapscott, Don 1998, *Growing Up Digital: The Rise of the Net Generation*, McGraw Hill, New York.

Taylor, Peter, Walker, D.R.F., and Beaverstock, Jonathon 2002, 'Firms and their Global Service Networks', in S. Sassen (ed.), *Global Networks, Linked Cities*, Routledge, New York, pp. 93–115.

Tellis, Gerard J., and Golder, Peter G. 1996, 'First to Market, First to Fail? Real Causes of Enduring Market Leadership', *Sloan Management Review* 37(2): 65–75.

Terranova, Tiziana 2004, *Network Culture: Politics for the Information Age*, Pluto Press, London.

Thompson, Grahame 2003, *Between Hierarchies and Markets: The Logic and Limits of Network Forms of Organization*, Oxford University Press, Oxford.

Thompson, John 1991, *Ideology and Modern Culture*, Polity Press, Cambridge.

——1995, *The Media and Modernity: A Social Theory of the Media*, Polity Press, Cambridge.

Throsby, David 2001, *Economics and Culture*, Cambridge University Press.

Thussu, Daya Kishan 2006, *International Communication: Continuity and Change*, Arnold, London.

Toffler, Alvin 1970, *Future Shock*, Random House, New York.

——1980, *The Third Wave*, Bantam Books, New York.

Tofts, Darren 2005, *Interzone: Media Arts in Australia*, Craftsman House, Melbourne.

Tsagarousianou, Roza, Tambini, Damian, and Bryan, Cathy (eds) 1998, *Cyberdemocracy: Technology, Cities and Civic Networks*, Routledge, London.

Turban, Efraim, Lee, Jae, Kung, David, and Chung, Michael 2000, *Electronic Commerce: A Managerial Perspective*, Prentice-Hall, Upper Saddle River NJ.

Turkle, Sherry 1995, *Life on the Screen: Identity in the Age of the Internet*, Simon & Schuster, New York.

Turner, Graeme 1990, *British Cultural Studies: An Introduction*, Unwin Hyman, Boston MA.

——1999, 'Tabloidisation, Journalism and the Possibility of Critique', *International Journal of Cultural Studies* 2(1): 59–76.

——2004, *Understanding Celebrity*, Sage, London.

——2005, *Ending the Affair: The Decline of Television Current Affairs in Australia*, UNSW Press, Sydney.

UNCTAD 2004, 'Creative Industries and Development', <www.unctad.org/en/docs/tdxibpd13_en.pdf>, accessed 10 May 2007.

——2005, *World Investment Report 2005: Transnational Corporations and the Internationalization of R & D*, United Nations, New York and Geneva.

UNESCO 2003, *Culture, Trade and Globalization: Questions and Answers*, <www.unesco.org/culture/industries/trade/html_eng>, accessed 4 June 2003.

United Nations 1948, *Universal Declaration of Human Rights*, adopted by the General Assembly of the United Nations, 10 December, <www.un.org/Overview/rights.html>, accessed 5 May 2007.

Vaidhyanathan, Siva 2001, *Copyrights and Copywrongs: The Rise of Intellectual Property and How it Threatens Creativity*, New York University Press, New York.

——2004, *The Anarchist in the Library: How the Clash between Freedom and Control is Hacking the Real World*, Basic Books, New York.

van Dijk, Jan 1999, *The Network Society*, Sage, London.

Vastag, Brian 2004, 'Does Video Game Violence Sow Aggression?', *Journal of the American Medical Association* 291(15): 1822–4.

Venturelli, Shalini 2005, 'Culture and the Creative Economy in the Information Age', in J. Hartley (ed.), *Creative Industries*, Blackwell, Oxford, pp. 391–8.

von Hippel, Eric 2005, *Democratizing Innovation*, MIT Press, Cambridge MA.

Wagstaff, Jeremy 2004, 'Korea's News Crusaders', *Far Eastern Economic Review*, 7 October, pp. 34–7.

Wang, Jing 2004, 'The Global Reach of a New Discourse: How Far Can "Creative Industries" Travel', *International Journal of Cultural Studies* 7(1): 9–19.

Ward, Ian 2003, 'An Australian PR State?', *Australian Journal of Communication* 30(1): 25–42.

Wasserman, Stanley, and Faust, Katharine 1994, *Social Network Analysis: Methods and Applications*, Cambridge University Press.

Webster, Frank, and Dimitriou, Basil 2003, *Manuel Castells*, 3 vols, *Sage Modern Masters in Social Thought Series*, Sage, London.

Weiss, Glenn 2007, 'Glenn Weiss: Architecture, Design and Public Art', <www.glennweiss.com>, accessed 5 May 2007.

Wellman, Barry 2001, 'Physical Place and Cyberspace: The Rise of Personalized Networking', *International Journal of Urban and Regional Research* 25(2): 227–52.

——2004, 'The Three Ages of Internet Studies: Ten, Five and Zero Years Ago', *New Media and Society* 6(1): 123–29.

——, and Guila, Milena 1998, 'Virtual Communities as Communities: Net Surfers Don't Ride Alone', in M.A. Smith and P. Kollock (eds), *Communities in Cyberspace*. Routledge, London, pp. 167–94.

——, and Haythornthwaite, Carolyn, 2002, 'Moving the Internet out of Cyberspace: The Internet in Everyday Life—An Introduction', in B. Wellman and C. Haythornthwaite (eds), *The Internet in Everyday Life*, Blackwell, Malden MA, pp. 3–41.

——, Haase, Anabel, Witte, James, and Hampton, Keith 2001, 'Does the Internet Increase, Decrease, or Supplement Social Capital? Social Networks, Participation, and Community Commitment, *American Behavioral Scientist* 45(3): 436–55.

Westerway, Peter 1990, *Electronic Highways: An Introduction to Telecommunications in the 1990s*, George Allen & Unwin, Sydney.

Wikipedia Contributors 2007, 'Mod (computer gaming)', *Wikipedia, The Free Encyclopedia*, <en.wikipedia.org/wiki/Mod_%28computer_gaming%29>, modified 6 April, accessed 7 April 2007.

Williams, Raymond 1965, *The Long Revolution*, Chatto & Windus, London.

——1974, *Television: Technology and Cultural Form*, Routledge, London.

——1976, *Keywords: A Vocabulary of Culture and Society*, Fontana, London.

Williams, Robin, and Edge, David 1996, 'The Social Shaping of Technology', *Research Policy* 25(4): 865–99.

Williamson, Oliver E. 1975, *Markets and Hierarchies*, Free Press, New York.

——1985, *The Economic Institutions of Capitalism*, Free Press, New York.

Windschuttle, Keith 2000, 'The Poverty of Cultural Studies', *Journalism Studies* 1(1): 145–59.

Winner, Langdon 1986a, 'Technologies as Forms of Life', in L. Winner, *The Whale and the Reactor: A Search for Limits in an Age of High Technology*, University of Chicago Press, pp. 3–18.

——1986b, 'Do Artifacts Have Politics?', in L. Winner, *The Whale and the Reactor: A Search for Limits in an Age of High Technology*, University of Chicago Press, pp. 19–37.

Winseck, Dwayne 2002, 'Wired Cities and Transnational Communications: New Forms of Governance for Telecommunicatons and the New Media', in L. Lievrouw and S. Livingstone (eds), *Handbook of New Media*, Sage, London, pp. 393–409.

Winston, Brian 1998, *Media Technology and Society—A History: From the Telegraph to the Internet*, Routledge, London.

WIPO (World Intellectual Property Organization) 2006, *WIPO Patent Report 2006: Statistics on Worldwide Patent Activities*, <www.wipo.int/ipstats/en/statistics/patents/pdf/patent_report_2006.pdf>, accessed 27 May 2007.

Witt, Leonard 2004, 'Is Public Journalism Morphing into the Public's Journalism?', *National Civic Review* Fall: 49–57.

Wolf, Gary 1996, 'The Wisdom of Saint Marshall, the Holy Fool', *WIRED* 4(1), <www.wired.com/wired/archive/4.01/saint.marshal.html>, accessed 29 May 2007.

Woods, Tim 1999, *Beginning Postmodernism*, Manchester University Press.

Woolcock, Michael 2001, 'The Place of Social Capital in Understanding Social and Economic Outcomes', *ISUMA: Canadian Journal of Policy Research* 2(1): 11–17.

Woolgar, Steve 2002, 'Five Rules of Virtuality', in S. Woolgar (ed.), *Virtual Society? Technology, Cyberbole, Reality*, Oxford University Press, Oxford, pp. 1–22.

World Bank 2003, 'Social Capital for Development', <www.worldbank.org/poverty/scapital/>, accessed 10 January 2004.

WSIS Civil Society Plenary 2003, 'Shaping Information Societies for Human Needs: Civil Society Declaration to the World Summit on the Information Society', Geneva, 8 December.

Yeon-Ho, Oh 2004, 'The Revolt of 727 News Guerillas', <http://english.ohmynews.com/articleview/article_view.asp?no=153109&rel_no=1>, published 19 February, accessed 5 May 2007.

——2007, '10 Preconditions for the Value of User-Generated Content', *OhMyNews* CEO Oh Yeon-ho's address on the 7th anniversary of *OhMyNews*, <english. ohmynews.com/articleview/article_view.asp?article_class=8&no=347268&rel_ no=1>, published 26 February, accessed 28 April 2007.

Young, Sally 2006, 'Not Biting the Hand that Feeds? Media Reporting of Government Advertising in Australia', *Journalism Studies* 7(4): 554–74.

Yúdice, George 2003, *The Expediency of Culture: Uses of Culture in the Global Era*, Duke University Press, Durham NC.

Zetie, Carl, 2004, 'Convergence or Divergence: What's Next for Mobile Devices?', *InformationWeek*, 15 May, <www.informationweek.com/story/showArticle.jhtml ?articleID=18311545>, accessed 12 December 2006.

Zelizer, Barbie 2004, *Taking Journalism Seriously: News and the Academy*, Sage, Thousand Oaks CA.

——2005, 'The Culture of Journalism', in J. Curran and M. Gurevitch (eds), *Mass Media and Society*, 4th edn, Arnold, London.

Zhang, Yonghua 2006, 'China's Efforts for International Cooperation in Copyright Protection', in P. Thomas and J. Servaes (eds), *Intellectual Property Rights and Communications in Asia*, Sage, New Delhi, pp. 149–63.

Zhang, Xiaoming 2006, 'From Institution to Industry: Reforms in Cultural Institutions in China', *International Journal of Cultural Studies* 9(3): 297–306.

index